THE BEST OF
Fly Rod & Reel

30 Years of Tips·Tricks·Patterns

flytying

Edited by Jim Butler
Introduction by Ted Leeson

Copyright 2010 by Down East Enterprise, Inc.

Photographs and illustrations are by the authors of the articles they accompany, except:

Greg Thomas (photo) Page 7

Martin Berinstein (photos): Pages 98, 99

Stephen Collector (photo): Page 41

Tim England (illustrations): Pages 24, 25, 50, 51, 85, 101, 106-109, 112-114, 125, 127, 128, 133, 141, 143, 144, 153-155, 157, 159, 161 (except top), 162-166, 170, 171, 173-175, 177-179, 181-183, 185-187

Ted Fauceglia: Tied and photographed Tap's Bug on pages 63, 65

Richard Procopio (photos): Pages 26, 27, 49, 83, 84, 87-90, 105, 107, 111

ISBN: 978-0-89272-908-1

Library of Congress Cataloging-in-Publication Data available upon request.

Printed in the USA

5 4 3 2 1

FlyRod&Reel Books

Distributed to the trade by National Book Network

Designed by Chad Hughes

Cover Photo by Barry Ord Clarke

THE BEST OF
Fly Rod & Reel

30 Years of **Tips • Tricks • Patterns**

fly tying

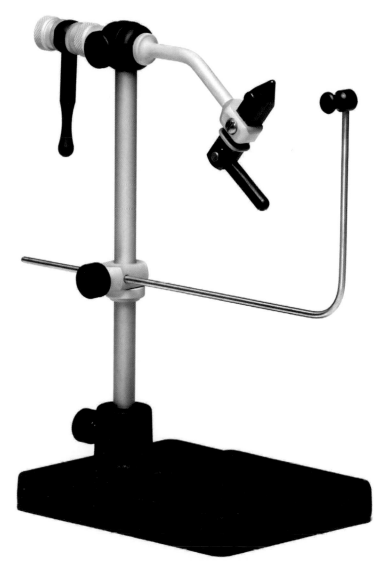

Edited by Jim Butler

Introduction by Ted Leeson

flytying Contents

FLY-TYING COLUMNS................................Darrel Martin

flytying Contents

{1⊙ Minute Ties} .... A. K. Best

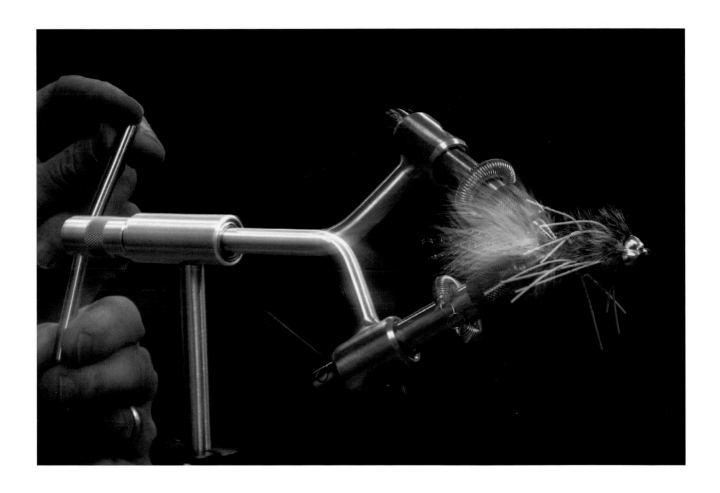

Introduction
Ted Leeson

The material in this book has been selected from the rich trove of fly-tying columns and feature articles that have appeared in *Fly Rod & Reel* Magazine over the past 30 years. In the world of modern tying, 30 years is a long time. Innovations in the craft—in patterns, materials and techniques—have accelerated during the past several decades at a rate that is arguably the fastest in the history of fly-tying. The information collected here represents a cross-section of this energetic, inventive period in the craft. Many of the contributions to this book not only capture that change but have helped to bring it about by introducing tiers to new dressings, tying methods, and approaches to representing natural food forms.

At the same time, though so much is new in fly-tying, its best practitioners never stray from certain immutable truths—rational design ideas, sound and efficient tying techniques and, above all, effective patterns. These fundamental principles at the heart of fly-tying are at the center of this book as well, and the instructional information here is marked by a solid practicality.

The breadth of material in these pages is unusual for a fly-tying book. You'll find not only traditional patterns that have been catching fish for centuries, but reinterpretations of those traditions that are more closely aligned with the way we fish and tie today. There are, of course, plenty of contemporary fly designs as well; and as a group, the patterns presented target a variety of species—trout, salmon, steelhead, warmwater fish and saltwater ones. But fly-tying is not exclusively about patterns, and some of the selections included here offer valuable information on choosing and using materials, while others profile noteworthy figures in tying, such as John Betts, who pioneered the use of many synthetic materials that have become fly-tying standards today.

Compiled from the work of many tiers, this book is essentially an anthology—comparatively rare in the literature of fly-tying—and its unique advantage lies in its range of voices, points of view, and varieties of fly-tying expertise. The work of some of the most the distinguished names in modern tying appear in these pages.

But two tiers in particular must be singled out. Not only are they among the best-known names in American tying and long-time contributors to *Fly Rod & Reel*; but taken together they bracket or bookend the broad spectrum of approaches to fly-tying represented in these pages.

The first is Darrel Martin, whose work is informed by an astonishing and encyclopedic knowledge of fly-tying history, patterns and, above all, fly-dressing methods. More than any other fly-tying authority in the past three decades, Darrel has been responsible for introducing American tiers to the dressings, design rationales, techniques and, in some cases, materials from European fly dressers, who have fueled much of the change that's taken place on the American tying scene. Experimental and inventive, Darrel is one of fly-tying's preeminent craftsmen, researching both historical and contemporary sources for tying ideas, and devising methods that enable tiers to create better flies or more innovative designs. Darrel Martin is a fly tier's tier.

The second contributor, A. K. Best, is a technician of a different sort. As a commercial fly tier for more than 35 years, A. K. has mastered what most of us are still working toward—clean, efficient tying with a minimum of waste in time, effort and materials. A. K. is a kind of professional perfectionist, with an exhaustive knowledge of materials and an inclination to more traditional fly designs that he has refined over the years. His contributions to this book give tiers the information they need to produce practical, durable, effective patterns in a minimum of time. A. K. is a fisherman's fly tier. Despite their differences, both men are phenomenally good at what they do, and like all the contributors to this book, have helped novices and advanced tiers alike improve their skills, increase the versatility of their tying, and fashion more productive flies, which in the end is what we all seek.

I learned a great deal from these tiers when their work first appeared in the pages of *Fly Rod & Reel*, and I'm delighted that the wealth of information they have to offer has at last been compiled into a single volume for the benefit of fly tiers everywhere.

On Proper Proportions
Nothing makes a fly more attractive

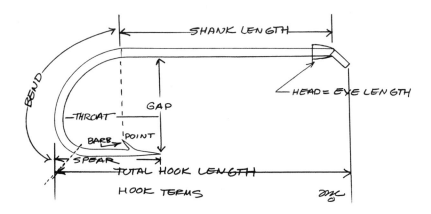

Darrel Martin
Nov/Dec 1998

The spinners dance—the bright, fluttering wings and the long, trembling tails fall and rise in the slanting sun. There is beauty in their delicate proportion. And nothing makes an imitation more attractive than proper proportions. Though there are personal proportions, all tiers should know standards of tying. Most modern proportions are, in fact, based upon a capricious tradition. Proportion has less effect upon fly function and fish than it does upon our tying aesthetics—the fragile beauty we capture tying.

Although proportion emphasizes material length, it may also include such elements as material quantity, shank location and mounting stance. Few proportions are actually based on fly performance or on the natural insect. J. Edson Leonard attempted to provide practical function to pattern design when he popularized the "ideal float line" in *Flies* (1950). He depicted the dry fly floating on its tail and hackle tips with the hook barely brushing the surface. Theoretically, the hook should not quite touch the float line. In actual use, of course, a dry fly quickly pierces the surface with portions of hook, body and barbs.

Tying proportions will always be debated and tiers will always test and modify tradition. No matter what scale is preferred, the tier must control the materials to create the proportions. If a proportion is not established and maintained, the fly may lack that stance and symmetry we so admire.

Though most tiers strive for conventional proportions, sometimes a slight variation may be attractive. Unconventional proportion can create interesting effects. As Francis Bacon once noted, "There is no excellent beauty that hath not some strangeness in the proportion." Competent tiers, however, have a consummate sense of proportion and can achieve a pleasing look no matter what the pattern size.

Traditional Fly-Tying Proportions

The proportion chart (above) is based on some traditional concepts. The hook shank (S) begins directly behind the hook eye and travels to a point on the shank directly above the rear of the barb. The hook bend usually begins at the rear of the shank. Not all tiers include the head space in the shank length. The slightly longer tail increases the delicacy of design. Hook length (H) is the distance between the total limits of eye and bend. Hook gap (G) is the distance between hook point and shank. The number of ribbing wraps depends upon ribbing width and hook length—on standard-length hooks, usually four or five wraps. The chart presents conventional proportions, including alternates, for future reference.

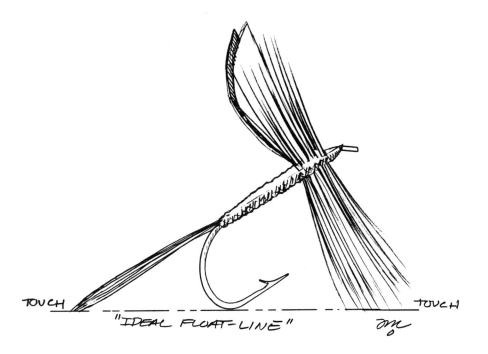

"IDEAL FLOAT-LINE"

TOUCH   TOUCH

❶ Traditional Dry

Tail: Hackle-barb tail equals hook shank, or 2½ hook gap. William Sturgis recommended that five or six hackle barbs are usually sufficient. Dun tails equal 1¼ shank length and the longer spinner tails are 1¾ shank length. Some tiers select tails slightly "proud" of the shank length.

Body: Slightly tapered body begins directly above rear of barb and ends behind wings. Body length equals ¾ shank length (Eric Leiser).

Wing: Quill wing length equals hook shank or 2X hook shank. Maximum wing length equals top hook length. Quill wing width may equal ¾ hook gap. Wing set begins at the front ⅕ or ¼ of hook shank.

Hackle: Hackle equals ¾ hook shank or 1½ to 2X hook gap.

❷ Catskill Dry

Tail: Sparse tail slightly longer than hook shank.

Body: Begins somewhere above rear of barb and hook point.

Wing: Slightly longer than shank length, and sometimes moderately canted forward, mounted ⅓ shank length behind the eye.

Hackle: A long, bare neck about three eye-lengths from the hook eye. Minimal wraps form a modest head. The bare neck seldom appears on modern commercial flies.

There are variations on the Catskill dry, and extended debate on the proportions of this graceful pattern.

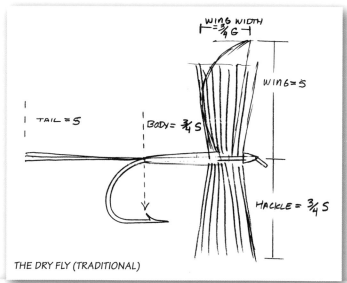

THE DRY FLY (TRADITIONAL)

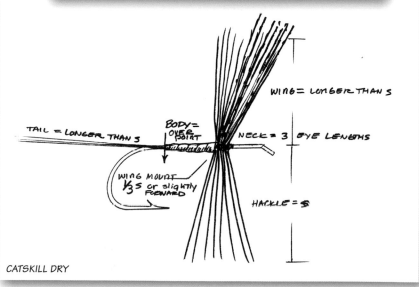

CATSKILL DRY

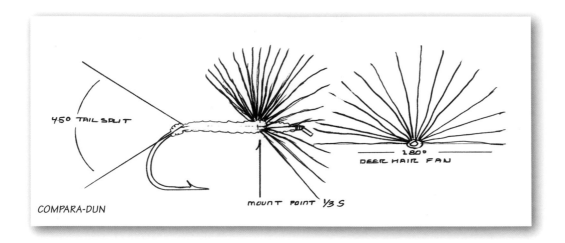

450 TAIL SPLIT

180° DEER HAIR FAN

MOUNT POINT ⅓ S

COMPARA-DUN

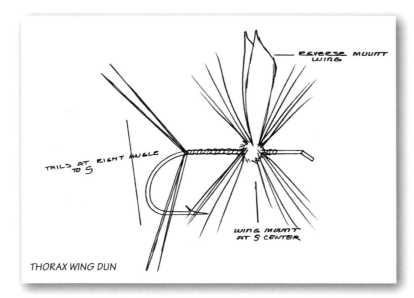

REVERSE MOUNT WING

TAILS AT RIGHT ANGLE TO S

WING MOUNT AT S CENTER

THORAX WING DUN

❸ Compara-Dun

Tail: Stiff hackles tied outrigger, divided by a small dubbing ball, split 45°.

Body: To support wings, dubbed body continues in front of wings.

Wing: Wing mount point is ⅓ shank length behind eye. The deerhair wing should be mounted on top and on both sides of the shank. The fan wing should extend 180° to support the fly.

❹ Thorax Wing Dun

Tail: Equal shank length, split at right angle to shank. Casting invariably reduces the spread. Marinaro used one tail barb per side on hook sizes 22 and 24, two barbs per side on size 18 to 22 and three barbs per side on size 14 to 16.

Body: No body, only small thoracic dubbing ball at wing base.

Wing: Wings mounted at shank center (Marinaro), or slightly forward. Thoracic wing set may also occur as far forward as ¼ of hook shank. Marinaro reverse-mounted quill wing for greater durability.

Hackle: When mounted, the hackle barbs should cloak the bottom of the hook.

❺ Hair-Wing Dry

Tail: Hair tail equals ¾ length or 2X hook gap.

Body: Directly over rear hub of barb to wing mount.

Wing: Wing equals hook-shank length.

Hackle: Hackle equals ¾ shank length. A flared and crimped hair tail may intercept the float line earlier than a straight hackle-barb tail. A dryfly hackle (with multiple wraps) may occupy half of the total shank length. So that the wings appear to emerge from the middle of the hackle, flies may have an equal number of wraps behind and in front of the wings.

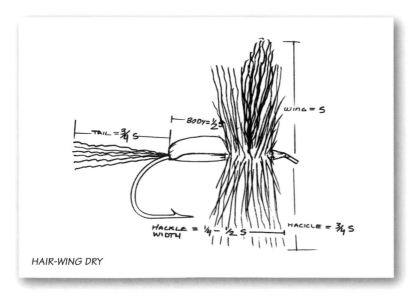

WING = S

BODY = ½ S

TAIL = ¾ S

HACKLE WIDTH = ¼ – ½ S

HACKLE = ¾ S

HAIR-WING DRY

❻ Quill Wing Wet

Tail: Tail equals ½ hook shank, or tail extends to rear extremity of the overwing. On some patterns tail length equals hook shank.

Body: Body occupies distance from rear of head to directly above rear of hook barb.

Wing: Wing length is "just proud of hook bend" or equals hook shank or 1¼ to 1½ hook shank. Wing length is variable. Wetfly wing width is ¾ hook gap. Wing mount point, a head length from the eye, is forward of the dryfly mount point. The illustration depicts the "sedge" mount that partially encloses the body. Despite the fact that some wet patterns may imitate ovipositing adults with extended wings, William Sturgis asserts that "the wings of the wet flies are . . . immature and lie closely along the body."

Hackle: Soft hackle just touches the hook point or hackle length equals hook gap. Hackle length may also equal ½ hook-shank length.

❼ Soft-Hackle

Body: Body length variable. Bodies may imitate the standard hook-shank length of dry and wet patterns. Body length may also conform to Scottish tying tradition:

Tweed style: Body ends midway above hook point and hook barb;

Clyde style: Body ends at midshank;

Tummel style: Body ends at front ¼ shank.

Hackle: Soft-hackle length equal to body length or equal to the rear extremity of the hook. Two or three wraps of hackle only.

Thorax: If present, the thoracic segment (slightly fuller than the body to give the hackle an open, pulsing movement) is ⅓ to ¼ hook shank.

❽ Nymph

Tail: Tails equal ½ hook shank. Stonefly tail equals ¾ hook-shank length (Sturgis).

Abdomen: Abdomen equals ½ hook shank. The head and thorax, on natural stonefly and mayfly nymphs, equals approximately ½ total body length.

Ribbing: Four or five equally spaced turns (½ hook shank).

Thorax: Thorax equals ½ hook shank.

Wing case: Wing case equals ½ hook shank.

Hackle legs: Hackle equals hook gap or ½ hook shank.

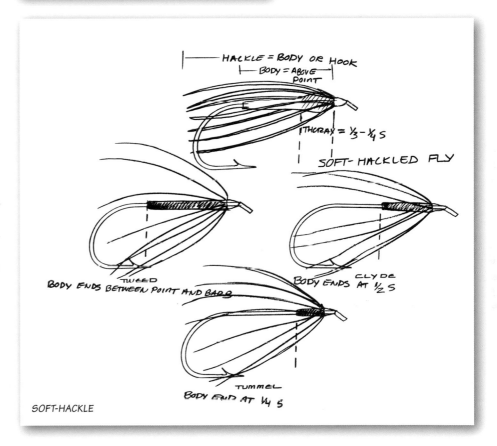

QUILL WING WET

SOFT-HACKLE

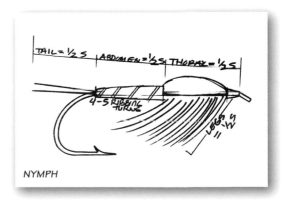

NYMPH

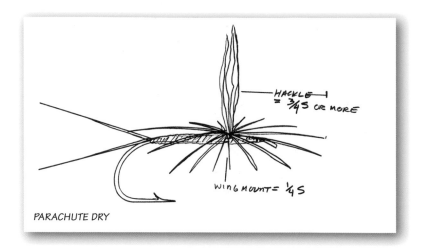

PARACHUTE DRY

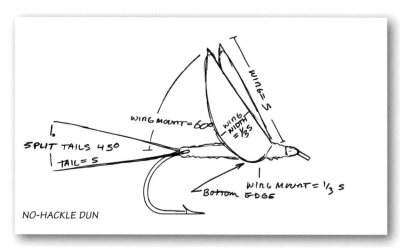

NO-HACKLE DUN

❾ Parachute dry
Wing: Wing mount point is ¼ shank
length from eye (Dick Talleur). Wing materials
include calf tail, calf body, goat and
various synthetics.
Hackle: For increased flotation, hackle
barbs may be slightly longer than standard.
Due to increased flotation, longer barbs
may have fewer wraps.

❿ No-Hackle Dun
Tail: Split with dubbing ball, equal shank
length.
Body: Equals shank length.
Wing: Wing length equals shank length.
Wing width equals approximately ⅓ shank
length (Swisher-Richards). Wing mount
point equals ⅓ shank. Lower edge of wing
acts as outrigger.

⓫ Hen Spinner
Tail: Tail equals 1½ shank length. Tail-split
angle equals 45°.
Body: Body equals shank length.
Wing: Wing equals shank length. Wing
width equals approximately ⅓ shank length.

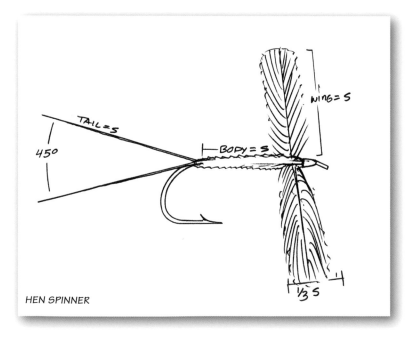

HEN SPINNER

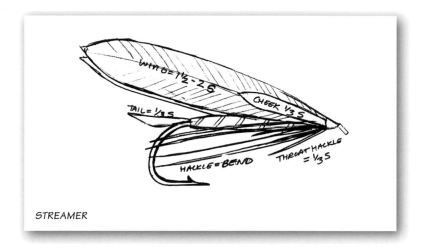

STREAMER

⑫ Streamer

Tail:: Tail, if present, is ⅓ shank length.

Body: The body, usually ribbed and divided, equals hook shank and terminates directly over the rear of barb. Ribbing turns variable depending upon shank length and ribbing width.

Wing: Wing is ⅓ longer than hook length or 1½ to 2X hook-shank length. Hair wing should extend beyond the bend equal to the gap of the hook (Sturgis).

Shoulder hackle: When wrapped, the hackle point just touches hook bend or extends ½ hook shank.

Throat hackle: Throat hackle equals ⅓ body length. On trolling patterns, the throat hackle may extend to the hook bend or wing limit.

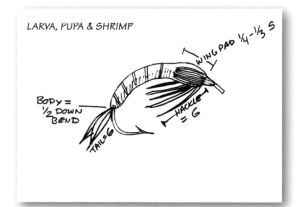

LARVA, PUPA & SHRIMP

⑬ Larva, Pupa & Shrimp

Tail: Short tails or gills approximately equal to hook gap.

Body: Body length may vary according to the particular hook bend. With rounded or circular bend, body generally extends halfway down the bend to take advantage of the circular form.

Wing pad: If present, the wing pad is ¼ to ⅓ body length.

Hackle: Leg hackle equals hook gap.

The larva and shrimp patterns often vary in proportions depending upon the hook shape and the natural. It is usually recommended that shrimp patterns be tied on straight-shank hooks.

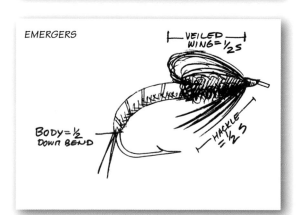

EMERGERS

⑭ Emergers

When tied on standard hooks, emergers usually assume the proportions of a dry fly. When tied on circular hooks, emergers usually adopt the proportions of a pupa or larva. To support the fly, float pod or veiled wings may be ½ hook shank.

Alaskan Trout Flies

Assembling the deadliest selection
for Alaska's rainbows and char

Will Rice
July/Oct 2002

It was one of those late-August days that epitomize Alaskan trout fishing. The river, a popular roadside stream, was gin clear and full of crimson sockeyes paired up and starting to spawn. Behind the salmon I could see the dark shadows of big rainbows and the bright flashes of arctic char. Another fisherman, looking a bit lost, stopped to watch me work a big 'bow that had been riding the pillow above a midstream rock. He walked up as I released the fish.

"Man, I haven't caught a fish like that all day," he said. "Nothin' but little ones. What are you using?" I glanced at the oversize egg pattern hooked in his keeper and showed him the fly I had just removed from the rainbow's jaw.

"You're kidding," he said. "I've got a whole damn box of those flies sitting on my desk back in Montana."

I had a pretty good idea of what the fly box he had with him now would look like. Every fly-shop catalog carries an "Alaskan selection." It invariably consists of egg flies, flesh flies, Egg-Sucking Leeches and deerhair mice. Many visitors, like my Montana friend, take the retailer's picks as a mandate, and fish with nothing else. While there is no question that these flies account for a lot of Alaskan rainbows and char, over the past 10 years, probably three quarters of my big fish—those over 20 inches—have been taken on other patterns.

I do most of my fishing on small, clear rivers, and I have about a dozen flies that I rely on over the course of the season. These include my own versions of the traditional four, together with some more unconventional selections. The appropriate patterns change over the course of the summer, and perhaps that is the best way to discuss them.

An analysis of trout behavior in Alaska always starts with the salmon, and in the early season that means alevins (just-hatched salmon still carrying the yolk sac), fry (first-year fish) and smolts (juveniles ready to migrate to sea). Alevins emerge from the gravel before the

season opens in most areas and are usually of limited interest. Fry and smolts, though, can provide heart-attack fishing.

The two most important salmon for trout streams are kings and sockeyes. With some exceptions, both species spend the first year in fresh water as fry and then migrate seaward in their second summer as smolts. King salmon fry rear in the rivers, but the much more numerous sockeyes migrate downstream to a lake. In June, clouds of sockeye fry haunt the edges and backwaters of their natal streams, making their dash for the safety of the lake under cloudy or twilight skies. The fry move in the upper inches of the water column, and those slashing rises you see are not trout chasing caddis.

Fry—both Chinook (kings) and sockeye—are about an inch long, largely silver with dark backs, have prominent eyes and exhibit a lot of movement when they swim. A number of streamers imitate them well, but all are measured against the effectiveness of a sparsely tied Thunder Creek, usually size 10. Fry patterns are effectively fished almost dead drift, with a bit of a downstream belly pulling them along just faster than the current. The fly is unweighted and fished on a floating line, so the imitation swims just under the surface film. When the fly reaches the end of the drift, mend upstream and let it swing across the current on

Thunder Creek

❶ Pinch the barb on the hook. Attach white 6/0 thread to hook shank behind eye. Tie in silver mylar tinsel and wrap back to bend and then forward.

❷ Cut a small bunch of white straight bucktail. You may need to roughly even up the ends, but do not use a stacker. Tie the bucktail, facing forward (tips extending beyond the hook eye, that is), underneath the hook shank. Prepare a sparse clump of brown bucktail in the same manner and tie it on top of the shank, again facing forward. Overwrap with the white thread, building up the head. Whip-finish and cut thread.

❸ Attach red thread (I like single-strand floss for this) just behind the head. Pull the brown bucktail back and secure with two wraps. Repeat with the white bucktail. Whip-finish. Coat head with head cement and let dry thoroughly. Using a round toothpick cut back to the appropriate diameter, paint a yellow eyespot on each side of the head. When dry, add a black pupil.

Hook: Tiemco 5262, size 10, 2X long
Thread: White 6/0, red 6/0
Body: Silver mylar tinsel
Upper wing: Very sparse brown bucktail, tied facing forward and pulled back
Lower wing: Very sparse white bucktail, tied facing forward and pulled back
Head: Bullet head created by pulling wings back and tying at throat with red thread
Eyes: Painted yellow with black pupil

Flashback Pheasant Tail Nymph

Hook: Tiemco 3769, size 12 to 14
Thread: Tan 8/0
Tail: Pheasant tail fibers
Rib: Fine copper wire
Underbody: Small amount of dubbing to give bulk to abdomen
Abdomen: Pheasant tail fibers wrapped over dubbing, counter-wrapped with copper wire
Thorax: Peacock hen
Shellback: Pearl Flashabou (the wide saltwater version works best)
Legs: Pheasant tail fiber tips

Guide's Special (Red)

Hook: Tiemco 7999, size 2 to 8
Thread: Fluorescent red 6/0
Weight: Lead wire or non-toxic substitute
Undertail: Red Flashabou, 8 to 10 strands, clipped shorter than tail
Tail: Black rabbit strip
Body: Palmered black rabbit strip
Head: Large thread head coated with epoxy mixed with fine red glitter
Note: This fly is equally effective tied with emerald green Flashabou, fluorescent green thread and green glitter.

a tight line until it hangs directly below you. Resist the urge to immediately pick up and cast again. Let it hang and maybe give it a short strip or two. A lot of fish can't resist the sight of that little morsel dancing in front of them. Strikes can be arm wrenching, and 3X tippet or better is mandatory.

Sockeye fry are found in the spawning streams above the lake in which they will spend their first winter. The following year, as smolts, both sockeyes and Chinooks head downstream to the ocean. Both migrations—of sockeye fry heading down to a lake, and sockeye and Chinook smolts migrating to the ocean—are brief and can be difficult to time correctly. The choice of pattern (fry or smolt) is largely a function of whether you are fishing above or below a lake in which young sockeyes rear.

In the larger rivers below the lakes, an out-migration of hefty, three-inch smolts will really bring the big fish up. The first notice of their arrival is often a flock of screaming terns and gulls moving downstream. As the birds get closer, you can see a frenzy of smashing strikes as the trout chase the fleeing smolts. Throw a size 2 or 4 white streamer into the middle of the frenzy and hold on. I like white Zonkers, gray-over-white double Bunnies, and white Woolly Buggers tied with a few strands of peacock over the back. A little weight will keep the fly a few inches deep. Fish smolt patterns like a more vigorous version of the fry.

Fry and smolt patterns are fun, but for truly big fish, try working big, dark streamers along the bottom. One of my favorites is a heavily weighted black Bunny Bugger with a twinkle of red or green Flashabou and a matching glitter head (mix the appropriate color of fine glitter with epoxy and coat the head). The best sculpin imitation that I have found is a rabbit-strip pattern developed by my friend Rich Chiappone. It is tied with stiff pectorals and a wide head, which combine to create enough turbulence to bring the bunny strip to life. The first fish that ever saw this fly was a big rainbow that came 20 feet out from under a floating bridge and almost beached itself with the strike.

Trout fishing generally slows during July because the sockeye runs push the rainbows into marginal water. Fish the side channels and the pocket water. This is dryfly and nymph time. You don't often see fish feeding steadily on the surface, but they will still come up for a dry. My selection is simple: Yellow Humpies, Elkhair Caddis and Parachute Adams in sizes 12 and 14 are probably all you need. I also carry a few big attractors like a Katmai Slider or Madam X in sizes 8 and 10. If you aren't getting strikes on a dead drift, try skating the flies. This is particularly effective on char, which seem to prefer a fly with action. Those deerhair mice can also be a lot of fun on the right water. A buddy of mine even tried one of those six-inch-long, jointed lemming flies that I thought people bought only as a joke. The Loch Ness monster came up, inhaled it whole and headed downstream without ever looking back.

As in most places, nymphs are generally more effective than dries. Beadheads are the order of the day for fishing pocket water. My favorite searching pattern is a beadhead Prince Nymph, in sizes 8 to 16. I also carry beadhead Hare's Ears, and some simple beadhead fur nymphs in green, brown and black. If you aren't getting strikes in the pockets, try moving your indicator closer to the fly—18 to 24 inches. The swirling currents of the pockets create slack in the tippet, and the trout can often spit out an imitation before the leader tightens.

Streamers, both dark sculpin patterns and bright smolt imitations, are also good in midsummer. If you are floating a riffle-and-pool stream, try them in the faster water. The trout will often move in there to feed and to escape from the sockeyes that are resting in the slower water.

This is the time everyone waits for: In late July, the kings begin to spawn. Look for those rust-red logs lying in midstream. By early August you will find wide, knee-deep runs measled with scarlet sockeye. It's not hard to locate trout. Just look about three feet behind every pair of spawners. There is no question that the trout are keyed on eggs, and egg patterns are the first choice. But they're not the only choice.

Before any spawning actually takes place the salmon pair up and begin digging their redds. This nest-building activity flushes insects from the gravel, and the trout are looking for nymphs and caddis larvae. My favorite fly for this period is a Flashback Pheasant Tail, size 14. Hare's Ears and caddis emergers are also effective.

Don't give up on those Pheasant Tails and Hare's Ears when the eggs hit the water. Egg-eating trout can become as selective of size and color as a spring-creek rainbow in a Baetis hatch, and in any stream that is heavily fished, they have seen every egg pattern in the catalog. You will get a lot of inspections and refusals, particularly from larger 'bows. Fishing a nymph, particularly sight fishing to an individual fish, is like using an ant or beetle pattern on those same spring creeks: They don't always work, but they will get you some big fish that you can't otherwise fool. In fact, it was a box of Pheasant Tail Nymphs that the Montana fisherman I mentioned earlier had left sitting on his desk.

If a trout is going to take an egg pattern, he will hit it on the first good drift. That is why eggs are such a great searching pattern— you can cover a lot of water. Nymphs, however, need to be fished differently. I like to spot a good fish and then work him hard. It may take 15 or 20 good drifts to get him to eat, but eventually most fish that are feeding will take the fly. If you are fishing one of the few streams that allow the use of a dropper, try a Pheasant Tail or Prince Nymph behind an egg pattern. While the egg will get their attention, you will be surprised how many fish reject the egg but take the nymph.

One fly that I don't use during this period is any type of streamer pattern. Not only will you foul-hook salmon on the swing, but the male sockeyes will hammer the little egg thieves, and you will spend all your time wrestling with over-the-hill spawners.

As the sockeyes begin to die, flesh flies become effective. My favorite is a mix of dirty-white and salmon-pink marabou roughly dubbed on a size 8 or 10 hook. The smaller size

Maggot Fly
Hook: Tiemco 2487 (scud hook), size 14
Thread: White 8/0
Body: White polypropylene yarn

provides a more realistic imitation of the scraps of flesh that drift loose. There are still eggs in the water, but at this point most are dead and attacked by fungus. Use cream or dull yellow patterns to imitate them. If the river has risen, it will have washed old salmon carcasses into the water and a maggot imitation (forgive me, Theodore Gordon) can be deadly, particularly along the stream edges. A curved-shank size 14 hook wrapped with white yarn or tight dubbing is all you need.

With the salmon gone, those big leech and streamer patterns work well again. Sculpins are rooting through the redds for eggs, and rabbit-strip imitations fished slowly along the bottom are most effective. By this time though, the trout are beginning to drop back down to their wintering grounds, and the upper parts of smaller streams will suddenly go blank. Be prepared to fish bigger water and go deeper.

Everyone who fishes for trout in Alaska remembers those died-and-gone-to-heaven days. But there are plenty of times, particularly on the more heavily fished streams, when Alaskan rainbows are as picky as big trout anywhere. When those days happen, you will be glad you brought something besides your local fly shop's Alaskan recommendations. That box of Pheasant Tails—don't leave home without it.

Chiappone Sculpin

❶ Pinch the barb on the hook. Attach thread and wrap to the bend. Wrap lead wire over the rear ⅔ of shank, leaving enough room to fit in tail and materials at rear. Leave the front ⅓ of shank bare to allow room for the head. Tie in a dozen strands of emerald green Flashabou at the tail and trim short.

❷ Tie in a black rabbit Zonker strip at rear of hook. The Flashabou should be shorter than the rabbit-fur tail. Tie in brown Crystal Chenille.

❸ Wrap the rear ⅔ of the shank with chenille. Bring the Zonker strip forward and tie off.

❹ Prepare pectoral fins by stripping the soft fibers from two small, sharply cupped feathers, such as the shoulder feathers from a grouse wing. Coat lightly with Flexament to stiffen. The purpose of the pectorals is not to imitate the sculpin fins as much as it is to create turbulence alongside the rabbit fur. Tie in the feathers concave side out.

❺ Tie in dark olive or brown ram's wool, allowing the tips to stream back on the top and bottom of the fly. Continue to tie in wool to build the rear half of head. You can use a mixture of colors and materials, including sculpin wool or McFlyfoam. Prepare a pair of medium mono nymph eyes by touching them with Superglue or head cement to give them some shine. Tie in with Figure-8 wraps. Add more wool to complete head. Whip-finish and cement.

❻ Trim head flat on bottom, wedge-shaped on top and sides. The head should be wide and stiffly packed, which helps create more turbulence.

Hook: Tiemco 5262, size 2 to 4, 2X long
Thread: Black 6/0 Monocord
Undertail: Emerald green Flashabou, trimmed shorter than rabbit-strip tail
Weight: Lead wire, .025" or .030", wrapped around rear ⅔ of hook shank, or non-toxic substitute
Tail: See wing
Body: Bronze Crystal Chenille, rear ⅔ of hook shank
Wing: Black or olive rabbit strip tied Zonker style (i.e. tied down at front and rear of body)
Pectorals: Small breast or partridge shoulder feathers, stiffened with Flexament, tied on with concave side facing out
Collar: Brown or olive natural wool
Head: Mix of brown and olive wools or Glo-Bug yarns, trimmed flat on bottom, wedge-shaped on top and sides. The head should be trimmed wide to create maximum turbulence around the rabbit strip
Eyes: Medium mono nymph eyes coated with superglue

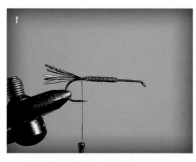

The Curious Corixa
. . . a water boatman, by another name

Darrel Martin
Sep/Oct 2000

Many years ago, when trout were very big and the summer days were very long, I scooped up a corixa, a water boatman, to examine it. As I admired its glistening wing case and long oar legs, it startled me with an abrupt flight. Stunned, I stared as it flew away and splatted into the water. I had never seen a corixa on the wing before. They filled the shallows of the lake, resting at the surface and then diving down among the weeds. Underwater, their bodies shimmered in a silver sheath of air. Here was an insect as curious as its tying history.

It was not until Charles Edward Walker's *Old Flies in New Dresses* (1898) that the corixa received proper tying attention. Walker devoted a full chapter to his pattern. The success of the fly, however, did not silence the criticism that the artificial corixa was "a lure which should not be allowed on waters" devoted to fly only. Walker considered such criticism an attack upon his ethics as well as his tying. To defend both his pattern and reputation, he listed the various reasons why the corixa was a legitimate fly: 1) corixae live in the water and are eaten by trout; 2) they possess wings and sometimes fly considerable distances; 3) the efficacy of the pattern depends upon imitating the movement of the insect. Walker even added that some noted

anglers used a similar short, jerky retrieve with the popular sunken, downstream alder pattern. Thus " . . . if the lure in question is the imitation of an insect which can and does fly, made of ordinary materials used in fly-making upon one hook, this lure has a perfect right to be called a legitimate trout-fly." Though it was not a true dry fly, it was a fly. Walker concluded that his corixa imitation had met, both in his hands and in those of others, "with greater success than any other form of wet fly."

Walker's corixa had a body of pale-yellow Berlin wool mixed with hare's mask dubbing ribbed with silver tinsel. The wing case was two woodcock quill sections, stacked and laid flat over the body. The paddle legs, each made from a quill feather of a starling wing, maintained their spring even when soaked for long periods. To make these legs, Walker stripped the barbs from one side of the feather and "nearly so on the other, leaving however a few short stumps at the end to represent the paddle shape of the legs." Walker mounted the legs with the stem butt to the rear, and then bent the legs out at right angles to the body. He believed that the flexible paddle legs were critical to any corixa imitation. "I have seen the hind legs of the corixae when the insects have been suspended motionless in mid-water, standing out at right angles on each side of the body."

The pattern was cast, allowed to sink and then retrieved in short jerks that flexed the legs. "Thus the movement of the legs of the natural insect when swimming is accurately imitated." Walker noted that the fly was often taken during the dive as well as during the retrieve. Walker's early imitation is still one of the best.

In 1921 Leonard West, in *The Natural Trout Fly and Its Imitation*, gave us another corixa in which he emphasized the wide head of the insect with brown wool eyes. The rest of the pattern, however, was far more conventional: merely a silver tinsel body, game-hen legs and a bustard wing case. In *Nymphs* (1973), Ernest Schwiebert offered a pattern with a hare-mask body and mottled-brown turkey wing case. Fine oval tinsel suggested the air bubble, while two pheasant-tail barbs imitated the swimming legs.

The insect

Though Walker's pattern appeared in June of 1897, it was recognized as early as 1888 that the corixa was preferred food for some fish. With well more than 100 species, they constitute the largest group of water bugs and are a principal fish food in late summer, fall and winter. The corixa, the water boatman (family Corixidae), is often confused with the similar backswimmer (family Notonectidae). As the name implies, backswimmers swim backside down. Both insects occupy shallow water and have a jerky, sculling motion, and both usually have oval bodies with whitish abdomens, though the abdomens of some corixae can be pale tan, brown or yellow. Corixae and backswimmers have four wings, tightly folded, with the hind wings resembling the leathery wing case of beetles. The wing case of the backswimmer is sometimes paler than a corixa case. Unlike the corixa, the highly predaceous backswimmer can inflict a stinging bite.

Backswimmers often rest at the surface with the body at an angle, head down and swimmer legs extended. Both insects are active in the shallows, rising and diving to replenish their oxygen. Fine hydrofuge hairs hold the bubble in place along the abdomen. When submerged, corixae cling to plants, often for some time. Mating and migration may be the cause for most flights. They splat into the water like hail drops. Though I have not been privy to their music, the curious corxiae even sing to each other. Due to the similarities of the boatman and backswimmer, a single pattern usually suffices.

The elements of imitation

Walker imitated the simple, oval body shape, the conspicuous paddle legs and, with tinsel, the body bubble. These remain the essential elements of water boatman imitation, though modern patterns usually incorporate glass or metal beads, silver tinsels, bright dubbings and synthetic or feather wing cases. The pattern requires little weight: Often a proper weight hook, 1X or 2X heavy, is sufficient. Because these are shallow-running bugs, a floating line or sink-tip is normally used. Following are two slightly different, fun and effective corixa patterns: one for the shallows and one for deeper running.

flytying

Corixa (Unweighted)
Hook: Daiichi 1560, Mustad AC3906B or Tiemco 3761BL, size 12 to 16
Thread: Bright white and dark brown or black
Dubbing: Master Bright pearl dubbing
Wing Case: Black or dark brown Swiss Straw
Swimmer Legs: A prepared quill feather

Corixa (Weighted)
Hook: Daiichi 1560, Mustad AC3906B or Tiemco 3761BL, size 12 to 16. The glass bead (see below) should slip over the hook eye.
Bead: Spirit River glass bead, pearl, size large fits a size 12 hook. Glass beads have more flash and less weight than metal beads. The pattern may be tied with one, two or more beads for depth control. Most corixae inhabit marginal waters less than three feet deep
Thread: Bright white and dark brown or black
Dubbing: Master Bright Pearl dubbing
Wing Case: Black or dark brown Swiss Straw
Swimmer Legs: A prepared quill feather

❶ Mount the hook securely in the vise and lay down a thread base. To preserve the flash of the beads and dubbing, I use a bright white thread. After the underbody is complete, I whip and remove the white thread. I then mount the darker thread for securing the wing case (i.e., the front of the wing case) and finishing the head.

❷ Mount the end of the Swiss Straw. I often fold the Swiss Straw in two to increase the bulk of the wing case. For a smooth case, iron (medium heat) the Straw prior to mounting. Other materials, such as oak turkey-wing panels, produce interesting wing cases. To ensure durability, spray Tuffilm on the wing panel material prior to mounting. Add a small pod of Master Bright dubbing to the rear half.

❸ Prepare the swimmer legs as illustrated. Select a hen body feather that has a rather rapid taper. This will create a small paddle tip at the end. With scissors, trim off the barbs on one side, leaving short barb stubble along the stem to create some width for the leg. On the other side, pull off all barbs except those at the very tip. These become the paddle. Extended leg length should be approximately ¾ body length. Now make an opposing duplicate leg for the other side. For increased durability (though decreased flexibility), coat each leg with a fast-drying nail polish.

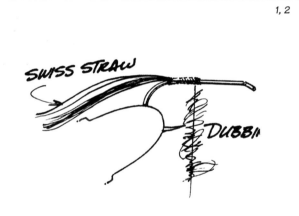

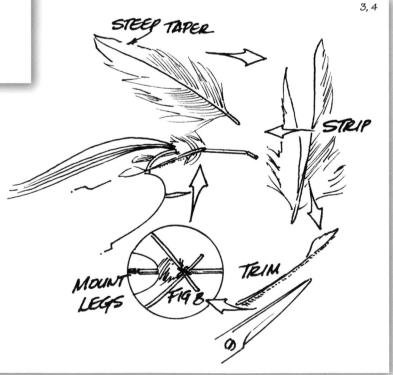

❹ With Figure-eight wraps, mount the legs on the shank immediately in front of the dubbing.

❺ Add dubbing in front of the legs and whip off the white thread. Now mount the dark thread. The dubbing should fill the wing case and create the oval body.

❻ Fold the wing case forward and overlap three times. Trim the excess and whip-finish the head. Add a coat or two of clear nail polish to the wing case. Let dry.

Begin the weighted corixa the same way as the unweighted, but add a small pod of rear dubbing. Mount the legs, prepared as before. Then slip on a pearl bead in front of the legs and add the forward dubbing. Again, change to the darker thread to secure the wing case and whip-finish the head. Note that a single bead makes a shallow-running bug. For even greater sink, add two or more glass or silver metal beads.

A final observation: Writers have emphasized the flicking legs of the pattern during the retrieve. During a rapid twitch, the legs do flex back. But when they spring forward they encounter the density of water. The forward flex is not truly imitative of the quick, pulsing paddle of the insect. In fact, flex is only apparent if the legs are long and supple. In corixa patterns, perhaps form is more important than function. In any case, these corixae are simple, attractive flies that can prove effective during slack summer hatches or winter ice. Trout know them well, and so should the tier.

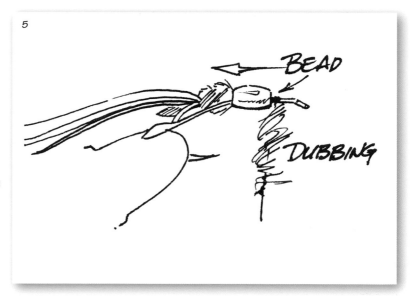

5

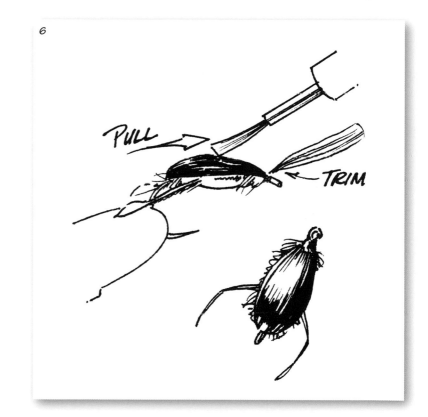

6

Hackles: Saddle or Neck?

A question for the ages, answered

A.K. Best
March 2001

When I began tying flies commercially, in the mid-1960s, I bought India rooster necks in lots of 300 to 500 for around a buck apiece. They were about all that was available at the time, they came in nearly all the colors I needed, I could dye the cream-white necks to several shades of dun, and they were cheap. The individual hackle fibers were pretty stiff (good), but the feathers were quite short (not so good). It was a rare neck that had size 16 or 18 feathers that would allow me to take more than two turns of hackle. It was tedious work to tie five or six dozen #16 Adams, often requiring more time to find a dozen #16 hackles than it did to tie the 12 flies. Size 18 and 20 dry flies were next to impossible. There were a lot of tiers then who simply wrapped the hackle collar and then trimmed it to size, since it was a lot quicker and the trout didn't seem to mind. It's not unusual these days to hackle a dozen #16 flies with one-and-a-half saddle hackle feathers.

The bulk India rooster necks I used to buy were "ungraded." That is to say, they weren't marked #1, #2 or #3 as most necks are today. My grading system evolved into a couple of boxes that I labeled "OK" and "bad." There were a few people raising roosters for fly-tying in those days, but if you weren't already on their list, you were out of luck. Those of us who were just getting started had to make do with what was available.

Most of the dryfly hackle available to me was what I now call Barnyard Quality. And I, like lots of other tiers, even tried my hand at raising some birds of my own. It was not entirely successful. Then along came Buck Metz, with his large-scale genetic-hackle breeding operation in Pennsylvania, and the lives of just about every fly tier in the country changed. There were a lot more smiling faces at the tying bench and a lot more really good-looking flies.

Buck Metz made the most important contribution to fly-tying in this century from the standpoint of good quality hackle available to the masses. Following closely behind in terms of production were Henry Hoffman and his famous Grizzly necks, Bill Keough of Keough Hackles and, lately, Dr. Tom Whiting of Whiting Farms; there are now too many to list. Suffice it to say that, in my opinion, Buck Metz and Henry Hoffman were the leaders in what has become a revolution in hackle quality.

Genetic control of the flocks and the occasional addition of new breeding stock have produced necks and saddles that are truly amazing. I've even heard of one major hackle grower who is attempting to raise roosters with longer legs to keep the saddle hackles from dragging on the ground. Where will it end?

SADDLE HACKLE

NECK (OR CAPE) HACKLE

Lately, it seems as if saddle hackles are being pushed on us by every hackle grower in the country. They are beautiful products. The colors are getting better each year and the length of the individual feathers is seldom shorter than 11 inches. Not only that, but the per-inch hackle-fiber count is increasing, which means you can now fully hackle a dry fly with only three or four turns of saddle hackle on a pattern that used to require six or seven turns of neck (cape) hackle (I remember having to use two neck hackles on some flies to get it right). And the ever-finer hackle quills (the center stems) are getting stronger.

The question has now become which to choose: necks or saddles? Or both? How do we get the most for our dollars? I hope some of the following will help you decide.

There are some problems with saddle hackle. First, there are usually no more than two or three different hackle sizes on any given saddle patch. Second (and I consider this the most frustrating), the traditional grading of #1, #2, #3, etc. that has been used for years for neck hackle does not necessarily indicate the size of flies you will be able to tie from a given saddle patch. The grading system for saddles seems to have more to do with length and quantity of the feathers than with their size.

Nearly as frustrating is the fact that you will often find that a single saddle hackle contains two (sometimes three) different lengths of hackle fibers. You simply must use a hackle guage when buying a saddle patch to determine that it indeed contains the size hackle you're looking for. Those long, skinny, thread-like hackles that appear to be size 18 and 20 are often size 16 and 14. When you begin tying, you must use a hackle guage for the entire length of each feather to prevent under-sizing or oversizing the hackle collar.

Considering the hundreds of necks and saddles that someone—who may not be a fly tier—has to grade every day, there will always be some error. And it's not easy to find a saddle patch that contains hackles that will allow you to tie size 12 and larger dry flies. I tie a lot of size 12 Colorado Green Drakes for several accounts, and I like to use olive-dyed grizzly

mixed with medium dun for the hackle collar. I have lots of size 12 medium-dun neck hackle left over from years of tying little Blue-Wing Olives, so that color isn't a problem. Grizzly is another matter, so I once ordered two dozen grade 4 grizzly saddle patches and was assured they would contain mostly size 12 and 10 hack-les, with a few in size 14. Of the 24 patches, only four had mostly size 12 hackle. The remaining 20 saddles all contained size 16 and 14 hackles, with only a few size 12.

I buy all my tying supplies from whole-salers, with the exception of saddles, which I prefer to use when hackling parachutes.

Then I go to one of the nearby fly shops with my hackle gauge, make my selections and pay retail. It's worth it in the long run because I get exactly what I want in the shortest amount of time. I once bought a #3 brown saddle whose hackles were mostly size 16 and 18, with a dozen or more size 20!

So we're back to that agonizing choice: Saddles or necks? Saddles do have a much greater yield in terms of the number of dry flies you can tie from one saddle (compared to one neck). The neck, however, will afford many more different sizes of hackles, plus the spades for tailing, and the neck butt feathers for streamer wings and quill bodies. You'll have to purchase several necks to equal the yield from one saddle per hook size. But you'll also have to purchase three or four saddle patches to find all the hackle sizes you can find on one neck. Add to this the fact that you're going to need at least the following basic colors: grizzly; brown; medium dun; light dun; ginger; cream; and black. That's a total of seven necks to tie almost any dry fly from size 22 through size 10. To achieve the same size range with saddles would require a minimum of three saddle patches per color, or 21 saddles! However, if you consider the number of flies you can tie from 21 saddle patches, you'll probably spend more money for necks to tie the same number of flies. You'll just be spending a little less a little more often. Cash flow can be a consideration.

Dryfly neck retail prices range from as much as $125 to as little as $25, with an average cost of $75 per neck if we use those high and low Figures. Saddles range from $90 to a low of $12, with an average cost of $51 per saddle. Generally speaking, you get about what you pay for. The more expensive necks will contain more feathers that are longer and in a wider range of hackle sizes, often down to 24 and 26, with a few 28 and possibly some 32. The top-of-the-line saddles will have much longer hackle feathers and more of them, but you will still be pretty much limited to two or three hook sizes per saddle.

It looks like a no-brainer: Saddles are cheaper and you get a greater yield of flies per dollar, right? Take another look at it.

Carefully decide what size flies you tie the most and what your budget will allow, and make your purchases very selectively. If you can afford the very best, seven top-quality dryfly necks (one of each color listed above) at $125 each will set you back $875. If we can agree that it will take three saddles to equal all the hook sizes available on one neck, then 21 top saddles will set you back a whopping $1,890. Or set your sites a little lower and buy medium grade; at $75 each, seven medium-grade necks will cost you $525, while 21 medium-grade saddles ($51 each) will dent your wallet to the tune of $1,071. But before you run out and start buying hackle, think about where you're going to find size 20 and smaller hackles.

What do I do? Except for grizzly, I order #3 cream-white necks and dye them to the colors I need. I can get all the hackle sizes I need from a single neck. Usually this means I need size 22 through 12. And there's the very important bonus of spade hackles for tailing, which I haven't been able to find on any saddle in the lengths I need without stacking. Some large streamer and bass-bug necks now available have some usable tailing material, but it adds to the cost of producing dry flies.

Individual neck hackles these days are beginning to contain hackle fibers of a consistent length almost to the tip of each feather. And the hackle-fiber count per inch is getting better on neck hackle, too. They are from the same birds as saddles, aren't they? If I order grade 3 necks, I am almost assured of some web on each hackle feather, which I prefer because I can achieve the illusion of a thicker thorax on the completed fly. When waterproofed with some kind of silicone-based fly flotant, the softer web does not soak up water. And I can even use some of the stripped butt hackle feathers for quill bodies. The quills on saddles are simply too thin for this.

You get the idea. My answer is to stay with what works best for me, which is #3 necks.

Or we could all take up nymphing and not have to worry about any of this!

The Magic of the Adams

A veteran angler rediscovers the very best of the good, old standbys

A.K. Best
March 2005

Why an article about the Adams? Because I recently rediscovered the Adams as a lifesaver during what could otherwise have been a very frustrating day.

A few weeks ago, my friends Mike Clark and John Gierach invited me to fish some trout ponds not far from Boulder that had been stocked with some rainbow/steelhead hybrids several years ago. We've fished these ponds several times over the past few years and knew the trout were large, very strong, extremely fast and would eagerly rise to midges. It was mid-April, so we assumed that midges would be the order of the day. I packed fly boxes loaded with midge adult, emerger and larva patterns in all the colors that had been successful in the past.

When we arrived the pond was glassy smooth, with no rises, so I tied on a size 16 Peacock & Black hackled wet fly, tossed it on the water and began to strip out line for my first cast. An enormous rainbow appeared from nowhere and inhaled the fly with such sudden viciousness that it snapped the 5X tippet as though it were 10X. I tied on an identical pattern, tossed it onto the water and the same thing happened again! I hadn't made a cast, yet had lost two flies in as many minutes, and I was beginning to think it was either going to be a great day or I was going to be frustrated for most of it. I tied on my third and last Peacock & Black and carefully stripped off some line before casting. Of course, this time the fly was totally ignored.

Forty-five minutes later I was still casting without so much as a refusal look at my fly. It was then that I began to notice rises all over the pond. Notice? Hell, I could hear them. The trout sounded like bass slurping frogs! I looked for midges in the air and on the water but there were none. Instead, there were hundreds of small, gray mayflies riding the surface. *Callibaetis*? I wondered.

It was way too early in the season for *Callibaetis*. But when I carefully waded a little deeper and scooped an insect from the surface, it was a perfect size 17 *Callibaetis*! Great. I had left my box of *Callibaetis* duns, parachutes and spinners at home. All I had with me were some size 16 and 14 Adams. To condense the next six hours of fishing into a few sentences: I went home with only one of the six size 16 Adams I started with. I lost the first three on 5X tippet, the second two on 4X tippet, and was finally able to land my first fish (which I estimated to be somewhere in excess of six pounds) on a size 16 Adams and 3X tippet. I lost count of the number of fish I caught on that last Adams after landing something like two or three more trout that took me into my backing on each hookup.

The number of fish didn't matter at this point, only their brute strength and what seemed like lightning speed. I likened the experience to hooking a BMW going 85 mph on my backcast. I finally clipped off my last Adams long before the hatch was over and the trout had stopped rising. I didn't want to lose it because I wanted to tie an exact copy when I got home. What was I thinking? An Adams is an Adams. Or is it?

I'll bet everyone who has fly-fished for more than a week has a few Adams in their dryfly box. It's a fly that has saved many a day for more than a few fly fishers. It has a special place in my fly box because I once lived in the state where the Adams was born. While I don't often use them these days because I've become one of those types who likes to match what's on the water as closely as possible, there are times when the Adams will work when nothing else will. In fact, sometimes the Adams works so well it almost seems like cheating.

I once watched a guy catch trout after trout on some heavily fished catch-and-release water during a size 18 Blue-Wing Olive hatch by fishing a size 18 Adams dun. This was mind-boggling to me, since I was fishing the same hatch with a perfectly matched size 18 Olive Quill Dun and only doing half as well. Go Figure. I kept telling myself that my neighbor was simply a

better fly fisher than I—after all I did have the perfect fly, so what else could it be? Yet, his backcast was a little sloppy . . . .

Some fly fishers and tiers believe there are magical qualities in the combination of materials used to tie the Adams. Others believe the magic is in the silhouette the fly presents on the water, and still others are convinced that presentation is the key factor. I'm of the opinion that it might be a combination of all three, with a little extra weight thrown toward the presentation theory. In a contest of skill versus equipment, skill is always supposed to win. But then again, there is that magical thing to consider.

Bobby Summers, formerly of the Paul Young Rod Co. and now building his own superb bamboo fly rods, took me to a pool on the Boardman River in Michigan years ago and told me, "The Adams was conceived here." We stood on an old iron bridge that spanned the Boardman and, as we watched the downstream pool for risers he added, "I think it was first tied on this bridge and fished in this pool—at least that's the local legend." I could almost feel the excitement and anticipation that Charles Adams must have felt as he tied on a new fly pattern and tried to determine how to fish it on the slowly boiling surface of this wide, flat pool.

Leonard Halladay, of Mayfield, Michigan, tied the first Adams and gave it to his friend, Charles F. Adams of Lorain, Ohio. In 1922, Adams became the first to fish the new pattern; hence the fly's name. Years ago I came across some very old, exquisitely tied dry flies at an estate sale near Michigan's Au Sable River. Among the large collection of flies were some Adams that I believe were tied after the original recipe, which Bobby told me was invented to represent a gray caddis.

I acquired those flies nearly 40 years ago and promptly put them in a separate box and labeled it "Old Adams." Alas, some damn little bugs got in there and chewed off most of the hackle. However, there is enough material remaining that I can give you the recipe and recreate the fly for photo purposes (see sidebar). It's a very different fly from most of the

Adams you'll see today in that each of the flies the bugs chewed on had golden pheasant tippets for the tails, and all of them were also tied on long-shank hooks.

I have no idea if the recipe on the facing page is really the original pattern or merely an adaptation of the original. The old man who died 40 years ago and whose estate was being liquidated was 80 years old when he passed on, so he was born before Leonard Halladay tied the first one. I Figure if the old man had a cabin on Michigan's Au Sable River, he must have been a devout trout fisherman and, if that is so, he was probably also aware of any new developments in fly-fishing just as we are today. I think it's rather nice that there remains some mystery about all this. But then, a lot about what we do holds many mysteries!

The same tail, body and hackle materials have been used on parachute versions of the Adams as well, with the exception that the wing post is usually white calftail, high-vis yarn or white turkey T-base segments. I'm not known as a mathematician, but if I remember correctly, to find the total number of possibilities for Adams dun variations using the list at right (see sidebar), you would multiply tails (9) x wings (7) x bodies (13) x hackles (5) for a total of 4,095 possible Adams variations, not counting hook sizes, parachutes or the female version! By the way, I was once given anatomically correct male and female Adams flies. I would never fish them because the identifying parts were made of monofilament and appropriately painted and I have this thing about using only natural materials on the flies I fish. I thought it very interesting that the identifying parts were more carefully constructed than the rest of the fly.

And of course we have all seen the Adams Irresistible. Incidentally, there are a number of tailing materials used for this fly as well. Some authors attribute the origin of the Irresistible to the creativity of Joe Messinger of Morgantown, West Virginia. Others say it was Harry Darbee of Livingston Manor, New York. I like to think it was Messinger, simply because I have become good friends with Joe, Jr., who ties them exactly as his father taught him.

Here, however, is the recipe I use to tie the Adams:

A.K.'s Adams:

Hook: Dryfly, size 10 to 22
Thread: Black 6/0 through size 18; 8/0 for size 20 and 22
Tail: Brown spade hackle fibers or brown dyed Coque de Leon
Body: Medium gray rabbit belly fur, very tightly dubbed and carrot-shaped
Wings: Pair of well marked grizzly hen hackle tips
Hackle: Brown and grizzly mixed

Given the number of possibilities for tying the Adams, coupled with the various hook sizes, we could easily fish an Adams and match damn near any mayfly hatch we're likely to encounter. Isn't that a wonderful tribute to Leonard Halladay?

And here's the recipe for those "original" Adams I bought at that estate sale:

"Original" Adams

Hook: 2X long, such as Mustad 94831 or 9672
Thread: Black 6/0
Tail: Small clump of golden pheasant tippets, slightly shorter than shank length
Body: Dark gray muskrat dubbing, tight and slender with very little body taper
Wings: Grizzly hackle tips tied delta-wing style and flat
Hackle: Very dark brown and grizzly mixed

There have been a few changes made in the way the Adams is tied since 1922, so I did a little research to try to find out how many different Adams pattern variations I could find in books, magazines, catalogs and Web archives. I even added some that I've seen in fly shops across the continent and in the fly boxes of fly fishers I've met along the stream. The list became so long I decided to construct a chart and list the various components. I'm pretty sure there are more than what follows, but I'd consider these the standard variations.

Tail:
Golden/pheasant tippets
Brown/grizzly mixed hackle fibers
Grizzly hackle fibers
Brown hackle fibers
Ginger hackle fibers
Dun hackle fibers
Black moose hair
Elk body hair
Deer body hair

Wings:
Grizzly hen tips
Light grizzly hen tips
Dark grizzly hen tips
Medium dun hen tips
Teal segments
White calf
Elk body

Hackle:
Light brown
Dark brown
Light grizzly
Dark grizzly
Black

Body:
Dark dun muskrat
Light dun muskrat
Brown muskrat
Stripped peacock herl
Stripped & dyed hackle quill
Yellow dubbing
Brown dubbing
Black dubbing
Dark olive dubbing
Light olive dubbing
Tan dubbing
Spun deer hair
Royal (peacock & red floss)

BLACK ADAMS

OLIVE ADAMS

YELLOW ADAMS

TAN ADAMS

BROWN TWISTED ADAMS

GRIZZLY-TAILED ADAMS

TEAL-WING ADAMS

HALF-SPENT ADAMS

ORIGINAL ADAMS

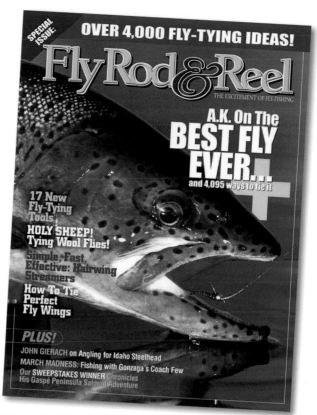

From the March 2005 issue

2006 Co-Angler of the Year:
Russell Blessing
The man behind the Woolly Bugger

Barry Beck
Jan/Feb 2006

One of the principal, if unspoken, rules of modern fly-fishing is: If everything else fails, try a Woolly Bugger. This was as true in 1967 as it is today.

On a hot August afternoon of that year, I found myself getting skunked by the trout of Pennsylvania's Little Lehigh River. I'd had some success during the morning Trico hatch, but as the sun climbed higher in the sky, the fish completely turned off. Now, this turn of events was far from unexpected—it was August in Pennsylvania, after all—and I dealt with the situation to the best of my abilities: I nymphed the heck out of a likely looking riffle with a cress bug imitation. But even this failed.

The half-dozen or so anglers who had been on the water for the morning hatch had sensibly departed hours earlier, and I was thinking of getting on my way as well, when I heard the sound of a fish being landed. I looked upstream and I watched as an angler released a large trout, and I remember thinking that he'd used up his luck for the day. But over the next 20 minutes the man led three more nice trout to the net.

By now I was totally fascinated (and flabbergasted); I couldn't imagine what sort of fly he was using. I intently watched his technique as he cast and began to retrieve his fly. Then it hit me: This guy was fishing a streamer, which was puzzling, as streamers rarely worked on this river. During a pause in his fishing I approached him, intent on learning his secret.

Our introduction was short and sweet. He said his name was Russ Blessing, and the fly he was using was a Woolly Bugger. I'd neither seen nor heard of such a pattern, so when he offered me one to try, I quickly tied it to my tippet. The Woolly Bugger worked like magic on the picky trout of the Little Lehigh that afternoon, and I proceeded to catch trout on it until the evening.

Back at the parking lot I ran into Russ again. He was parked next to my old Land Rover, and as we took apart our tackle Russ

36

filled me in on the details of his miraculous fly. He had come up with the pattern while trying to imitate the dobsonfly larva, experimenting with various designs and materials before settling on a fly that combined a chenille body with a marabou tail and a black hackle palmered over the chenille.

Strange as it now may seem, for a long time after that the Woolly Bugger still was known only to a small circle of anglers. But in 1984 I wrote an article for a fly-fishing magazine that officially introduced the Woolly Bugger to the public, and the rest, as they say, is history.

Fast forward to 2005. It scares me to think that 38 years have passed since that first encounter, and yet I am once again on the water, fishing with Russell Blessing. We are on my home stream, Fishing Creek, and Russ is here because I called him and said the fishing was not to be missed. He has no idea that what I really want to do (besides fish) is interview him for *FR&R*'s 2006 Angler of the Year profile.

Russ has always been a graceful caster, and I admire his presentation as I watch the leader and tippet turn over the tiny black beetle he is using. The trout's refusal simply urges Russell on and he tries again. I teasingly suggest that maybe he should try a Bugger. Russ replies that he's going to rest the water a bit and he joins me on the bank.

I awkwardly converse with him, not wanting to give anything away, and the conversation goes something like this:

BARRY: So, you're retired. Since when?
RUSS: 1996.
BARRY: What do you do with all the spare time?
RUSS: I fish.
BARRY: Did you ever think that the Woolly Bugger would become as popular as it is?
RUSS: Not initially, but after the story about it came out in '84 it soon became apparent that it had a universal appeal. Not only for trout but for other species as well.

BARRY: Your first design on the Bugger had a trimmed hackle and no tail, is that right?

RUSS: That's right, but I wanted to add more movement to the fly, so I added the marabou tail and after a few experiments I decided not to trim the hackle. What I liked most about the fly was that it looked alive in the water. Even if I dead-drifted it, the fly still had movement.

BARRY: Today you can find Buggers tied in almost any color scheme that you can think of. What's your favorite color?

RUSS: It's still the black hackle and the olive chenille body version.

BARRY: What hook sizes do you prefer?

RUSS: You'll probably be surprised, but I fish Buggers tied in sizes 12 through 16 a lot, and there are times when I fish them in even smaller sizes. But on big water it's not uncommon to tie on a size 4 or 6.

BARRY: You were friends and traveled with the late Vincent Marinaro, who by his own admission was a dryfly purist. What did Vince think of the Bugger?

RUSS: You know the answer to that. He despised it.

BARRY: What do you think about all of the alternative ideas that other fly tiers have come up with on the Bugger?

RUSS: Fly tiers are creative by nature, so slightly changing a pattern or incorporating new ideas into an existing pattern is a common practice. Besides, most modern patterns are based on an earlier design. Why all the questions?

BARRY: Just asking. No, actually I thought about doing another piece on the Woolly Bugger some day, and like all writers I'm just looking for information.

RUSS: That trout is back up, think I'll give him another try.

There were still questions left unanswered, but I gave in to Russell's desire to catch that fish. I wondered, as Russ entered the water, whether things would be vastly different for him if he had put his name on the Bugger. He could have named it the "Blessing Bugger" and chiseled his name into the annals of fly-fishing history, as well as turning a pretty penny from royalties.

But at the end of the day, as we talked more about the subject, Russ showed no regret or disappointment. Indeed, he seems quite content and pleased that his fly pattern has found its place not only in our fly boxes but in the history of our sport. To those of us lucky enough to know Russell we would expect nothing less, for he is a gentleman who has always shared his knowledge of fly-fishing and fly-tying with everyone he meets.

2006 Co-Angler of the Year:
John Betts

Historian, craftsman, conversationalist, author, artisan and angler

Darrel Martin
Jan/Feb 2006

Contemporary fly tiers are now so completely accustomed to working with a vast array of synthetic dressings that many of us have all but forgotten the not-so-distant days when few man-made materials had yet been incorporated into our ever-evolving craft. It took creativity and a number of long leaps of the imagination on the part of some late 20th Century fly-tying innovators to move us out of the relatively black-and-white world of all-natural tying materials and into the Technicolor universe of synthetic options. (Of course, many tiers still claim that natural materials are superior for a number of reasons, but that is a debate for another day . . . .)

Of those early innovators, none was more influential than a fly-fishing renaissance man named John Betts. Not only did Betts introduce a number of still-popular synthetic tying materials in the 1970's, but his 1980 book, *Synthetic Flies*, served to open the eyes of fly tiers around the globe. *FR&R*'s Darrel Martin caught up with Betts, one of the fly-fishing world's most unusual personalities, at the Colorado home from which he continues to fish, tinker and dream . . . .

John Betts continues to be a curiosity, a person in search of himself. Born in 1937 in Short Hills, New Jersey, he began his angling,

at age nine, with a $20 Montague rod, an Avon reel, a William Mills silk line, gut leaders and a dozen flies. His first casts were at an old Cape Cod fishing club, and his first fish was a 10-inch brook trout caught on a Black Gnat. He quickly lost that Gnat, so he took a Pflueger bait hook, mounted it in his father's bench vise and wrapped a pattern with feathers molted from his mother's pet, a bobwhite quail that lived in the front room.

After attending private schools, John entered Washington and Lee University in Lexington, Virginia. He took with him a 25-cent fly-tying kit, which included *The Noll Guide to Trout Flies and How to Tie Them*, a stamped aluminum F-vise, hooks and materials. The vise screw stripped out immediately, but he solved the problem with a clamped hemostat. From then on, tying traveled with John wherever he went.

At the university, John desperately wanted his name on the front page of *The New York Times* sports section. He wanted people to know his name and he wanted to excel in swimming (as his father had done at Yale). He broke into the swimming pool at night and swam countless laps to make the swim team. About the time he finally made the front page of the sports section, he flunked out of college; as he said, "You cannot swim at that level and study at the

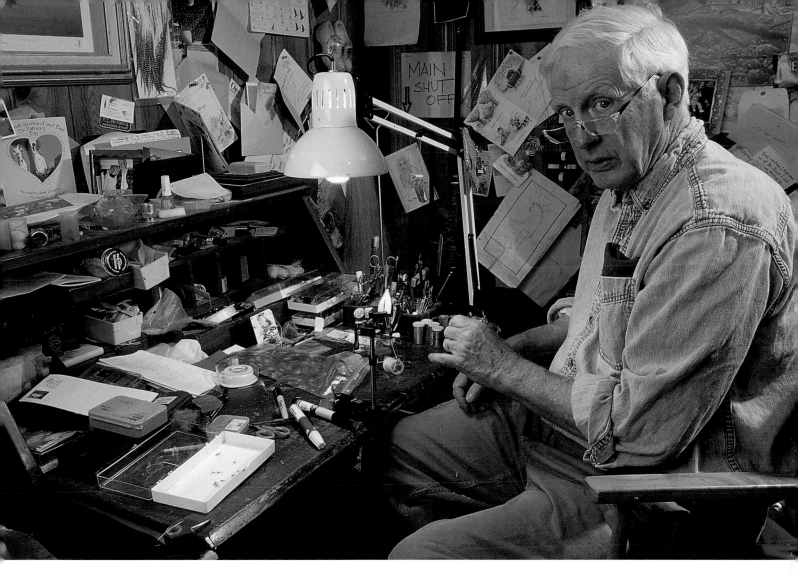

same time." John then enlisted in the Air Force.

Part of his Air Force duties included medical research for the Mercury and Apollo programs. He met the first astronauts, Werner von Braun and other notables. In flight medicine, John worked on white-out research, the Mercury capsules' artificial horizon system, and protective lenses for radiation and atomic flash. Part of his training included parachute qualification. John recalls, "There's nowhere anybody who had flunked out of college in his first semester would ever have a job like that in civilian life. It was a wonderful opportunity and I loved every moment." After the Air Force, John briefly returned to college; but again, it wasn't a good fit. The only thing left now was finding employment.

He subsequently worked at a variety of jobs—making concrete pipe in Wyoming, working briefly for the Bromley Mountain Ski Corporation in Vermont, and as a loan collector in Denver repossessing cars, clothes and televisions. As John recalls: "The worst job I ever had . . . God, it was just awful . . . the dumbest damn job!" Soon his father would offer a solution.

John's father was a director of Cheeseborough Ponds, the cosmetics company, and the president of International Pipe and Ceramics (Interpace). While traveling around the world to visit various Interpace branches, the elder Betts visited the Wildfowl Trust, in Gloucestershire, England. Impressed by the experience, he thought of John and encouraged him to be part of it. John quickly quit his summer job making concrete pipe, drove from Cheyenne to New Jersey nonstop, sold his car and bought a ticket to England.

He worked at the Wildfowl Trust for room and board plus 4-pounds-10 a week. With his car money, he bought a season's rod on the Coln, a lovely chalkstream at Fairford, outside of Cirencester. James Ogden, sometimes regarded as the best angler of the 19th Century, had frequented these waters. John saw Ogden's name in the game book, many pages before his own, but never realized until later who Ogden was. (Ogden wrote the 1879 book *Ogden on Fly Tying*, and was instrumental in the development and promulgation of the dry fly.) Nearly every night at "Ogden's Bar" in the Bull Inn, John watched the old tiers sip their pints and wrap fly patterns. Some of the old men, perhaps in their 80's, may even have known Ogden. Though John did not realize the opportunity before him, he would later make up for it. For him, fishing an English chalkstream was a new world of angling and history.

After his return to the States, John worked at Orvis in the early 1960s in Manchester, Vermont. He ran errands, did line splices, worked in sales and rod-making. John and Orvis soon parted company. "Getting fired in Manchester in the winter is no fun," he says. But Dick Finley, his good friend at Orvis, had done him a favor: His dismissal became the best thing that ever happened to him because it forced him to return to his education.

John drove to the University of Vermont. When college admissions asked him what he wanted to study, he replied, "I don't know. What is there?" They went down through the list until John spied forestry. It was then that he decided he had found his future. He finished the program with a forestry degree in three and a half years and never missed a class. There isn't a day that goes by that John is not aware of the education he was given, not necessarily about trees, but about how to learn.

After graduating, he opened his own business as a landscape designer, and it was then that he began to tie flies in earnest. He took advantage of some savings and a long seasonal layoff—November through May—in order to retreat to his cellar and do nothing but tie for the entire winter. The word went out, and the phone rang; he soon had an order for four dozen flies. Within the hour, another order arrived for more than 100 dozen. He filled the orders, and for three years John

laid bricks in the summer and tied flies in the winter. He also began to write about fly-tying, and experimenting with unconventional materials.

John first introduced a synthetic tailing fiber, later known as Microfibetts, in 1976. Other synthetics followed: Organza (a wing material), and then in 1985, Zelon (a tail, wing and body material). Of the latter John comments, "God, I don't know how many units of that I sold, perhaps three- or four-hundred thousand, I guess." In the mid-1980's John, now know as "Mr. Synthetics," did a series of six magazine articles on manmade materials.

From 1995 to 1999 John published another series of 15 articles called "Traditions," a history of fly-tying. By then his privately printed books on fly-fishing included: *Synthetic Flies* (1980); *Flies with an Edited Hackle* (1981); and *Catch the Hatch* (with hand-painted mayflies, 1984; a second edition appeared in 2000). He illustrated all the titles himself.

Currently, John Betts publishes regularly in *The American Fly Fisher*, a quarterly put out by the American Museum of Fly Fishing, and he continues to be a creative craftsman. For instance, after learning that the six-strip fly rod was fully established by 1850 and that four-strip, solid-wood fly rods once were made, he began to wonder how a six-strip, solid-wood rod would work. So he set about making them. Creating many of his own unique tools for the job, John began to produce solid-wood rods, making his own brass ferrules, guides, reel seats and slip rings. John also makes his own tapered fly lines by pulling various lengths of nylon through a 40-pound braided line. The taper is created by staggering four-pound-test monofilament within the braid. The resulting fly line has the same weight and properties as silk line and, when impregnated with flotant, John finds them to be remarkably durable and pleasant to cast.

In 1987, John also began to handcraft his own fly reels: brass single-action and aluminum anti-reverse. His most recent reel has a dogwood spool and the brass back-plate design is the dogwood flower. The crank handle is mountain laurel: dogwood and laurel live together on the reel as they do in nature. These reels are made the old-fashioned way, with hacksaws, files and hand drills.

When John showed me pictures of his dogwood reel, he also shared the myth of the dogwood. In the beginning the dogwood was tall. Mankind used the dogwood for the tree of crucifixion. God decided then that this would never happen again and made the dogwood a small tree. The flower petals have a reddish-brown stain at each tip to signify the wounds of Christ. The blood-red center is the crown of thorns. This is vintage Betts—everything connects to everything else.

Betsy, John's gracious wife, has a doctorate in clinical psychology. She puts things into perspective. She once asked John, "How many fish have to die before you become famous?" To John this is a question that all anglers must face. Part of John's answer is his Tag hook, made by Partridge of Redditch. The Tag ("touch-and-go") hook has a ring or eye in place of the point. The object of the game now is the strike itself, like counting coup, rather than taking the fish. According to one commentator, "This changes the whole point of fishing."

John received the Hans de Groot Award from the Dutch Fly Fair for contributions to international fly tying. In 1998, he garnered The Austen-Hogan Award for writing from the American Museum of Fly-Fishing. And he was a featured artist of flies and reels in the American Craft Museum. His watercolor, "The Bubble," was chosen by the museum for their 30th-anniversary print. It also won fourth place in the prestigious printing competition, the International Gold Ink Awards.

Let John take you into his basement, his sanctum sanctorum of old books, piled rods, stacks of papers and publications—the tools that create his rich angling life. Then take one of his solid-wood rods out to the front street and make a cast—a smooth, responsive cast. John's discourse on books, rods and reels will enchant. He loves to share his knowledge, his experience, and himself. John, a cancer survivor, also participates in the Reel Recovery Program, a national non-profit organization that conducts fly-fishing retreats for men recovering from life-threatening cancer. John's gift is sharing.

Kathleen Achor, editor of *The American Fly Fisher*, notes that John is a living reminder that learning is as much play as work. She adds that "John studies how one thing leads to another—how advances in thought and technology in any field might ultimately set the stage for change, however subtle or grand, in our sport." And she recognizes, "Fly-fishing is lucky to have the likes of John Betts paying attention."

Gordon Wickstrom, author of *Notes from an Old Fly Book* and *Late in an Angler's Life*, knows John well: "He frightens the insecure and offends the self-assured." And he adds that, "If you are not teachable, stay away from him." I would add that John is just as tough on himself: He recognizes his own limitations. Wickstrom continues, "John has never played the bourgeois citizen. I think he has rarely, and not for long, been gainfully employed in the conventional sense. He is utterly independent. . . . John has enabled me to see how lying at the core of fly-fishing is what I want to call 'the principle of contingency.' That is, in its every aspect, fly-fishing is the expression and scion of some greater and abiding factor in human culture. And that this is the richest thing about our sport and its legacy . . . ." Wickstrom admires John's respect for the past. "He refuses ever to think that the ancients were in any way inferior in their angling technologies. He strongly holds for the efficiency and elegance of their solutions."

In Japan, there are people regarded as national treasures—artisans who devote themselves to perfection. John Betts is such a treasure. His mark on American angling is at once subtle and pervasive. John not only glories in angling history, but he enjoys sharing that knowledge and the peripheral minutiae of our sport. A tribute then to John Betts—historian, craftsman, conversationalist, author, artisan and angler. It is an honor to call John Betts a friend and Angler of the Year.

Don Quixote de la Michigan

Chasing giant mayflies on the Rogue and Muskegon rivers

Chad Mason
June 2007

Making a date to fish the *Hexagenia* hatch can feel like arranging to swap contraband. "Take a nap in the afternoon," Glen said. "Then eat a good supper and meet me in the asphalt lot behind the warehouse, ready to fish, at 8:45." Glen Blackwood operates Great Lakes Fly Fishing Company, a fine little fly shop near the Rogue River in Rockford, Michigan. We had met only a few minutes earlier, when I walked into Glen's shop for the first time. I had been in Michigan for less than 24 hours and my first order of business was locating a first-rate fly shop. I found what I was looking for at GLFFC.

Shortly before 9:00 PM we left our cars in a vacant parking lot, crossed a bike trail and descended a steep, slippery slope to the Rogue. It was early June and we found the river swollen and nearly opaque from recent rain. The conditions were less than auspicious, but hope springs eternal in the angler's heart. We waded into the upper end of a shallow riffle and stood there with our hands in the chest pockets of our waders, and our rods tucked under our arms. "Hurry up and wait," said Glen.

We watched the sky for bugs while we talked sporadically about our families, bird dogs, and the things we used to do for gainful employment. There in the hospitable space that opens wherever men stand in a river without fishing, we discovered that we had a few mutual friends and learned something of each other's ways. Then a long, companionable silence enveloped us until Glen finally raised a finger to the sky and broke it.

"There's a drake," he said.

It was 9:20 PM, and the first Brown Drake spinner had left the hardwood boughs to search for a mate above the Rogue. This single insect was soon joined by a few others, and then their numbers became like the leaves on the trees. They descended with darkness on the river, a veritable storm of mayflies so numerous we could actually hear them over the sounds of the Rogue, and the most obvious thing about the world was not the water below but the wings above.

"Still no Hexes," Glen said.

"And no rises," I replied.

Our rods were tucked into our armpits, partly from lack of rising trout, but partly from awe of the sheer immensity of the spinner fall. Up and down the river not another human soul was visible. Fishing drakes and Hexes is often lonelier than you might expect, when you consider that the density of these hatches very often lives up to the legends about them. This kind of thing should draw a crowd. Perhaps it is the darkness that keeps people away.

"A few weeks ago I saw a big sow bear and her cub right here," said Glen.

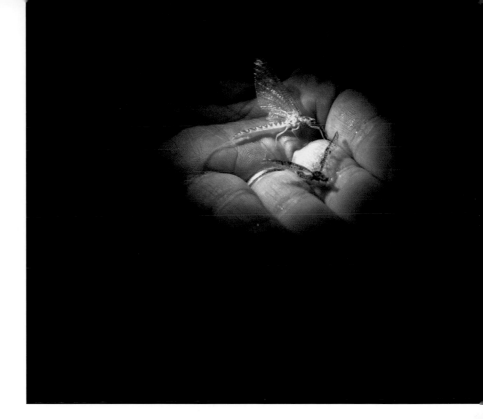

Whatever the reason, very few people—even among fly fishers—have ever witnessed this bug event that so defies belief. It gives you a feeling at once pleasurable and sad to stand there in the river knowing that you are but one of a few people in the world who know or care about what is happening. Amid so fecund a swarm of doomed creatures, it strikes me that the universality of death and the profligacy of life are not easily disentangled, and that most of our tribe is oblivious to the thoughts inspired by such a spectacle.

Sometimes the trout are oblivious, too. With the Rogue showing less than a foot of visibility, I imagined the fish lying lazily on the bottom, no more aware of the buzzing drakes than people watching television in their homes in Grand Rapids. Then I heard a splash and turned around to see Glen fighting a small trout. All color had drained from the river, and his red jacket looked gray.

I worked out some line myself, blindly feeling the rod loading and unloading. When it seemed that enough line was off the rod tip, I let it lie on the river. I heard a small splash out there and raised the rod into a fish that felt none too large for the few seconds that it was on. Then the night became very dark, and I had no more strikes for a long while.

"The Hexes are on," Glen said.

He was shining his flashlight onto the river, and in its beam uncountable bugs flopped and fluttered on the water. Many were the same Brown Drakes we had been watching for an hour, but some were absurdly large and meaty *Hexagenia* spinners, often called "the Giant Michigan Mayfly." The river's surface was alive with dying things, a rich conveyance of entomological triple cheeseburgers. But nowhere did a trout rise.

We watched the bugs and listened to them for another hour, breathing carefully to avoid inhaling them, and never caught another fish. When we left the river at midnight, Glen apologized for the lack of trout. He said the catching had been brisk until the recent rains discolored the river.

Perhaps here is another reason why so many people ignore the Hex hatch: A big hatch does not necessarily equal a big catch. Late May and early June are ripe with rain, which can throw the whole thing off. But if you want to chase Hexes, you can't be the kind of person who pursues only those things in life that are easily obtainable. This hatch, like few others, calls for the spirit of a windmill chaser, a Don Quixote de la Michigan.

I told Glen there was no need to be sorry, and thanked him for the great bug-watching safari. The hatch had become an end to itself and not a means to an end.

"There's always the Muskegon," he said.

The next afternoon I returned to Glen's shop to meet up with Don Graham, a guide who books clients through GLFFC. Don worked more than 30 years as a sales rep for a food company before "retiring" to guide anglers on the Muskegon. Don showed me numerous jaw-dropping photos of his clients with steelhead and salmon caught during the spring and fall runs. Anadromous fish are all well and good if that's what you like, but I would rather catch a 14-inch resident trout rising to a mayfly than a 14-pound steelhead after deep-drifting an egg pattern 50 times through the same run with frozen fingers.

Thankfully, you can do either on the Muskegon. This broad, deep and muscular river has few Hexes, since it lacks the soft, mucky-bottomed areas needed by the burrowing Hex nymph. But the Muskegon boasts a wonderful hatch of Gray Drakes, another large mayfly that dances at dusk.

After launching the boat from a steep concrete ramp, Don and I motored a few miles up the Muskegon. It was about 4:00 PM, and we passed the evening hours ripping streamers cross-current on medium-density shooting heads. We connected with a few fish that way, but we were only killing time until the drakes appeared.

Flowing at almost 2,400 cubic feet per second (about 30 percent above normal) the Muskegon looked like the sort of river you don't want to fall into. Though high and fast, the water was gin-clear. We could easily see our blue-and-white streamers racing through the depths. Infiltration by zebra mussels has clarified the Muskegon considerably, allowing sunlight to penetrate the depths and energize a number of abundant insect hatches that previously had barely existed. To an already rich Muskegon River forage base of baitfish—imitated by our streamers—the usually pernicious mollusk has added large numbers of Sulphurs, caddis, Mahogany Duns, Blue-Wing Olives, Light Cahills, midges and Gray Drakes. It's hard to know what to think when an ecological disaster turns out so well.

The first Gray Drake duns lifted from the water shortly after 8:00 PM, and spinners were on the water an hour later. We found a pod of eager risers in a swift midstream run, just downstream from a dark pool at the base of a cliff. While Don anchored the boat within casting distance of the fish, I began to cast.

In addition to Gray Drakes, tan caddis and Sulphurs were coming off in considerable numbers. I managed to land a couple of smaller fish on a size 14 Elkhair Caddis before a large fish rose almost directly downstream from the boat. After watching a couple more rises from the same fish, we decided two facts were certain: It was a hell of a fish, and it was taking the drake duns.

Don handed me a simple dun pattern in size 10. I dropped it a few inches upstream of the fish's presumed location, and it promptly disappeared as the fish rose dolphin-like and engulfed it. I could not tell exactly how big the fish was, but Don—who spends 130 days a year on the Muskegon—said "Oh my God" when he saw it, and I remember thinking that I'd need both hands to hold it for a picture.

The reel screamed and Don hurriedly pulled anchor to follow the fish. But this trout was broad and long and deep and full of the kind of brawn that fish everywhere gain from living in strong rivers, and I couldn't do anything with it. The fish played me for several minutes, never showing itself, and then the rod finally went straight and still. Dejected, I pulled in the line to find the tattered dun pattern still hanging at the end of my 5X tippet. I looked wistfully downriver after the windmill that I had glimpsed for only a moment.

Minutes later, I landed a husky brown of 17 inches as dusk fell on the river. This one also took the Gray Drake dun pattern, and fought with all the fury of a much larger fish. It wasn't quite the trout I had come for, but that's just as well. If you ever land the fish that you came for, the quest is over.

If you want to chase Hexes, you can't be the kind of person who pursues only those things in life that are easily obtainable. This hatch, like few others, calls for the spirit of a windmill chaser, a Don Quixote de la Michigan.

Hook: Mustad 94831, size 6
Thread: Brown 6/0
Tail: Moose body hairs
Ribbing: Furnace saddle hackle, tied in by the tip at rear of shank and wound forward over body
Body: Yellow deer hair, tied reverse at front of body, folded back along shank, and held down with ribbing. Measure to ensure tips extend slightly behind bend of shank
Wing: White calftail, upright and divided
Hackle: Brown saddle hackle; heavily hackled for good flotation

Hairwing Hex

Brown Para-Drake

Hook: Mustad 94840, size 10
Thread: Brown 6/0
Tail: Pheasant tail fibers or moose body hairs
Body: Yellow deer hair, tied reverse at front of body, folded back along shank, and held down with ribbing. Measure to ensure tips extend slightly behind bend of shank
Rib: Tying thread
Wing: Gray poly yarn
Hackle: Brown saddle hackle, parachute-style

Hook: Mustad 94849, size 10
Thread: Gray 8/0
Tail: Moose body hairs
Body: Gray muskrat fur, guard hairs removed
Wing: Mallard flank, upright and divided (Cahill style)
Hackle: Grizzly saddle hackle; heavily hackled for good flotation

Gray Drake

The T.P. Stickleback Streamer

Jay "Fishy" Fullum
Nov/Dec 1996

Thirty years of pursuing stream trout has been a strong influence on my fly-tying. Even when I am tying flies that are meant to imitate things other than aquatic insects, I am always very much aware of the importance of matching the imitation to the natural. If a well-tied fly can convince a wary brown trout that the combination of steel, fur and feathers that just drifted by is a specific insect, then why shouldn't the tier make the same effort to produce a streamer that looks like the real thing?

Down through the years I've tied thousands of streamers. Some of these patterns were concocted of brightly colored materials, the final product resembling nothing that ever swam in fresh or salt water. But while most of the streamers I've tied and fished were created to imitate specific baitfish, including shiners, sculpin, dace, smelt, even adult herring, I'd never come across a fly that would imitate the small fish that struggling smallmouth sometimes spat up into the bottom of my boat.

After identifying these small fish as sticklebacks, I tried fishing a few of the established patterns that vaguely resembled the naturals. I took a few fish, but I was not convinced that any of the flies really looked like a stickleback. The overall shape of conventional streamers just didn't have the extended body and tail of the real thing.

It was the distinctive body and tail that presented the main problem when I first attempted to come up with a stickleback imitation. But since developing the "toothpick method" used to extend the body of these streamers, I have successfully fished this pattern in waters containing resident populations of sticklebacks, especially one of my favorite lakes in southern Québec. Success on this lake was not a surprise, since I developed the fly soon after several bass I caught there regurgitated a mess of the naturals into the bottom of my boat. What has surprised me is that this streamer has also been very productive when fished in waters that do not even contain sticklebacks. Numerous warmwater and cold-water species have been taken on the T.P. (toothpick) Stickleback since I developed it, including some gamefish that I am sure have never seen an example of the real thing.

Although it is "merely" a baitfish, the stickleback is an interesting creature in its own right. The sticklebacks, members of the family Gasterosteidae, are inhabitants of the North Temperate Zone, with most species found in North America. The brook stickleback occurs only in fresh water, while the threespine and the fourspine species are common to both fresh and salt water. (The fourspine stickleback prefers salt water.) All species of sticklebacks may be found in many of the waters that we fish and are commonly preyed upon

by the larger fish that we hope to catch, especially during the sticklebacks' spring spawn.

Breeding habits may vary slightly from species to species, but all of these little nest builders are fascinating to watch during their time of courtship and breeding. The male builds a nest, cementing together bits of algae or plant detritus with a substance discharged from his kidneys. Once the nest is completed the female stickleback enters it, deposits her eggs and squirms out the other side. The male then enters the nest, fertilizes the spawn and cares for the eggs by fanning them, keeping the nest repaired and driving off intruders. After the eggs hatch the male herds the fry around the nest until the new generation becomes too active to retrieve, at which time he abandons them.

I apologize for the extra steps required to make the extended body and tail on the T.P. Stickleback. I generally prefer simple ties with fewer steps but, in this case, the complications are well worth the trouble, and I recommend that you tie up a selection of these streamers and try them on your favorite water. You may vary the overall color of the streamer, tying additional sticklebacks in mottled shades of tan and olive; I've had success fishing this fly in a variety of colors. I'm convinced that the extended body and the tail are the primary reasons why this particular streamer is so productive.

Tying the T.P. Stickleback

❶ Tie a section of a round toothpick onto the top of the hook. The point of the toothpick should extend ⅜" beyond the hook bend.

❷ Select a matched pair of light-brown partridge or hen pheasant feathers. Place the two feathers back-to-back and trim them to the shape of the tail (see illustrations). Don't cut the tail from the tips of these feathers; cut off the first third of the feathers, then cut them to shape. Using a portion closer to the butt strengthens the tail, as the quill is thicker there. With the hook reversed in the vice, tie on the tail sections and add a drop of head cement.

❸ Cover the extended portion of the body with light-brown dubbing. Return the hook to its normal position in the vise and tie in a length of silver oval tinsel. Finish off the body using more of the dubbing. The body should cover only the first ⅔ of the hook shank. Color the top of the dubbed body with a reddish-brown marker.

❹ Select a pair of dyed brown grizzly hackles for the wing and strip the hackle barbs from them until you have the length you want. Choose feathers with pointed tips rather than round; the pointed tips improve the shape of the body once the wing is attached. Attach the front of the

Hook: #4 straight-eye streamer
Thread: 3/0 white
Extended Body: Section of a round toothpick
Tail: Two partridge or hen pheasant feathers trimmed to shape
Body: Any coarse, light-brown dubbing
Ribbing: Silver oval tinsel
Wing: A matched pair of dyed brown grizzly hackles
Head: Trimmed lamb's wool, colored with marker
Eyes: Very small doll eyes, attached with 5-minute epoxy

wing with several wraps of thread and remove the excess, then pull the wing tight and make the first wrap around the body and through the wing using the gold tinsel. Continue the rib forward to complete the Matuka-style wing, then tie off the tinsel and remove the excess.

❺ Tie in the lamb's wool head, then tie off the head and add a drop of head cement before trimming it to shape with scissors. Color both sides of the wool head with a light brown marker, then color the top of the head with a black marker. Color the bottom portion with a bright red marker.

❻ Attach the doll eyes with 5-minute epoxy.

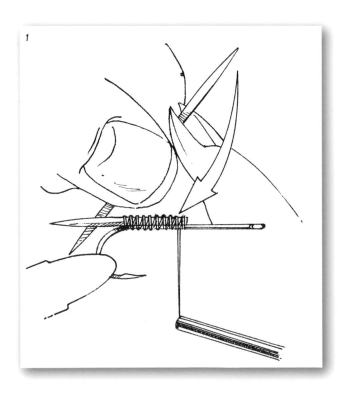

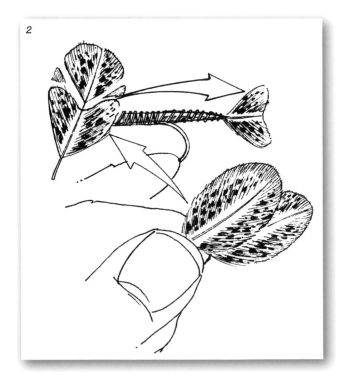

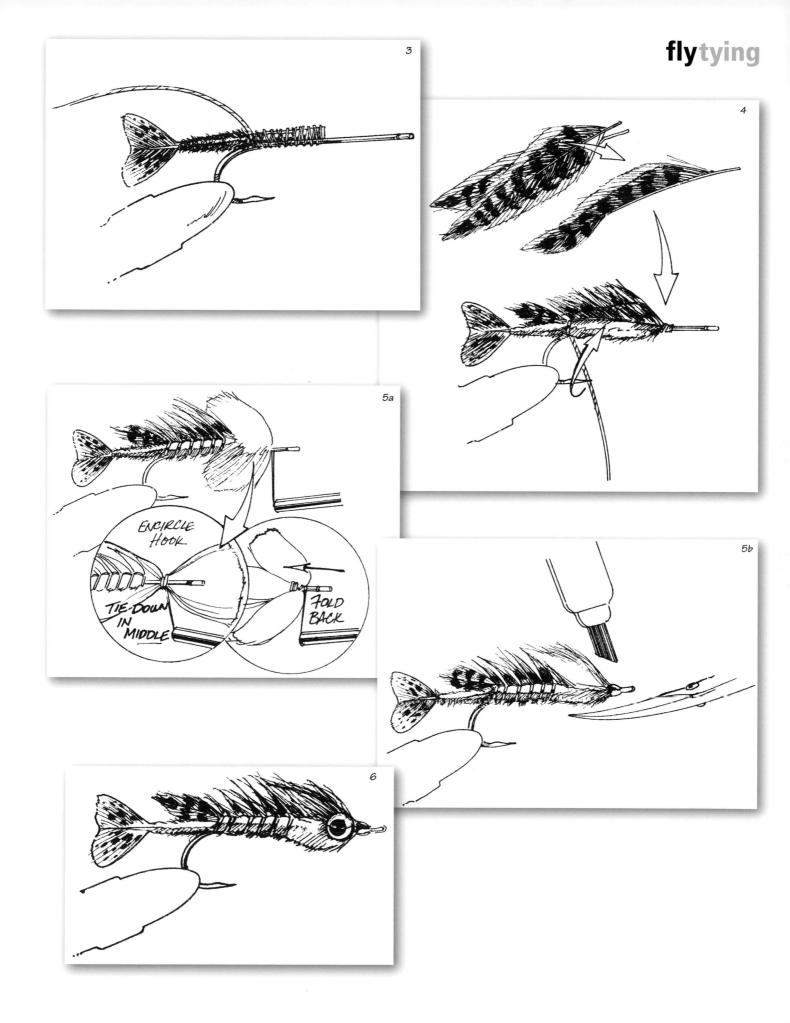

3

4

5a

ENCIRCLE
HOOK

TIE DOWN
IN
MIDDLE

FOLD
BACK

5b

6

From the Mind of Matarelli

Tying tools made with passion and perfection

Darrel Martin
Jan/Feb 1997

Years ago, in West Yellowstone, Montana, I gave a program on streamside tying for the Federation of Fly Fishers. I demonstrated my compact tying kit, complete with a shortened Matarelli bobbin. After the talk, a gentleman with a wry smile took me to task for mutilating such an elegant tool. He was Frank Matarelli.

Weeks later, Matarelli sent me several specially shortened fine-tube midge bobbins. An enclosed note informed me that I would never have to mutilate a Matarelli again. He also added that he would never make more because they were too damn hard to form. They were a gift.

Frank Matarelli received his machinist apprenticeship at the Caterpillar Tractor Co., in Peoria, Illinois. In the early days of World War II he worked for Studebaker, in South Bend, Indiana, and later as a machinist supervisor at the Higgins-Tucker plant in New Orleans.

Matarelli felt like a "damn Yankee" in New Orleans. Finally, he and his wife, Helen, decided to move to her hometown, San Francisco. In San Francisco, he worked at the US Pipe Bending Co., making pipe for the Navy. As the War deepened, Matarelli began work at the UC Berkeley radiation laboratory. He stayed there through the war. His work was part of the Manhattan Project, the venture that created the atom bomb.

His experimentation work with exotic metals produced some interesting tales. One day he was asked to mill some bronze-like bar stock. To test the hardness, he scratched it. His scribe created flying sparks that popped like brilliant star bursts. Years later, he recognized that his "tubaloy" bar stock was metallic uranium.

After the war Matarelli went to work as maintenance machinist for the San Francisco *Examiner*; he continued with the newspaper for 36 years. Now there was time for other things—things that would bring him into the world of fly-fishing and fly-tying. It was just a short distance from his home on Irving Street to the casting ponds of the Golden Gate Angling and Casting Club. The GGACC, established in 1933 as an offshoot of the San Francisco Fly Casting Club (itself founded in 1894), was instrumental in producing many innovations in fly-tying and fly-fishing. It was the right time and place for Matarelli. Some members of the club quickly discovered that he was gifted at splicing lines and repairing fly reels. He soon became a member. Jack Horner, creator of the Horner Deer Hair Fly, taught Frank to tie flies. Under Horner's tutelage and with the help of other club talent, Matarelli himself became a tier. Unknowingly, Jack Horner thereby did an immense service to every American tier.

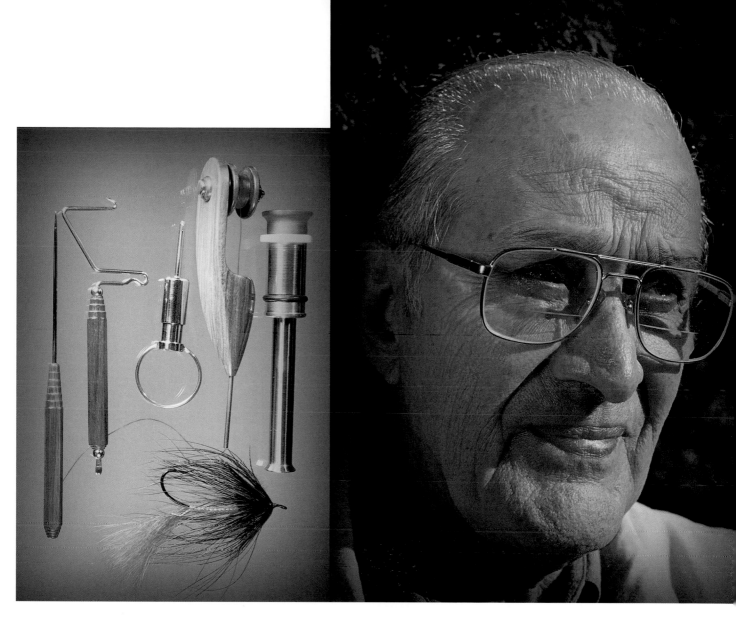

Horner never used a bobbin; he instead caught his tying thread on a mounted rubber button when he had to release it. Matarelli tried Horner's method, but his rough machinist's hands snagged the thread. He needed a bobbin. And so he solved the problem as a machinist would: He made one. His first bobbins appeared about 1952. When Cal Bird opened his San Francisco fly shop, in 1966, he sold Frank's bobbins. Bird would soon sell them to other shops and the word slowly spread. No bobbin matched the craftsmanship of a Matarelli. Matarelli produced high-quality, hand-polished stainless-steel tools, as opposed to the chromed tools so prevalent in the early days.

Horner also introduced Matarelli to fly-fishing the waters of Yellowstone National Park. Since 1951, Frank has only missed one year (1995) of fishing there.

In those early years Matarelli explored the Yellowstone country and he fell in love with the Firehole. Those were the days, he recalls, when large trout commonly rose to dry flies. Once, while fishing the Firehole, Matarelli met an angler who had snagged his plug and wanted Matarelli, who was in waders, to retrieve it. Matarelli waded out, broke off the plug and informed the angler that the Firehole was fly-fishing-only. Matarelli recalls his Firehole years as some of his best angling. To affirm his love of the place, he bought a cabin in West Yellowstone.

And he continued to tie. But he never could work the whip-finishers then available. He always pulled the thread off the head of the fly. He visualized what his fingers did when wrapping a whip-finish and then designed, in the late 1950s, an ingenious yet simple tool to duplicate this action. Unlike the English whip-finisher, which rotated on the head of the fly, the Matarelli whip-finisher does not touch the fly. The tip hook of the Matarelli tool prevents the thread from escaping. Furthermore, the Matarelli whip can be rocked back and forth, extending the thread for continuous wrapping. Only the thread touches the fly. Frank's whip-finisher, patent #RE 29,604, finally made whipping simple and fast. Few tying tools match the simple, elegant beauty of the Matarelli whip-finisher.

The tools commercially made by Matarelli include a standard whip-finisher, an extended-reach whip-finisher, a standard bobbin, a midge bobbin, a long-tube bobbin, a material bobbin, standard bobbin thread cleaner, midge bobbin thread cleaner and shepherd hook (dubbing twister). Matarelli's tools are a family affair. His wife Helen and his son Frank, Jr. both work in the family business, making, packaging or shipping.

Matarelli has, through the years, made many unique tying tools, tools too expensive for commercial production. Perhaps his most coveted custom tool is his brass and stainless-steel hackle pliers; they've sold for as much as $100 at auction. No, don't call him for any non-commercial custom tool. Such tools are rare and only given to friends and worthy causes.

Only an enormous amount of handwork produces a Matarelli tool. He forms and polishes each hook and bend by hand. The bobbin tubes alone undergo cutting, burnishing of the ends, grinding to precise length, radial chamfering, a tumble polish, buffing of the ends, hand polishing, buffing of the soldering and a final tumble polish. Hand-polishing the bobbin tube includes buffing the inside of each tube with a special tool. Not only does Frank create the tools, he also creates the tools that create the tools.

When buffing, Frank must take great care that the tool does not snag the buffing wheel and become a weed-whacker.

(Matarelli has had a stainless-steel rod put through his finger this way.) Wherever the thread touches a tool, including the finely tapered hooks, must be polished to a glassy smoothness. A long, hard day produces about 280 whip-finishers.

According to tier Ted Niemeyer, Matarelli loves a challenge. He is a perfectionist, intrigued by mechanical problems. In the early 1970s Keith Fulsher showed Niemeyer a Matarelli bobbin. The quality enthralled him. This was the first time he had heard the Matarelli name. Later, Niemeyer presented a tying demonstration at Jack Mickiewicz's shop, in Phoenixville, Pennsylvania. Mickiewicz carried various sporting goods, including archery products. Niemeyer watched burners shape the fletching on arrows. Perhaps, he thought, feathers could be burnt to form wings and wing cases. He dissected stoneflies from the Beaverkill and Battenkill. He detached the wings, dried and then traced them. Niemeyer wrote to Matarelli, sending the drawings of the various wing patterns. In time, Matarelli sent back some wing burners. The Matarelli wing burners were bowed to keep the tips closed and, if narrow, had alignment pins. They were so complicated that Matarelli never made a set for himself.

Months later, at a sportsmen's show in New Jersey, Niemeyer demonstrated his burners. Enthusiastic tiers traced the burners and, within the year, various wing burners appeared on the market. There was never a mention of Matarelli. According to Niemeyer, no manufacturer has ever matched the original quality of Matarelli's burners. Niemeyer concludes, as many tiers can, "Matarelli made my fly-tying days very rich."

Recognition of Frank's inventiveness and craftsmanship grows steadily. In 1987 he received a coveted *Fly Rod & Reel* Kudo award for his tools and craftsmanship. He is also a charter member of the Federation of Fly Fishers. And, in January of 1996, Frank Matarelli was inducted into the Federation of Fly Fishers' Northern California Council Hall of Fame. Lorna Carriveau, president of the

Northern California Council, sums up the achievements of a lifetime: "Frank Matarelli is inducted into the Hall of Fame for his insight and inventiveness in solving fly-tying problems. His tools have enhanced the enjoyment and abilities of novice and professional fly tiers alike. At a very personal level, Frank has made available to his colleagues his genius in dealing with materials and stubborn mechanical problems. This generosity has enabled master tiers and anglers to advance their personal expertise and elevate the art of fly-fishing and fly-tying." Today there are few tiers who do not own a Matarelli tool and fewer still who have not heard his name.

Frank has never advertised his tools or himself. He has never had to. Because of his quiet modesty, I had to spend several months just to convince him to do an interview with me. He said that he was not worthy of such interest. He only wanted to pursue his quiet art. Matarelli continues to produce as many as 25,000 tools a year. Though he talks of retirement, he has made no decisions yet—and he turned 80 this past June.

Through the years Matarelli has helped me in various ways. Not only did he make that special tool I sought, but he did it with bright enthusiasm. Truly, his ability to conceive spatially and to solve mechanical problems has significantly advanced American fly-tying. The modern tier today is a better tier because of Frank. To the true craftsman like Matarelli, "life is so short, the craft so long to learn." There are imitators of his tools, but all imitators fall short. They fail to copy the passion found in the buffed and burnished detail of a fine tool made in a garage shop in the city by the bay.

Streamers for Big Smallies

These half-dozen patterns are guaranteed to attract trophy bronzebacks, nationwide

Harry Murray
April 2008

For their brute strength and aerial acrobatics, smallmouth bass have a well-deserved place high in the rankings of gamefish. And their ubiquity across our nation means no matter where you live, you're never too far from smallmouth water. Sure, nothing beats catching a smallmouth on a topwater bass bug; but to consistently catch trophy smallmouth, I recommend tying and fishing one of the streamers you see here. The reason is simple: As smallmouth bass grow larger, they feed primarily on minnows. I've found that these six streamers will catch smallmouth in every river and lake in which I've tried them.

Tying tip: To make these streamers more durable, use a 22-gauge hypodermic syringe to place a small drop of head cement at each tie-in and tie-off spot.

Ed Shenk's White Streamer

This is one of the finest chub minnow patterns we have. A very effective tactic for this pattern (and all streamers in general) is to wade below a riffle and make a 40-foot cast across the stream. Every five seconds or so, make a six-inch strip until the fly is 20 feet away. Extend each subsequent cast by 10 feet until you cover all the water within your range, and then wade downstream in 10-foot intervals and begin the casting sequence again. This method will present your streamer to every bass in the pool. Be ready for some explosive takes.

Shenk's White Streamer is also effective for smallmouth in lakes and ponds. From a boat, canoe or float tube, cruise parallel to the shore 50 feet out and cast your streamer tight against the bank and slowly strip it back for 10 feet before picking up and casting farther down the shore. Systematically covering the shore with this tactic will catch many large bass.

Hook: Mustad 9672, size 4 to 8
Thread: Gray 3/0 prewaxed Monocord
Weight: Lead-free wire, 0.020"
Tail: White marabou
Body: White rabbit fur

❶ Cover the hook shank with thread. Wrap the lead-free wire over the middle third of the hook shank. Tie in a clump of white marabou equal in length to the hook shank over the hook bend.

❷ Form a dubbing loop at mid-shank with the tying thread. Insert the spinning tool in the loop and allow it to hang straight down. Trim the white rabbit fur from the hide and place it in the dubbing loop so it lies perpendicular to the loop.

❸ Spin the spinning tool to lock the rabbit fur inside the thread loop.

❹ Starting at the hook bend, wind the dubbing loop forward in snug adjacent wraps to the hook eye, and then tie it off with thread. Trim off any excess dubbing. Use a dubbing needle or bodkin to pluck out the rabbit fur so it sticks out at right angles to the hook shank. Note: Depending on the size of the hook and the amount of fur you place in the loop in Step 3, you may need two dubbing loops of fur to reach the hook shank.

❺ Whip-finish and trim the thread. Use scissors to trim the fly to a minnow shape, and apply a drop of cement to the thread head.

Murray's Mad Tom

Madtoms, those ugly minnows that look like baby catfish, just might be the favorite food of river smallmouths. I grew up fishing Virginia's Shenandoah River and the top winners in the local Big Fish Contests were always caught on live madtoms.

Madtoms live beneath softball- to basketball-size stones on the riverbed. During low-light periods such as dusk and dawn, and in slightly discolored water, madtoms feed on insects and small minnows, and this is when the smallmouths pounce on them. The tails of pools are particularly good areas to target.

Here's how I fish this pattern: Wade into the river 200 feet upstream of the lower riffle and cast a Murray's Mad Tom across the current and swim it slowly across the stream bottom by stripping it four inches every 10 seconds. Do this as you work your way down to the end of the pool.

Hook: Mustad 9672, size 4 to 8
Thread: Black 3/0 prewaxed Monocord
Weight: Lead-free wire, 0.020"
Eyes: Metallic barbell eyes, ³⁄₁₆"
Tail: Black rabbit fur strip
Fins: Black rabbit fur
Body: Black rabbit fur

❶ Cover the hook shank with thread. Place 10 wraps of lead-free wire mid-shank, and tie in the metallic eyes on top of the shank ¼" behind the hook eye.

❷ Tie in a hook-shank-length strip of rabbit fur at the hook bend.

❸ Form a dubbing loop with the tying thread mid-shank, and insert the spinning tool into the loop, allowing it to hang straight down. Trim a large pinch of rabbit fur from the hide and insert it evenly into the dubbing loop. Spin the loop to lock the fur in place and use a dubbing needle or bodkin to pluck out the fur so much of it stands out at right angles to the loop.

❹ Starting at the hook bend, wind the dubbing loop all the way to the hook eye and tie off, trim the extra and whip-finish. Again, use a dubbing needle to tease out the rabbit fur so it sticks out at right angles to the hook shank. Note: Depending on the size of the hook and the amount of fur you place in the loop in Step 3, you may needed two dubbing loops of fur to reach the hook shank.

❺ Trim off the body, pectoral fins and head into a madtom shape. Cement the thread head.

Silver Outcast Streamer

Shiners are schooling minnows, and great numbers of them can be found over shallow gravel bars in water one to two feet deep. Smallmouths often prowl the edges where the gravel bars taper off into deeper water and feed on any shiners that stray away from the school. So you'll want to cast into the deep water and strip the streamer back toward the gravel bar. Expect to get the take in the interface where the deep water meets the gravel bar.

Once the aquatic grassbeds form along the bank in the summer, many shiners will congregate there. Casting a Silver Outcast Streamer against the grass and stripping it slowly out about 10 feet works great. The most productive areas are right beside the grass, so keep alert for the strike in the first several seconds after the fly touches down.

❶ Cover the hook shank with thread and coat with cement. Tie in a 6" piece of tinsel ¼" behind the hook eye and wind this to the hook bend and back to the tie-in spot with smooth, adjacent wraps. Tie off and trim.

❷ Form the wing by tying in the white bucktail over the hook shank so it extends about ½" behind the hook bend. Next tie in the yellow bucktail and finally the blue bucktail on top of the white. All three colors should be the same length. Trim the butts.

❸ Tie in three or four strands of peacock herl ⅛" behind the hook eye so they extend slightly beyond the bucktail to form the overwing. Trim the butts.

❹ Build up a head with the thread, whip-finish and add cement to the thread.

Hook: Mustad 9672, size 4 to 8
Thread: Black 3/0 prewaxed Monocord
Body: Medium flat mylar silver tinsel
Wing: White, yellow and blue bucktail
Overwing: Peacock herl

Murray's Perch Bucktail

This pattern imitates the fry of perch, bluegill and other panfish that congregate over marble-size gravel in one to two feet of water along riverbanks and islands. Target the lower end of the islands where these fry are found and systematically fan your casts over the shallows as you wade. Dawn and dusk are the best times to hit these spots.

Hook: Mustad 9672, size 4 to 8
Thread: Orange 3/0 prewaxed Monocord
Weight: Lead-free wire, 0.020"
Tail: Yellow and orange bucktail; copper Krystal Flash
Wing: Yellow and orange bucktail; copper Krystal Flash
Body: Yellow Crystal Chenille

❶ Wrap the hook shank with thread. Wrap the middle third of the shank with lead-free wire.

❷ Tie in the tail at the hook bend. The tail consists of hook-shank lengths of Krystal Flash over the orange bucktail over the yellow deer tail. Trim off the hair butts.

❸ Tie in a 6" piece of yellow Crystal Chenille over the bend of the hook and wind it forward in adjacent wraps to ¼" behind the hook eye. Tie off and trim.

❹ Tie in the wing (copper Krystal Flash over orange bucktail over yellow bucktail) ¼" behind the hook eye so it extends even with the end of the tail. Whip-finish and apply head cement.

Murray's Black Marauder

This is one of the most effective smallmouth flies we have, possibly because it simply looks like a big mouthful of something good to eat. Its ostrich herl tail produces a more realistic swimming action than marabou when fished across mixed currents or upstream into fast currents; and its uniform body shape, with no highly contrasting back and belly, makes it irresistible to bass. This pattern is particularly effective in deep pools.

Hook: Mustad 9672, size 4 to 8
Thread: Black 3/0 prewaxed Monocord
Eyes: Metallic barbell eyes, ³⁄₁₆" size
Tail: Black ostrich herl and black pearlescent Krystal Flash
Hackle: Black rooster saddle
Body: Opalescent black Estaz

❶ Cover the hook shank with thread and tie in the metallic eyes ¼" behind the hook eye.

❷ Tie in approximately 30 strands of ostrich herl over the hook bend so they extend a hook-shank length beyond the bend. Tie in six strands of Krystal Flash over the ostrich herl.

❸ Tie in a black saddle hackle over the hook point, followed by a 6" strip of Estaz.

❹ Wind the Estaz forward in snug wraps to the hook eye and tie it off. Trim off the excess Estaz. Wind the hackle forward in six to eight evenly spaced wraps to the hook eye and tie it off. Trim the excess hackle, build a neat head, whip-finish and cement the head.

Clouser Deep Sculpin Minnow

Sculpin are a mainstay on most rivers across the country and the Clouser Deep Sculpin Minnow will work for bass (and trout) just about anywhere. Sculpin live beneath cobblestones and although they do not school, if you find one sculpin you'll usually find more. A good tactic is to wade to where the riffle empties into the main part of the pool and cast straight across the current and strip the fly back slowly just above the streambed.

A floating line with a 9-foot, 2X leader will be suitable for fishing most sculpin patterns below riffles. However, if the current is exceptionally strong, rig up a moderately fast sink-tip fly line (with a 10- to 15-feet-per-second sink rate) with a 5-foot, 10-pound-test leader.

Hook: Mustad 3366, size 2 to 6
Thread: Brown 3/0 prewaxed Monocord
Eyes: ³⁄₁₆" metallic barbell eyes, red with black pupils
Belly: Tan bucktail
Back: Dark brown bucktail and copper Krystal Flash

1 Use the tying thread to build a bump of 20 wraps one-third of the way down the hook shank from the hook eye. Tie in the metallic eyes behind the bump.

2 Take a bunch of tan bucktail two hook-shanks in length and tie it in behind the hook eye. Hold this down between the metallic eyes and spiral the tying thread over it back to the hook bend, then back to the hook eye. Trim off the butts.

3 Tie in about 20 strands of Krystal Flash under the hook and cut them so they extend an inch beyond the tips of the bucktail.

4 Tie in under the hook shank a bunch of dark brown bucktail two hook-shanks in length; this bunch should be slightly thicker than the tan bucktail. Trim the excess hair and Krystal Flash and build a neat head with the tying thread. Whip-finish and coat the head with cement.

Tap's Bug
A bass bug that's among the all-time best

Jim Dean
November 2008

I'll bet I'm not the only warmwater angler whose fly boxes are crammed with new deer-hair bass bugs that will never get wet. They would catch bass, too. But, oh, how those bugs suffer for their creator's art. Many are ungainly to cast, or so stunningly realistic and time-consuming to tie (expensive, too, if you buy them) that I hold them in reserve like traveling exhibitions in a clear, plastic museum. Alas, the occasion to use them never seems quite worthy.

Look more closely, though, and you'll find a few compartments crammed with well-chewed bass bugs that seem very much out of place amid all the pristine glamour. These hard-fished bugs all share the same very simple design, and their beauty is apparent only when I fish them.

What makes this relatively nondescript surface pattern so special? I like to think of it as having been designed backwards—from fish to angler—a near-perfect, and wonderfully versatile, example of fly-fishing form following function. Fished with an occasional tremble, it looks like a half-drowned moth. Worked moderately, it delivers a delicious, bubble-trailing burble. Popped vigorously, it demands attention on big, wind-ripped waters. Even in large sizes, its flat bottom and streamlined shape make it easy to pick up at the end of a long cast, and it flies true to its target without

sailing, buzzing, whistling, twisting your leader or landing upside down—rare qualities where utility has been sacrificed to display the tier's skill.

The flat bottom and wasp-waisted design also expose a generous gap between the point of the hook and the body of the bug to ensure solid hookups and fewer lost fish—insufficient hook gap is a major flaw in many bugs. Furthermore, this deceptively simple bug is easy to tie and very durable. Best of all, no floating pattern I've ever used will outfish it for largemouths or smallmouths.

What innovator has developed such a bug? His name is H.G. Tapply, and his contribution to bass bugging is nearing its 70th anniversary. If that name sounds familiar it should. Tapply was a long-time editor, writer and originator of "The Sportsman's Notebook" (which included "Tap's Tips"), a monthly feature that he began writing for *Field & Stream* in 1950. Indeed, "Tap's Tips" was so popular that it continued to be reprinted in the magazine for many years following Tapply's retirement as associate editor in 1985. It was, however, in the late 1930s while he was editor of *Hunting and Fishing* Magazine that he developed his now-classic bug.

At that time, Tapply frequently fished the wide, tranquil meanders of the Charles River between Waltham and Auburndale,

Massachusetts, well upstream from where it flows into Boston Harbor. On lazy summer afternoons, he liked to cull his 12-foot, canvas-covered Penn Yann with one hand and cast with the other, his 8-foot split-cane fly rod flashing in the waning light, the greased silk line gently dropping a bug beside lily pads along the shore. When I spoke with him shortly before his passing, he recalled catching largemouths up to 4 pounds, and some nice chain pickerel, too.

"At that time," Tapply said, "I was using Joe Messinger's handsome deer-hair frogs, and although they caught fish, the splayed legs made them difficult to cast and they seemed almost too pretty to use. Then, Roy Yates, of Toledo, Ohio, sent me some bass bugs he had developed. He called his bug the Deacon. It had a floss body and closely trimmed head of deer hair about the size of an acorn. It cast beautifully, but it didn't create enough disturbance on the water to suit me. I began to fiddle with the pattern, and the bug I developed evolved from that."

Tapply tied some of his first variations with four flared hackles as tails, but he didn't like the way they buzzed past his ear, so he swapped the flared hackles for deer hair, which also improved the bug's buoyancy. He soon abandoned the floss for a body tied entirely out of spun, tightly packed deer hair, trimming it to a triangular shape with a flat face.

The first Tapply bugs I ever saw were given to me about 25 years ago by Matthew Hodgsdon, at that time director of The University of North Carolina Press, in Chapel Hill, and an old friend of Tapply's. As an avid bass-bugging enthusiast and student of early bass-bug history, Matt had been tying and fishing with replicas of many older bug patterns, and he thought the Tapply bugs were the best of the bunch.

Late one afternoon a few days later, I launched my 12-foot johnboat on the dark waters of an ancient mill pond rimmed with arrowroot and studded with stumps. Out of habit, I began fishing with a large cork popper, but it attracted little attention beyond an occasional bulge that indicated a possible refusal.

Thinking I needed something a bit more subtle, I knotted one of the Tapply bugs to my leader and began to fish it along the edge of the arrowroot. I had made only a couple of casts when the bug simply disappeared—subtle strikes are not uncommon on calm water—and I set the hook half-heartedly thinking that a small bluegill had grabbed the tail and pulled it under. The leader sliced the water in an audible sizzle, and the line burned a groove across my index finger. At the end of a 20-foot dash, there was a massive boil, and I could see the long, pale belly of a bass. A moment later, six ponderous pounds of largemouth cleared the water. That bass towed me around the lower end of the pond for what seemed an eternity until I finally got my fingers locked on its lower lip. Before dark, I landed several more nice bass, and my appreciation for Mr. Tapply's accomplishment began to grow.

Over the years, I've fished with countless patterns, both old and new, but I've never found another floating bass bug that incorporates so many desirable features quite so well. You can easily learn to tie your own, and that's good because commercial versions of Tap's Bugs that were once offered in a variety of colors are no longer available. The bug's originator, however, had a definite favorite.

"Any color will catch bass a long as it's yellow," Tapply told me, perhaps with tongue in cheek. "Actually, I don't think color makes much difference, and the only reason I tie my bugs in so many colors is to avoid boredom. I believe action is more important, and I think these bugs work best when yanked hard so they make a real loud 'glug'. A sink-tip fly line helps the bug create even more disturbance, a

trick I learned when I began using such lines so that I could quickly change to a streamer when that was more appropriate."

One of the greatest assets of Tap's Bug is its versatility. If you're on a big lake or river, especially if the water is choppy or muddy, a colorful bug that can create lots of noise will often bring those smallmouths and largemouths to the top. No deer-hair bug I know of will kick up more fuss that Tapply's creation, and his favorite tactic was to fish it in a sequence of vigorous pops with intermittent pauses.

On small lakes, millponds, farm ponds and sedate rivers, largemouths may sometimes prefer a more subtle approach, and I've generally had better luck working Tapply's bugs a bit more gently—even sometimes leaving them motionless for long pauses.

Smallmouths also sometimes prefer a quieter presentation. And I seem to have better luck with subdued colors on relatively calm waters, and my favorite Tapply bugs are tied with either an all-white or all-natural, gray-brown deer body hair on a size 2 hook. One modern variation that you may want to add is a monofilament weed guard. These work quite well, and will reduce frustration if you fish weedy waters.

If you don't tie flies often, this is a bug for you: Simply tie in a deer-hair tail, and spin clumps of deer hair up the hook shank. Tie off, and clip the bug to Tapply's inventive wedge shape. That's it.

Like most bugging enthusiasts, I fish diving and sinking flies when necessary, but I prefer to catch bass when they're eating their meals on top where I can keep an eye on their table manners. And of all the surface bugs I've used—classic or modern—I've never found a more popular snack to serve them than H.G. Tapply's simple little deer-hair bass bug.

1 Tie in the deer-hair tail.

2 Spin the first clump of deer hair.

3 Pack hair tightly with pen body or some other tube.

4 Keep spinning deer hair up the hook shank.

5 Add the red (or other color) deer hair.

6 Begin to trim the deer hair to shape.

7 A razor blade will help you groom the fly.

8 The finished Tap's Bug

A Hairy Problem

Dr. Deerhair, the guru of bass bugs, imparts his knowledge

Tim England
January/February 1996

I enjoy fishing bass bugs. Holding one in my hand conjures visions of warm summer evenings. In my mind I can see the lengthening shadows that bring stillness with them. The only sounds are the creak of an oar and the droning of frogs. A nighthawk dips its wings before me, and my senses are filled with the rhythm of my fly line carrying its cargo to some inviting target. My eyes strain to make out the form that I think is my bug. Suddenly, the mirror surface of the water is shattered. My rod is pulled into a straining arc, and I can feel the power behind my bug's demise. The feeling is electric.

Bass bugs are made out of a variety of materials. Cork, plastic, foam, balsa and deer hair all have their place. While I have bugs made of all these materials, my favorites are those of deer hair. You can purchase all manner of deerhair flies for bass these days and I think most of those available are excellent. Yet, if you tie trout flies for the pleasure of catching fish on them, why not do the same with bass bugs? Stick with me and I will give you not only the basics of making a simple deerhair bass bug, I'll share the steps to make anything out of hair. I will first caution you, however, that you must bring the right attitude to the table. If you are like me, you will struggle at first. But

do not despair. If you don't learn anything else from this article, learn these two things: Most good things in life require effort; and practice, practice, practice does a good bugmaker make.

I cannot, of course, even begin to cover every aspect of this subject here. I will assume you have basic tying skills, say intermediate level. If you do not, go out and get them. Then come on back.

The first thing you will need is a strong vise capable of holding a large hook. The next—surprise—is the proper hook. Many styles are available, but for this purpose use a Tiemco 8089 in a #6.

There are lots of opinions out there regarding thread; take it from me, you only need one for most deerhair work, and that's size A rod-winding thread, in white. I do use 3/0 Monocord in both white and red for some steps, as you'll see.

Let's see, you've got the vise, hooks, thread . . . . Now you need a large hair stacker, a comb or toothbrush to remove underhair and a pair of sturdy scissors like Thompson's ICE scissors. You will also need a bodkin, tweezers, the body from a ballpoint pen and single-edge razor blades (I like the GEM brand). Last, but not least, you will need a steam kettle.

There are some basic concepts you need to understand before we get started. The first is that you should not tie on a bare hook shank. "What?" you say. "But all the big boys of tying say otherwise." Trust me on this one, too; piles of deerhair flies (not to mention deer hair) have brought me to this conclusion, and I'll explain more later. Next is this thing called "spinning." It's a goofy term that says little about what you're really doing when you tie deer hair onto a hook. I do not know where the term comes from, yet it has become the accepted way of describing what we do when we encircle a hook shank with deer hair.

Which brings me to my next point: In order to master deer hair as a material, you must understand how to distribute it on a hook. Distribution of the hair is a function of thread control. The act of distributing the hair is a deliberate motion or set of motions. Speed has little to do with it. Thread type has everything to do with it, as does a wrapped hook shank. You will not always want to encircle a hook shank, for instance; instead you may want to distribute hair on only a portion of the shank. When you tie deer hair onto a hook, you are encompassing it with thread to keep it from flying off into space and then you are folding the hair in two by collapsing the wall of the hair with thread tension. How and when you apply the tension will determine whether or not the hair encircles the hook shank or only covers a portion of it. Thread torque is the force you must learn to control—it can work for or against you.

It really comes down to two basic methods of application. Once you encircle the hair bunch and the hook shank with thread, you can flare or fold the hair and then distribute it, or you can distribute the hair and *then* flare or fold it. Are you with me? Let's try a couple of simple exercises as illustration. Mount a hook in your vise and wrap the center of the shank with size A thread for ¼", allowing each turn to touch the other. Wind the thread back over itself toward the hook eye to the center of the tie-down area.

Exercise 1

❶ Cut a bundle of hair, ¼" in diameter, from a piece of deer hide (cut the hair off close to the hide). Clean the underhair out with your comb or toothbrush. Keeping the hair butts even, place the bundle in your other hand and trim the tips to make them even, leaving a bunch of hair approximately ¾" to 1" long.

❷ Place the prepared hair bunch over the hook shank. Encircle the hair bundle twice with thread at a point halfway down its length, going around the hook shank as you do so; the second turn should be on top of the first. Continue to hold onto the hair bundle.

❸ Pull straight down on your bobbin, tightening the thread. The hair bunch will flare, but do not let go. Take a third turn of thread, placing it over the top of the previous two. Let go of the hair bundle as you tighten. The bundle will rotate under the hook shank as you torque the thread.

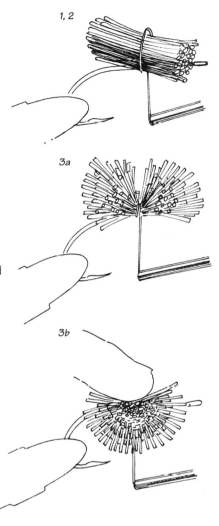

You will now have a flared bundle of hair occupying the lower half of the hook shank. It will look like half a ball or sphere. You have just folded the hair and then distributed it. You might be saying, "Great, now I have hair on half a hook—so what do I do with it?" Good question, Grasshopper. This technique allows you to do a couple of things. For one, it is the basis for "stacking." You could put another hair bundle on top of this one; if you used a different color, you would end up with a two-tone effect, and you would double the number of hairs per square inch (provided both bundles were of the same diameter). Second, if you used the same color you would have a single color but twice the fiber count, resulting in a denser body and greater flotation. Understand? Great. Let's move on to the second exercise. Once you have mastered this one, we'll tie a bug.

flytying

Exercise 2

❶ Untie the hair bundle you just applied. Notice how the hair has seemed to lock itself around the thread. Take a look at the hair fibers: they should look like little Vs. That is because the wall collapsed at a single point and folded in two against the thread. Prepare another bundle of hair, and place it over the hook shank.

❷ Encircle both the hair bundle and the hook shank as you did before.

❸ Now, instead of pulling down on the thread start another turn with the thread. As you do so, tighten down against the hair, but do not flare it; if it's straight, it will make distributing it easier (a slight flare will occur). As you feel the tension build, let go of the hair bunch and the torque of your thread will carry it around the hook shank. Keep your thread moving just ahead of the hair bunch. The hair fibers are sliding and rolling around the hook shank within the confines of the wrap of thread.

The thread base on the hook shank is actually aiding the process, as it creates a greater diameter and a more secure anchoring point. The hair fibers end up trapped and folded between the thread base and the thread encircling them. This is why it's important to always wrap the shank. (It is like securing an anchor point for wildland firefighting or rope rescue—I never attempt either one without anchoring first!) Tighten your thread as you complete the third turn, flaring the hair. You should now have a ball or sphere of flared hair completely encircling the hook shank. You have just distributed the hair and then flared it. Take a "soft loop" of thread through it and tighten. Check your work: The hair bunch should be secure and not twist on the hook shank. The turns of thread should all be in the middle and locked up against the thread base (which, again, is why we wrap the hook shank).

1, 2

3a

3b

There you go—the two application techniques for deer hair. By repeating and/or combining the two, and varying the color and size of your hair bundles, you can create single- or multi-colored bugs, adding bands or spots of color as you desire. Join the bunches of hair together by pushing them back with a ballpoint pen body after tying them in. Advance your thread out onto the hook shank after you have pushed the bundle back. Don't worry, the thread won't slip; remember how difficult it was to undo the hair in the first exercise? If you bring the thread out and wrap the shank before you push, it will not be as tight (it would be like trying to push your car with the brake on). Be sure to place a couple of wraps at the base of the hair bunch you just pushed back. Use your index and middle fingers and thumb to pull back on the hair as you do this. Practice these two exercises until you have them down, and then we will move on to a simple, single-colored bass bugs.

Basic Bug Design

The next thing you need to know is what a bug should look like. Figure A shows a typical hair bug. Note lines A, B and C. Line A marks the hook's barb. Line B denotes the end of the hook point. Line C is the lower contour of the bug's body. See how the bulk of the body is above the hook shank. Do not attach your tailing material any farther back than the section of the hook shank between lines A and B; the body of the bug should begin at Line B. If you keep all of this in mind as you construct your bugs, they will perform well. The gap of the hook will not be obstructed and the attitude of the bug on the water will be correct for good surface disturbance (popping). And note the "shape" of this angle; the oval contours will also assure the proper attitude on the water.

FIG. A

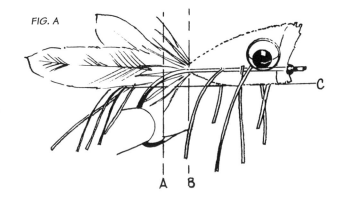

Weed guard

If you are going to fish for bass in their back yard, you are best served by installing a weed or snag guard on your fly. The one illustrated in Figure B is called a parallel loop, first popularized by Ted Trueblood in the 1950s. I like to use a stiff monofilament like Mason; Trilene XT also works well. An accepted rule of thumb is that the diameter of the mono should equal that of the hook shank.

Be sure to wind your thread at least halfway down the hook bend to ensure the guard stays lined up with the hook. I use white 3/0 Monocord for this. Bringing the mono up through the hook eye also helps keep it in line. Do this after you have completed your bug. To reduce the area the mono takes up in the hook eye, flatten it with a pair of pliers. I usually do several hooks and then coat the thread with a two-part rod finish.

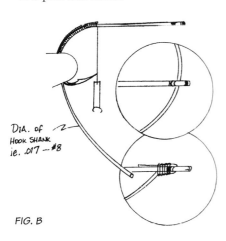

DIA. of HOOK SHANK ie. .017 — #8

FIG. B

A simple bug

Let's begin with a simple, effective deerhair concoction. Besides thread, you will need only two materials—deer hair and rubber hackle. Our focus will be on the techniques of distributing, then folding or flaring. Use any color of hair you like; I suggest black and white, with black rubber hackle in fine and medium.

But first, a word on materials: I use hair from Rocky Mountain Dubbing, period. I'm not a paid spokesman; it's just good stuff. Fine and medium rubber hackle is available from any retailer who carries Umpqua Feather Merchants products. Well, enough of that, let's move on to some tying.

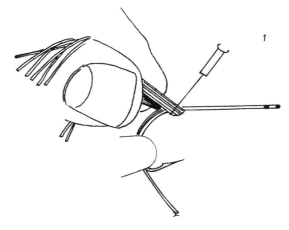

❶ Attach your thread to the hook shank behind the eye and wrap back to where you will tie in the tail (see Figure A). Fold 12 to 15 strands of six- to eight-inch black rubber hackle in two. Grasping the free ends of the rubber hackle, slip the looped ends under the hook shank and slide the tailing back to the tie-down area. Keeping the hackle grouped together, pull up and back on the rubber, stretching it slightly. Catch the hackle with your thread as shown. Wrap thread evenly around the rubber hackle, keeping it in the tie-down area. Apply some cement to the thread. You should have a nice full skirt that flares out at the sides. Do not trim it yet. The extra length will help keep the tail out of the way as you tie the rest of the fly. Bring your thread to the front of the tail tie-down area.

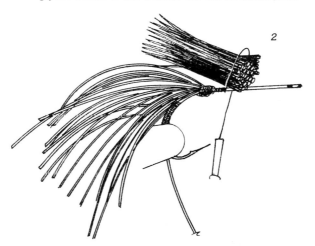

❷ A collar nicely bridges the gap between the tail and the body of the bug, and adds to the action. Cut off, close to the hide, a bunch of black deer hair ⁵⁄₁₆" in diameter. Clean the underhair from it, and place it, tips down, in your stacker. Tap the stacker several times to even the tips. Trim even the butt ends of the hair; when you're finished, the hair should ¾" to 1" long. Place the hair bundle, with the tips to the rear, over the hook and in front of the tailing. Distribute and fold the hair, encircling the hook completely. Bring your thread out to the hook shank to ready it for the next hair bunch, placing a couple of thread wraps at the base of the collar.

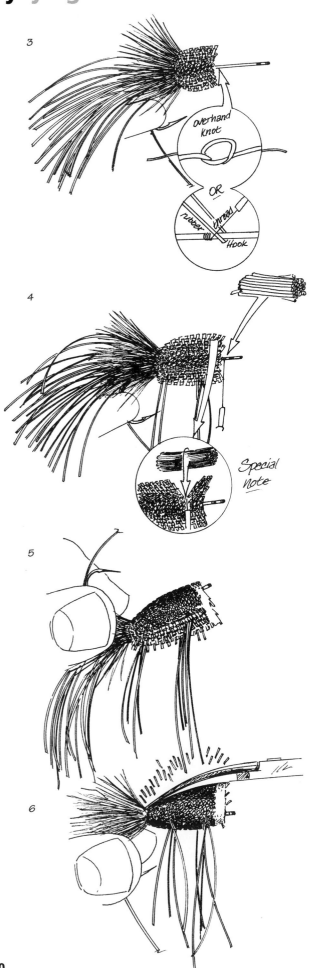

3 Prepare another bunch of black hair the same size as before, but this time trim the tips off.

Distribute and fold this hair into place. Push it back with your pen body and secure it with a couple of wraps. At this point, we want to attach a couple of strands of rubber hackle to make legs. You can attach them two ways. One is to tie a loose overhand knot in the middle of the strand, slip the knot over the hook eye and slide the strand into place. The other method is to loop it as you did the tailing and catch it with your thread. We need two strands here.

4 Put in three more ⁵⁄₁₆" bunches of black hair and add three more strands of rubber hackle. Add one more bunch of black hair. Now we will change to white or bleached deer hair. We want to create a "face" on our bug. The purpose of the face is to make the bug more visible to you; it's also aesthetically pleasing. (If you want a more pronounced slope to the face, add a small bunch of black hair onto the top of the last black hair bunch you just put in, as illustrated. Do not advance your thread until you have done so.) Now put in two ⁵⁄₁₆" bundles of white hair. We'll use two bundles, rather than one, because you want to overbuild the face, as we will be trimming part of it away. After you put in the white hair, finish off by half-hitching your thread and then cutting it. Remove the bug from your vise.

5 Who said fly-tying wasn't work? Now you're ready to trim your dust ball into a finished bug. Look at the illustrations and get a mental picture of what the finished product should look like. It is sort of like Zen. Relax, flip your bug over and, starting at the belly, slide your open scissors into the hair, down the center. Stop short of the collar, and don't cut the rubber legs off. Visualize the line; if you are satisfied, squeeze the scissors together. It is said that taking a little at first is much better than taking too much. If you are a little shallow, just cut a little deeper until you are satisfied. Once you have perfected this cut, use it as a guide to trim with. You will keep one blade of the scissors on the trimmed portion and the other in the long hair as you work your way around the fly to where the rubber legs stick out. (We'll do the same thing on the back before trimming the sides.) Scissors are used to rough out the bug; don't try to make it perfect at this point.

6 Flip your bug over and position the open scissor blades where you want the outline of your bug's back to be. You should have more hair between the scissors and the hook shank than you did at the belly. (Remember our basic design? Check Figure A again.) Be sure you stop short of the collar and that all the rubber hackle is out of the way. Trim to the rubber legs as you did with the belly.

❼ The trick here is to trim the hair without cutting off the legs. Grasp the bug by the hook bend. At the same time, hold the rubber legs down and out of the way with your index finger and thumb. With the rubber out of the way, slide your scissors along the side, position them to the desired contour and cut.

❽ Take a rest and put on the steam kettle. When the water boils, hold your bug with pliers or hemostats, stick it in the steam and watch what happens. The hair will appear to grow.

This is because the hair was sitting at a transverse angle to the hook shank instead of 90 degrees (perpendicular). I always steam my flies before the final trimming; if you don't, when you fish the water will do the same thing as the steam and your bug will change shape when you fish it. Now that the hairs are straight up, you can trim them to their proper length. This is probably not critical with a popping bug, but it is with other designs that are more complex.

❾ Notice how the "face" is flared forward. This will also happen when you fish the bug. Some tiers like to use glue here, but it doesn't work that well and will eventually come off unless you saturate the hair with it, in which case you might as well tie on a cork bug.

The hair is doing this because it wants to form a sphere—remember the exercises? Pull out a razor blade and we will address the face as we do the rest of the final trim. Hold the razor blade 90 degrees to the hook shank and trim around the circumference of the face. The hair closest to the hook's eye will become short, and the rest will be long. The shorter hair holds the longer hair back. The hair closest to the hook eye and shank cannot stick forward because it is now trimmed off. Is that clear as mud? OK—trim the rest of your bug with the razor blade. You can get it very smooth, which is not possible with scissors.

Once you are finished trimming, put the bug back in the vise. Be careful not to catch the weed guard in the jaws. Attach red Monocord to the hook shank right behind the eye and bring the monofilament guard forward and tie it off. If you keep your thread short—right up against the bobbin tube—you won't catch any of the hairs as you wrap the guard. Finish off with a whip-finish and coat the thread with cement using your bodkin.

The last thing you need to do is trim the rubber hackle to length. Hold our bug straight up with the face toward the sky. As the rubber hackle hangs down, trim it all to length with one cut of your scissors. I prefer hackle that is 1½ times the body length.

Congratulations! You're now a bugmaker.

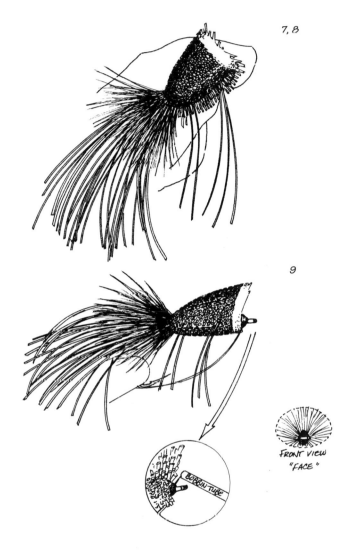

7, 8

9

FRONT VIEW "FACE"

BOBBIN TUBE

The San Juan Worm Ball

What could be better than one San Juan Worm? A bunch of them

Dan Fink
March 2008

The San Juan Worm has been a standard fly pattern for years now, because it's simple to tie and it works. So I thought, *Why not take it one step further?* If one worm is good, a bunch must be better. And it's true. The San Juan Worm Ball is a very fishable and effective pattern no matter what the purists might say.

To mess with your more closed-minded buddies, I recommend carrying your stash of newly tied San Juan Worm Balls to the river in a plastic bait container. The K-Mart sticker is optional, as is any sort of pre-presentation dip in stinkbait juice.

Seriously, though, this fly works quite well for trout and panfish, despite its origins during a four-foot snowstorm that I spent in the company of a bottle of good bourbon. Drift it just like a San Juan Worm, with an occasional twitch to imitate a mass of irritated, doomed nightcrawlers.

❶ Crimp the hook barb. Slip the tungsten bead over the hook point and slide it to the eye, then place hook in vise. Attach the red thread and wrap a smooth, thin body back to the bend of the hook, only one layer thick. Coat with head cement.

❷ Cut three pieces out of both regular diameter and micro thin chenille for a total of six segments. The two pieces for the back are two inches long, the middle pieces are 1½", and the front pieces are one inch each.

❸ Tie on the two long pieces of chenille at the back of the hook. Wrap thread neatly and evenly up to the middle of the hook and make some worm-like loops with the chenille. Tie off at the middle of the chenille, leaving ½" to 1" ends.

Hook: Mustad 37160, size 10	
Bead: ⅛" tungsten	
Thread: 6/0 red Uni	
Body: Thread	
Tentacles: Worm-colored Ultrachenille, both regular and micro diameter	

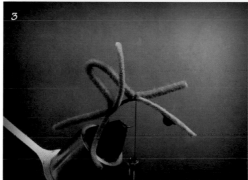

❹ Tie the two mid-length pieces of chenille on at the mid-point of the hook shank. Wrap thread up to just behind the bead. Make more worm-like loops in one or both of the middle pieces of chenille, and tie off right behind the bead head.

❺ Tie on the remaining two pieces of chenille right behind the bead head.

❻ Carefully flame every protruding end of the chenille with a cigarette lighter or match, tapering the ends so they look like the ends of worms. A rotary vise will help you avoid torching parts that shouldn't be torched.

❼ Didn't step 6 above just tell you to be careful? This is what happens if you are not! Remember, only you can prevent fly-vise fires.

❽ The aftermath. Go back to Step 1 and start over!

The Pheasant Tail Emerger
A classic steps out

Chad Mason
March 2008

Frank Sawyer devoted much of his life to maintaining the River Avon, in Salisbury, England. The job of a river keeper, as you might imagine, fires the mind at the tying vise. More than half a century ago, Sawyer developed a nondescript mayfly nymph imitation that now ranks, perhaps, second only to the Gold Ribbed Hare's Ear on the list of all-time favorite nymphs. Its inventor called it Sawyer's Pheasant Tail Nymph, but many of us have come to call it, affectionately, the "PT."

Like all great patterns, the PT is more than a recipe; it is a basis for many fruitful variations. Few American fly tiers follow (or even know) Sawyer's original recipe. Sawyer started with a tail of pheasant tail fiber tips. Then he twisted the butts of those fibers around fine copper wire and wrapped them over the shank for both abdomen and thorax. He used a second bunch of pheasant fibers for a wing case. And that's all. No ribbing, no peacock herl, no legs, no shiny "flashback." Though Sawyer's original tie remains effective, you'd be hard pressed to find such a PT in American fly shops. We Yanks like our nymphs full-Figured, leggy and a little on the trashy side.

One of my favorite variations on the PT is not a nymph at all but an emerger. Inside a mayfly nymph is a dun waiting to come out. Between sub-aquatic life and that which flies in the open air, there is an awkward, vulnerable, ephemeral struggle to emerge. To imitate this critical stage of the mayfly cycle, the Pheasant Tail Emerger (PTE) joins the stern of a nymph to the bow of a winged adult. Tied in sizes 12 through 22, the PTE can imitate almost any kind of mayfly emerger. Drakes, Sulphurs, Pale Morning Duns, Blue-Wing Olives and even Tricos can be matched with an appropriately sized PTE.

> ❝ Like all great patterns, the PT is more than a recipe; it is a basis for many fruitful variations. ❞

❶ Select a small bunch of pheasant tail fibers. Even the tips with your fingers, and clip them from the plume. Attach them to the hook shank, extending one hook-shank length behind the bend. Wind the thread back to the bend, then wind it forward to the mid-point of the shank. (Use 3 to 4 fibers for smaller flies, 5 to 7 fibers for larger ones.)

❷ Double the fibers back on top of the shank and wrap back over them to the base of the tail. Then wrap thread forward again to the mid-point of the shank.

❸ Grasp the fibers with your hackle pliers and twist them into a rope. Wind the rope forward over the shank to the mid-point, forming a segmented abdomen. Tie down securely and clip excess. Put a small drop of cement at the tie-down point.

❹ For the wing, grasp a small bunch of fur from a snowshoe hare's foot and clip it close to the hide. The base of the wing should be almost as thick as the abdomen of the fly. Tie the wing onto the top of the hook shank with the fur tips facing to the rear. Clip the butts and wrap securely over them.

The PTE is comprised of only three materials: pheasant tail fibers, snowshoe hare fur and muskrat fur. Not all pheasant tails are created equal. Look for plumes with long, fuzzy, brown fibers. These are generally the fibers located near the center of the bird's tail fan. Since I'm a hunter, I sift through the birds taken during the season and keep the best plumes. If you're not a hunter, shop accordingly.

The varying hare, or snowshoe hare, is a North American hare that changes its color from a mottled brown in summer to solid white in winter. In summer pelage, the hare's feet are cream-colored. This, apparently, is when the captive variety is harvested for fly-tying. Although dyed feet are available, I prefer the unbleached, non-dyed, natural cream-colored feet. Their color is perfect, and their natural oils are intact. Those oils give the hair good natural buoyancy.

For dubbing, I like solid patches of natural, non-dyed muskrat fur in medium gray. Muskrat fur also has natural oils, and is the traditional material for the Adams dry fly. To dub this material, clip a small patch of fur close to the hide. Then grasp the fuzzy bases in your right hand, and pull out the long guard hairs with your left and discard them. What remains is the soft, supple, gray fur. Roll the soft fur in the palm of your hand briefly to blend it. At that point, it is ready to dub.

❺ Prepare a small bunch of muskrat fur, wax your thread and attach the fur to the thread.

❻ Dub a fat head, whip-finish the fly and clip thread.

❼ Pull the wing back and clip it at an angle with your scissors, so the top edge of the wing is approximately even with the base of the tail.

❽ Admire the finished fly, give thanks to Frank Sawyer, and go fishing.

Hook: Mustad 94840, size 14 to 18; or Mustad 94859, size 20 to 22
Thread: 8/0 Uni, camel
Tail: Pheasant tail fibers
Abdomen: Pheasant tail fibers, twisted and palmered
Wing: Natural cream snowshoe hare's foot, clipped
Head: Natural gray muskrat fur

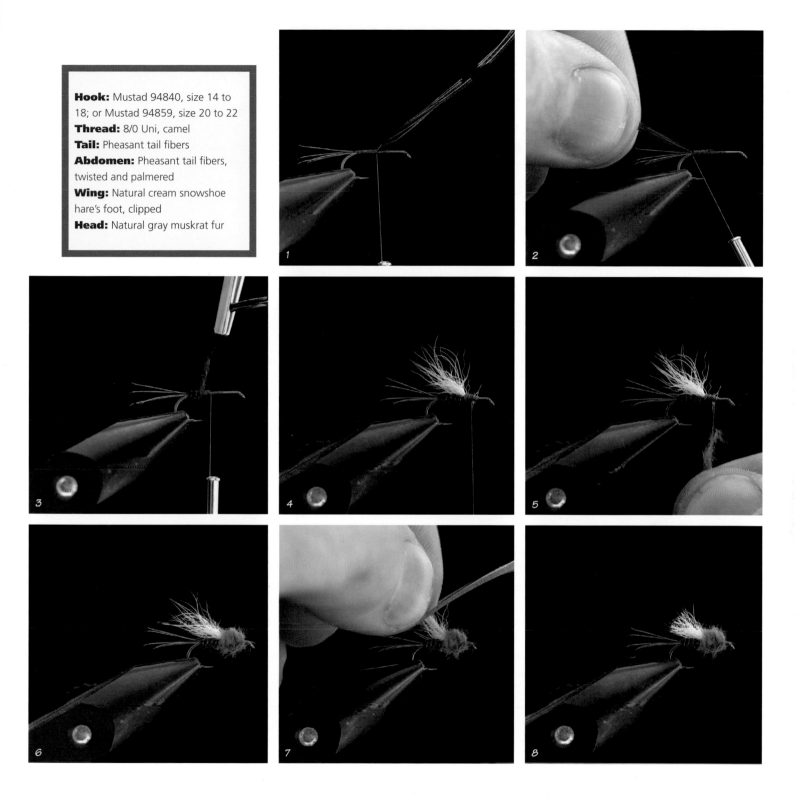

Spinners and Soft-Hackles

Are they the same?

Sylvester Nemes
Jan/Feb 2000

I will admit there is a great deal of resemblance between a Partridge & Orange soft-hackle with a rabbit-fur thorax and the *Heptagenia solitaria*, one of the orange-bodied spinner patterns in my 1995 book, *Spinners*. I have searched for years—and so have many other anglers—for the reasons soft-hackle flies, particularly that pattern, are so effective in so many different fly-fishing situations, so it might prove worthwhile to study the two styles side by side, at least in theory, to see why both flies work as well as they do. First, let's compare the two flies and see why my wife, Hazel, upon seeing my first patterns for *Spinners* before the book was published, promptly said, "They look just like soft-hackles."

Here's the Partridge & Orange soft-hackle with fur thorax: Body: Pearsall's gossamer tying thread (that's the classic tie, although the body could be made with nylon or synthetic thread or floss); Thorax: Hare's fur; Hackle: Partridge, no more than two wraps.

Here's the *solitaria* spinner tie from the book: Body: Orange Flymaster 6X nylon thread tapered into a thin body. Then fine gold ribbing; Tail: Three or four barbs of a golden pheasant topping feather, curved jauntily upward; Thorax: Dark orange dubbing; Hackle: Rusty, which has a dun or light dun center with gold tips; Body finish: A coating of fast-drying clear nail polish. This was an attempt to obtain the

highly reflective brilliance I had been seeing on many natural spinner bodies.

The bodies on some spinners—like the smaller Baetis, for example—were so reflective and shiny that I included a pattern called Syl's Gold Plated Spinner, with a body made entirely of ultra-thin gold wire. For a few of the patterns, I even suggested painting the hook shanks with white paint before wrapping the body, in an effort to make them less visible through the relative transparency of the thin, light-colored bodies.

The hackle on the Partridge & Orange is left natural and outspread, while the hackle on the *solitaria* is divided and squeezed by the tier's thumb and forefinger into a relatively flat plane on both sides of the hook. I arrived at this design for all 30 spinner patterns after studying the writings on spinners of Vince Marinaro and Roger Woolley, the latter a British professional tier who wrote two small guides on his tying methods.

Marinaro instructed the tier to wind the hackle around the hook five or six times in turns next to each other, the rest of the turns splitting the previous turns in two. Then the tying thread was tied in Figure-8s on the top of the hook, which was then turned over and the thread wrapped again in the same manner on the bottom of the hook. Woolley first wound the hackle around the front of the hook and, after cutting off the stem, he flattened the barbs by squeezing them with his thumb and forefinger. He then "fixed" them in that position by Figure-8s above and below, as Marinaro did. Woolley used the name "hackle fibre wings" to describe his spinners. Woolley also noticed, as I did, that spinner bodies were shiny and highly reflective, and suggested a spinner body tied with celluloid wrapped over the tying silk. I coat thread spinner bodies with fast-drying nail polish. The polish never seems to dry fast enough, so I recommend you coat the bodies after dubbing the thoraxes, setting the flies aside to dry thoroughly before hackling.

Woolley also complained he had a hard time finding enough "glassy" dun hackles. Today, thanks to the genetic pioneering of growers like Hoffman and Metz, glassy hackles from hens and roosters are available in practically every fly shop in the country. For my spinners, I prefer hen hackles to cock because they seem to be not only finer in texture—that is, with thinner stems and barbs—but offer more than one color or density of color in the hackles. The hackle is called rusty edge. The center of the hackle is off white or dun, while the edge is rusty or golden. Other suitable hackles have dark dun centers with lighter dun edges, or dun centers with white or silver edges. Some hackles will be spotted slightly, which I don't find objectionable.

The wings on these new spinners make use of a revolutionary fly-tying technique. Tie the hackle in by the stem, in front of the dubbed thorax. With the hackle tip in the jaws of the pliers, I pull the hackle into a perpendicular position (right angle to the hook shank for easier winding) and wind it five or six times around the hook. I've pushed the tying thread, by the way, to the rear of the fly by winding, and now bring it forward over the tops of the wound hackle barbs, which begins to split the hackle points on to one side and the other. Tie off.

I turn the jaws of the vice toward me, where I can see clearly every barb of the hackle radiating around the hook. I aim the forefinger of my right hand into the middle

of the wound hackle, and press it firmly there. This begins to push half the barbs on to one side and half on the other. Now, I wet my thumbs and forefingers of both hands and, with the jaws of the vice still facing me, I bend, pull and flatten the two bunches of wound hackle away from each other until they are quite flat and spreading away from the shaft of the hook. (Dabbing your fingers on fly-tying wax helps, too.)

There are only two or three tails on mayflies and they are, on average, two to three times the length of the bodies. Trico spinner tails are up to four times the length of the bodies. Tails are of two types, either spotted, or highly reflective like gold. Each pattern in my book suggests the kind of tail for the fly. It is advisable to tie the flies with three or four tail barbs because one or more of them will invariably break off with use. A tail of four barbs also helps to keep the fly up and on the surface longer.

The 30 fly patterns in *Spinners* were not designed to make it easy for the angler to see where the fly is on the water, but to make it convincing to the trout that what they're seeing is the real thing. As in my fishing of the soft-hackle fly, I have learned to know where the fly is practically every moment without gluing my eyes to a "bobber." To help in this, I have one simple tip: Never change the length of your leader.

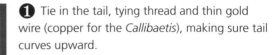

Ephemerella inermis (Pale Morning Dun)
Hook: Tiemco 100, size 16
Abdomen: Light olive
Thorax: Pale yellow
Ribbing: Gold wire
Hackle: Rusty or reddish ginger
Tail: Golden pheasant topping feather

Baetis No. 1
Hook: Tiemco 100, size 16 to 18
Abdomen: Rusty brown
Thorax: Reddish brown
Ribbing: Gold wire
Hackle: Rusty or ginger
Tail: Wood duck flank feather

Callibaetis
Hook: Tiemco 100, size 14 to 16
Abdomen: Gray
Thorax: Reddish brown
Ribbing: Copper wire
Hackle: White or rusty, with one wrap of partridge in front
Tail: Wood duck flank feather

Stenonema canadensis (Light Cahill)
Hook: Tiemco 109 BL, size 15
Abdomen: Yellow, dabbed with brown marker
Thorax: Dark amber
Ribbing: Gold wire
Hackle: Honey dun, plus partridge in front
Tail: Wood duck flank feather

❶ Tie in the tail, tying thread and thin gold wire (copper for the *Callibaetis*), making sure tail curves upward.

❷ Build spinner body into a slight taper with tying thread (Flymaster lies flat and can be un-spun from time to time to retain the flatness).

❸ Bring up the gold wire rib. I recommend Lagartun, fine or extra fine, which is no more than 0.500mm.

❹ Tie off and coat body with clear, fast-drying nail polish and set aside to dry.

❺ Remount thread at head of body and tie in the thorax, which is usually a slightly darker shade of the same color as the thread body.

❻ Prepare hackle by holding the tip of the hackle in one hand and pulling the barbs away from the top of the feather.

❼ Tie in stem of hackle a slight distance in front of the thorax to make room for five or six wraps (allow enough room for one wind of the partridge hackle on the patterns asking for it). Leave tying thread behind or in back of wraps, and it will be pushed backward with every one of the wraps.

❽ Cut off excess hackle and bring tying thread forward over the top of the wound hackle, helping to divide it into two even parts. Whip-finish.

❾ Turn vice toward you and press forefinger on top of the middle of the hackle.

❿ Wet both thumbs and forefingers, reach in and grab both sides of the wing and forcibly squeeze, pull, bend and flatten the two sides of the wing (sometimes I dab my fingers on fly-tying wax. And I am now trying Mucilin, which not only helps to flatten the wing, but adds a little flotant).

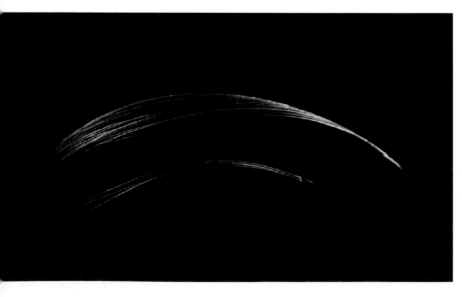

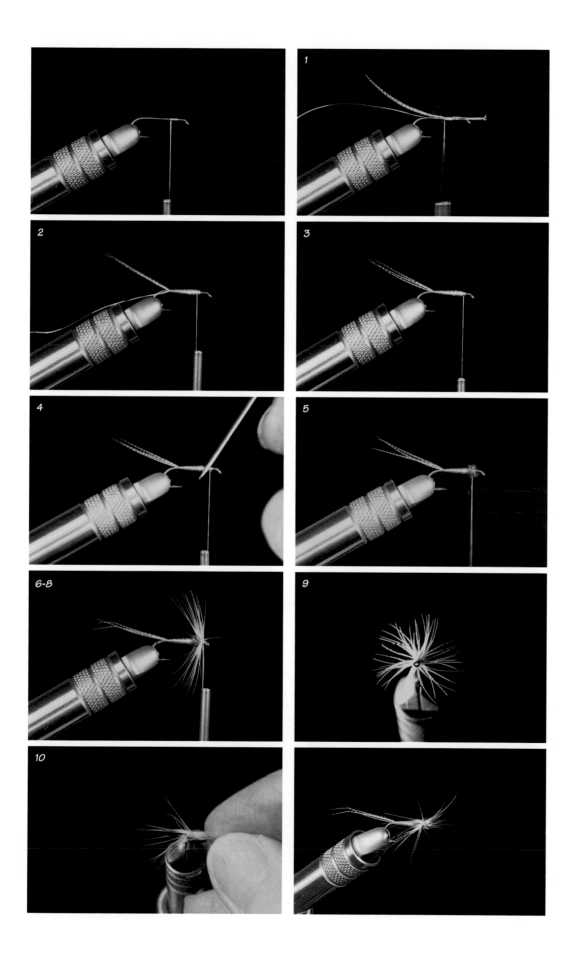

Tying Variants
The simple flies

Jeffrey Ripple
Jan/Feb 1997

The sun was fading behind the Catskill Mountains as we sat on a rock along the boulder-strewn river that we had been fishing throughout the day. A gentle breeze started up the river valley, carrying with it the fragrance of hemlock trees and the late-spring wildflowers that were in full bloom. After roasting all day in our neoprene waders, until we both imagined we knew what it felt like to be a littleneck at a clam bake, we were finally getting some relief. We sat on that rock, dangling our feet in the cool waters of the mountain river, smoking fine cigars and reminiscing about the day's adventures while waiting for the grand finale.

The evening before, we had witnessed a multiple hatch that included Sulphur Duns and Olives. This was what we had expected to find when we arrived in the Catskills several days earlier, because prior trips at this time of year had provided some of the best Sulphur fishing we had ever encountered. But the fish completely ignored our Sulphur imitations while gorging themselves on large *Isonychia* mayflies that resembled small bombers flying low to avoid radar.

Like a couple of bumbling fools, we were unprepared and had no imitations for these insects. Needless to say, later that night in our cottage we dug into our fly-tying stash to assemble a few choice patterns.

And now, as we sat waiting for the evening's festivities, we began to see a few flies buzzing upriver. But we resisted the urge to leave our rest spot until the fish started to work. Our discipline finally paid off; soon the fish started to show themselves, and there were some decent ones among them. We knew that, with a good deal of daylight remaining, we were in store for a fantastic evening.

We prepared our outfits, both tying on Dun Variants, and waded into casting position. The large air-resistant flies landed on the water with all the grace of the naturals that would occasionally drop to the surface. It was during these brief rests that the browns could dine on what must have seemed like filet mignon. I cast to a spot just below a large rock in mid-river where I had been watching a good fish enjoying its evening meal. The fly landed precisely where I had intended it to (this doesn't happen all the time) and the healthy brown slowly rose to the surface. While my heart beat hard, my hopes diminished as it scrutinized my offering. But then the fish slowly poked its nose out of the water, opened its mouth and engulfed the variant; I raised the rod and hooked up.

I looked over my shoulder to catch my partner's attention, only to find him extracting a variant from the reward of his own efforts. My large brown fought hard, making

some notable runs and for a long time refusing to surrender.

The remainder of the evening was just as eventful, bringing fish to the fly time after time, but nothing could surpass the satisfaction of that first fish. Spending the two minutes apiece required to tie these wingless wonders had certainly proven worthwhile.

A history lesson

Sometime during the late 1800s, Dr. William Baigent, of Yorkshire, England, set out to create a fly that he thought would attract trout better than an exact imitation of the natural. This new fly was intended to stimulate the trout's investigatory reflex. His "Baigent flies" were an immediate success; their appearance was thought to mimic the optical effect that water has on a trout's perception of a floating insect.

These flies soon found their way into the Hardy Brothers catalog and thereby to faraway countries. Soon letters of praise for their fish-killing powers poured in from all over the world.

One such letter came from Catskill angler Preston Jennings, who was pleased with their performance on the Esopus River. He was so pleased, in fact, that he devoted an entire chapter of his 1935 book, *A Book of Trout Flies*, to the Baigent flies, which by then had become known as variants. The original variants were dressed with oversize hackle and gold or silver tinsel bodies. Jennings noted in his book that these flies were particularly suited to fishing for brown trout in placid waters because of the delicate manner in which they landed.

In 1934 Art Flick arrived in the Schoharie River Valley to take over the Westkill Tavern from his parents. Flick envisioned the tavern as a haven for fly fishermen. At that time Jennings was identifying insects for his forthcoming book, and he recruited Flick to help gather information. Under Jennings' influence and tutelage Flick became a fly tier of extraordinary talents. His first original pattern was the Red Quill, an imitation of the male Hendrickson; it incorporated a quill body.

Following the success of the Red Quill, Flick tried a red quill hackle stem on Jennings' Blue Variant-Gold Body. That hybrid became known as the Dun Variant. His substitutions of the hackle-quill body on Jennings's other variants were also successful, even though the names for those flies—the Grey Fox Variant and the Cream Variant—remained unchanged. Flick noted that quill-bodied flies were easier to tie, more durable and easier to float than their predecessors with tinsel bodies. These revised dressings first appeared in print in 1947 in *Art Flick's Streamside Guide to Naturals and Their Imitations.*

Variants are much easier and quicker to tie than a standard dry fly because they omit the dryfly wing and use the oversize hackle

of the spider. These versatile imitations fish well in quiet water because of the gentle way they land; they also can be skated across the water in imitation of the natural as it tries to break the surface tension and become airborne. And you can make subtle modifications to the variant, even while fishing, to enhance the fly's performance. For instance, by clipping the hackle on the bottom of the fly you can change it from a dun to a spinner. And by clipping the hackle on top of the fly you can make a fully spent spinner. Imagine that: Using a single fly to fish several phases of a hatch without changing patterns. Talk about simplicity.

Tying the variant is a simple matter too; the fly consists of only a tail, a body and hackle. However, some tiers have difficulty finding hackle of the proper size. Good, web-free, oversize hackle is hard to find in today's era of genetically bred birds. Thrifty tiers can often find good hackle on Indian or Chinese necks if they are willing to spend some time rummaging at their local fly shop. In fact, sometimes those $5 to $15 necks provide a better value than $65 to $85 genetic capes, especially in the most common hackle sizes (inexpensive necks often have a lot of #12 and #14 hackles). And you can often find some unusual color variations that you wouldn't find otherwise.

Variant hackle size is on par with that of the skater variety of flies. The Neversink Skater, designed by the late E. R. Hewitt, was a good two to 2½ inches in diameter. As noted by the Walt and Winnie Dette, also of Catskill fame, a Variant on a #12 hook requires a #4 hackle; a size 14 fly calls for a size 6 hackle and a size 16 fly needs a size 8 hackle.

A word of caution here: Personally, I think it's risky to mail-order your necks unless absolutely necessary; better to examine your hackles before you buy. If you still have problems obtaining hackle of proper size, a good alternative is to use the Spey hackles from the outside edges of a neck. These feathers are scarce, but each neck holds at least a few of them. Once you have the material, the rest is a relatively simple affair.

Tying the Dun Variant

1 Secure the thread about mid-shank and wind it back to a point opposite the barb. Strip a few barbules from a dark dun hackle and tie them in for the tail. Do not trim the excess; the butt ends of the tail fibers will add bulk to the quill body and should be left long enough to reach the tie-in point for the hackle. The tail should be the same length as the hackle.

2 Select a brown-stemmed hackle from a brown neck and remove all the barbules. The bare stem should be reddish-brown. Tie in the stem at the bend of the hook; the base of the stem should extend beyond the tail and the tip/tag end should be long enough to reach the tie-in point for the hackle. This tag end also contributes to the bulk of the quill body; if you trim it too short the body will have a bump in it. Placing the hackle stem in a glass of water for a few minutes will make it more pliable for winding.

3 Bring the thread forward to just past the center of the hook shank. Wind the hackle stem to the midpoint of the hook shank, completely covering the hackle tip and the tail-fiber butt ends, and taking care not to overlap any turns. Tie off and clip away the excess stem. Wind the thread in a quick spiral back to the tail and forward again to the front of the body. Then place a small drop of thin lacquer on the body. The lacquer not only adds strength to the body but will help make the crisscrossing thread wraps disappear. You can also apply lacquer after the fly is finished, to secure the hackle and speed up your tying.

4 Select two dark dun hackles of the proper size and tie them in at mid-shank. Wind the thread to a point just behind the hook eye. Wind the first hackle forward to the tying thread, being careful to place each turn of hackle right in front of the last, and tie it off with two turns of thread. Do not clip the excess. As you wind the second hackle, you will need to wiggle it a bit so that it will not crush the first one as it falls into place. Tie off the second hackle with two turns of thread. With this double hackle, your fly will have a much fuller appearance.

5 Clip off both hackle points and whip-finish. Trim away any stray hackle barbules.

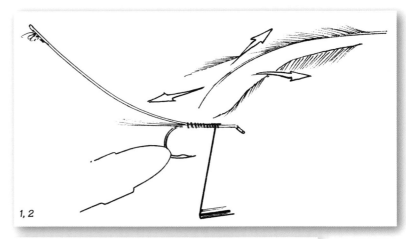

1, 2

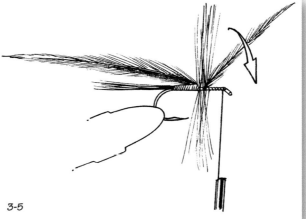

3-5

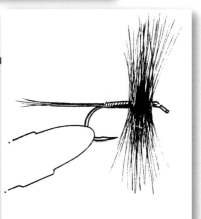

Dun Variant
Hook: Standard dryfly, size 12 to 16
Thread: Cream
Tail: Dark blue dun
Body: Stripped brown hackle stem
Hackle: Dark blue dun

Cream Variant
Hook: Standard dryfly, size 12 to 16
Thread: Cream
Tail: Cream hackle barbules
Body: Cream hackle stem
Hackle: Two cream hackles

Grey Fox Variant
Hook: Standard dryfly, size 12 to 16
Thread: Cream
Tail: Medium ginger hackle barbules
Body: Cream hackle stem
Hackle: Grizzly, brown and light ginger

Half-Dun Flies
Four floating nymphs

A.J. Somerset
July/Aug 2000

When it comes to trout flies, fly fishers fall neatly into two camps. The first group believes the mayfly life cycle consists of three stages: Hare's Ear Nymph, dun (color irrelevant) and spinner. The opposing camp stoutly maintains that trout recognize six or seven life stages and are expert taxonomists.

Both approaches catch fish, which is why the debate has persisted as long as it has. The success of either school of thought has probably had less to do with the nature of trout than it does with where and how you like to fish. Some rivers seem to fish better with emergers than with duns, and on those rivers the best emerger pattern is often a floating nymph.

Many fly fishers underrate the importance of floating nymphs, concentrating instead on duns and winged emergers. Winged emergers—usually just dun imitations with trailing shucks added—catch fish, but actually are poor representations of emerging mayflies. Most stream mayflies emerge in the surface film; the nymph rises from the river bottom until it reaches the water's surface, where surface tension holds it in the film as the nymphal shuck splits open and the dun begins crawling out. At this point, the wings remain trapped. Because the low-floating naturals are difficult to see, many anglers assume that emergence is quicker than it is. In fact, emerging mayflies may drift for yards, half in and half out of their shucks, completely vulnerable. Trout key in on the half-emerged floating nymphs.

An exact imitation of a floating nymph would be designed to float low in the film, with its abdomen dangling below the surface. The fly would be longer than the natural, perhaps by a hook size, to resemble a dun partially escaped from a still-intact shuck. The front third of the body would match the color of the dun, and the rear the color of the nymph. The fly, like the natural, would not have a visible wing.

Such a fly would be difficult to see on the water, and probably would not float very well. It would be useless in all but the flat water of slow pools. Fortunately, trout don't demand exact imitations, so we can compromise with flies that are easier to see and float well in a variety of situations. Each of the following four flies—the Swisher/Richards Floating Nymph, the CDC Floating Nymph, the XT Emerger and the Klinkhamer Special—represents one solution to floating-nymph design.

Hook: Dryfly, size 12 to 20
Thread: Yellow
Tail: Grizzly hackle barbs, splayed
Body: Yellow fur dubbing
Wing case: Mole fur, dubbed in a ball

❶ Build a thread base on the hook. Make a small ball of dubbing—one or two wraps—at the rear of the abdomen. Tie in the tails, splayed on either side of the ball of dubbing, and dub the body forward to the eye.

❷ Dub enough mole fur on the thread to make a thin noodle of fur about one inch long. Form the dubbing into a ball by compressing it with a rolling motion of the thumb and forefinger along the thread. Repeat, alternately rolling the fur into a noodle shape and compressing it into a ball until you have formed a tight, wing-case-size ball of fur on the thread.

❸ Wind the thread back over the body to the center of the thorax. Hold the thread above the fly and slide the ball-shape wing case into place on the back of the thorax.

❹ Secure the ball of dubbing in place with a few turns of thread. If the thread matches the body color, the extra turns of thread will not show. Otherwise, lightly dub over the wraps to hide the thread. Advance to the eye and whip-finish.

The Swisher/Richards Floating Nymph

Until the publication of Doug Swisher and Carl Richards' *Selective Trout* in 1971, American fly fishers fished nymphs and hackled dry flies that had remained fundamentally unchanged since the turn of the century. Beset by the problem of trout feeding selectively in slow, flat water, Swisher and Richards rejected traditional fly designs and introduced a series of patterns that more precisely imitated natural mayflies. The best known of their flies, the No-Hackle, remains popular for its realistic silhouette. Their other designs included emerger imitations with stubby wings of various materials, and their Floating Nymph.

Like the No-Hackle, the Swisher/Richards Floating Nymph lacks legs, relying on its body silhouette alone to imitate the natural. The wide-splayed tails do more to support the hook than to imitate the tail of a nymph. Its originators intended the fly to resemble a mayfly that has not yet begun emerging from its shuck, and it lacks the half-nymph, half-dun body of the natural. In other respects, the Swisher/Richards Floating Nymph closely resembles the real thing, reflecting its creators' belief in exact imitation.

It also suffers the disadvantages that might be expected of a close imitation: It is hard to see, and doesn't float well in larger sizes. Nevertheless, it is an effective emerger in flat water.

It is also a quick, easy-to-tie fly. The key to keeping the Swisher/Richards Floating Nymph afloat is to splay the tails. The tails should form a 90-degree angle, separated by a small ball of dubbing at the rear of the hook. Separate the individual fibers by using plenty of thread tension when tying them in. If the fibers are tied in a clump, they will suck in water by capillary action. To make a version that floats in rougher water, wrap a hackle parachute-style around the bottom of the wing case. Vary the color of the fly to match natural mayfly nymphs, in shades of brown, tan and yellow.

CDC Floating Nymph

The problem with floating nymphs is making them float, so it was inevitable that fly tiers would experiment with CDC solutions. Cul-de-canard feathers, or CDC, are probably the most popular new fly-tying material of the past decade. Touted for its buoyancy and lifelike movement, CDC is an ideal material for floating-nymph imitations, and several fly tiers have used it to create new patterns. Many of these flies, such as René Harrop's Transitional Emerger and the Barr Emerger, are essentially similar. This generic CDC Floating Nymph is based loosely on these popular patterns.

The CDC Floating Nymph uses a curved hook so that the abdomen will hang below the surface while the CDC of the legs and wing case suspends the thorax in the surface film. It works best in flat water, where air bubbles trapped in the wing case are sufficient to keep it afloat. In fast

Hook: Curved-shank nymph or emerger hook in appropriate size, 2X long
Trailing shuck: Tan Antron dubbing
Abdomen: Tan Antron dubbing
Wing case: Blue dun or natural CDC
Thorax: Rust-color fur dubbing
Legs: Tips of the wing case CDC pulled to the sides

water, it is difficult to see because it rides low in the water, and it may also sink as it soaks up water.

Proportion is important when tying this fly. The CDC feathers that form the wing case and legs must be long enough to leave an air space under the wing case and enough length in the legs. A rust abdomen and yellowish thorax is "near enough" to the colors of many mayflies, but other colors can be substituted to match naturals.

❶ Start the thread and lay a thread base on the hook. Tie in the trailing shuck and dub the body forward over the rear two thirds of the hook.

❷ Select four CDC feathers to form the wing case and legs. On smaller flies, two may be sufficient. Align the tips of the feathers and tie them in at the front of the abdomen so that the tips of the feathers reach slightly beyond the trailing shuck.

❸ Trim the butts of the CDC feathers. Dub the thorax.

❹ Pull the CDC feathers forward over the thorax, leaving an air space underneath them, and then secure them in position. Separate the tips and stroke them back to form legs at each side of the fly. Make several wraps of thread immediately in front to secure them. Form a neat head and whip-finish.

The XT Emerger

This unusual floating nymph is the brainchild of fly tier Ray Dolling, whose XT series includes the XT Dun and XT Spinner. Dolling originally created the XT Emerger to imitate the Slate Drake (*Isonychia*). Contrary to popular belief, Slate Drakes do not always crawl out on streamside rocks to emerge; many hatch in the surface film like other mayflies. Because adult Slate Drakes don't rest long on the water, most anglers don't think to fish this hatch with dry flies. But the adults do take longer than most to struggle out of the shuck, and trout often key in on the floating nymphs.

Floating nymphs in larger sizes usually do not float well because of the weight of the hook. But the extended-body design of the XT Emerger makes it an ideal choice to imitate large mayflies like the Slate Drake, Brown Drake or Green Drake because it allows the use of a smaller, lighter hook, and the deerhair underbody provides buoyancy. Darker deer hair makes a more natural fly, but light-colored deer hair makes it more visible on the water. A brown abdomen and yellow thorax is a good generic color scheme, but as always, vary the colors to match the natural mayflies.

Hook: Wide-gap dryfly hook
Underbody: Bleached deer or elk hair, with the tips extending to form tails
Abdomen: Brown fur dubbing
Thorax: Yellow fur dubbing
Wing case: Butts of the underbody hair, pulled over the thorax to form a wing case

Use the narrowest needle possible when tying the body. A thicker needle will leave a space inside the body, resulting in a less durable fly. When starting the thread on a needle, use only a few turns. If you wrap a full thread base on the needle, you'll find it almost impossible to remove the completed body. Always take care when tying extended bodies on needles—impaling a finger on the needle is both easier and more painful than you might think! I prefer to use a very thin beading needle with a small eye. I can then bury the point in the jaws of my vise, and pull the body over the eye of the needle to remove it. By tying up the extended bodies in advance, you'll find this pattern as quick to tie as any standard trout fly.

❶ Position a beading needle in the vise. Start the thread on the needle and tie in the underbody. Take care not to compress the underbody material too tightly. Air trapped in the hollow deer hair helps to float the fly.

❷ Coat the underbody with superglue and then dub over it. The glue makes for a more durable fly. Without it, the dubbing may pull off the underbody and unravel after a few fish. Whip-finish at the front of the abdomen, and leave the butts of the underbody material untrimmed. Remove the completed abdomen from the needle.

❸ Position the hook in the vise. Build a thread base on the hook, and secure the abdomen at the bend of the hook with a few turns of thread.

❹ Dub over the thread you used to secure the abdomen to the hook, then lift the butts of the deer hair out of the way to dub the thorax. Pull the butts of the deer hair forward over the thorax to form a wing case. Tie off and trim the deer hair, form a head and whip-finish.

❶ Tie in the wing on top of the shank. Make several wraps around the base of the wing to secure it in the upright position. Tie in the hackle, securing it to the base of the wing so that it stands up parallel to the wing post.

❷ Dub the abdomen over the rear two thirds of the hook shank.

❸ Tie in two or three strands of peacock herl to form the thorax. Twist the peacock herl to form a rope, wrap forward to the eye and tie off.

❹ Wind three turns of hackle around the base of the wing post, counter-clockwise. Secure the hackle by laying the hackle stem along the top of the thorax and tying it in at the head. Wrapping the hackle counter-clockwise ensures that the thread wraps tighten, rather than loosen, the hackle. Whip-finish, and trim post.

Hook: Curved-shank nymph or emerger hook, 2X long
Abdomen: Yellow synthetic dubbing
Thorax: Peacock herl
Wings: White polypropylene yarn
Hackle: Brown

Klinkhamer Special

This fly seems out of place in an article on floating nymphs—after all, it's a parachute dry fly, not a nymph at all. On the other hand, the Klinkhamer Special has all the characteristics of a floating nymph: an abdomen that hangs suspended below the surface; a two-color body to mimic the adult escaping from the shuck; and a design that lets the thorax sit flush in the surface film. But it also has a wing, which a floating nymph does not.

In this case, however, the wing is an advantage. While most floating nymphs are difficult to see on the water, the Klinkhamer Special's wing post stands out. In small sizes or on faster water, the Klinkhamer Special is an excellent emerger.

The Klinkhamer Special is the creation of fly tier Hans van Klinken, who originally designed it to imitate an emerging caddisfly. It looks enough like an emerging mayfly to serve double duty—trout don't seem to care that it doesn't have tails. They do care, however, about the shape of the hook. The hook must be shaped so that the abdomen hangs below the surface, suspended by parachute hackle. Originally, Hans van Klinken used pliers to bend the hook to the correct shape. I prefer to use a hook with a strongly curved shank so that I don't have to get out the pliers.

Triple Threat Caddis
European imports for North
American caddis hatches

Barry Ord Clarke
April 2009

Here are three caddis patterns you've likely never heard of but are worth a place in your fly boxes this season—and surely worth casting wherever trout are feeding on caddisflies. The Streaking Caddis, as its name suggests, is a trout fly that imitates an adult *Phryganea grandis*, which is the largest caddisfly found in Europe (where I live and fish). Along with the Super Pupa, it's from the tying bench of Swedish fly-tying guru Lennart Berqvist; these are probably the two most popular caddisfly patterns in Scandinavia and it's high time that anglers in the States knew about them. The European 12 rounds out our caddis trilogy.

I believe that many great trout patterns have common attributes: they are quick and easy to tie, with no special techniques or tools required; the materials are easy to obtain, meaning you could find them in most fly shops; they cast without problems; and of course they catch fish. The flies we'll tie here fit the bill on all counts.

Super Pupa

This is a floating caddis-pupa imitation that works just as well in running water as it does in still. Made to imitate a swimming pupa, it can be tied in a variety of colors to match specific hatches. But this pattern also fishes well as an attractor. The original pattern uses only Fly-Rite dubbing; the variation shown here uses any poly dubbing for the body and peacock herl for the thorax. You can dress it with flotant and fish it high and dry, or without flotant just under the surface. When fish are feeding selectively, this fly stands above most others. The normal method of fishing the Super Pupa is to present it to a rising fish and let the fly sit still in the rings of the rise. Just be patient: Sometimes it takes a few minutes before the fish is tempted. Another technique is to twitch the fly on the surface every now and then.

Hook: Mustad 94833, size 12
Thread: Dyneema (gel-spun poly)
Hackle: Dark dun clipped under and over
Body: Yellow poly dubbing
Thorax: Peacock herl

❶ Place your hook in the vise and run the tying thread along the shank. Select a dark dun cock hackle and prepare it by trimming the lower hackle fibers. Tie in the hackle at the bend of the hook.

❷ Apply some yellow dubbing to the tying thread and dub an even body. The rear part of the dubbed body should cover three-fifths of the hook shank. Tie in two strong strands of peacock herl. The best (strongest) are found just under the eye of the peacock tail feather.

❸ Wind the herl on to form the thorax, making sure that while winding you don't trap the small fibers of the herl, and tie off.

❹ Wind on the hackle, palmer style, approximately 10 turns. Tie off and trim the excess hackle. Whip-finish. The fly should now look like photo #4.

❺ With a pair of sharp scissors, trim off the top side of the hackle, taking care not to trim off too much. When correctly trimmed the fly should look like photo #5.

❻ Follow step 5 again, this time clipping the hackle fibers on the underside of the fly. Be sure you don't trim the hackle on the sides of the fly; you want to maintain the "winged" aspect of the pupa pattern. Now you have a finished Super Pupa.

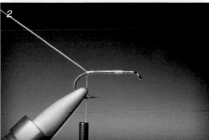

European 12

The E12, as it is also known, has its origins in France. Who developed it, I can't be sure, but it was one pattern from a series of flies that didn't have names, only numbers; this was fly number 12. As far as I'm aware, this is the only remaining pattern from that series still in popular use. Without doubt, this is Scandinavia's most-used caddis pattern for river fishing, being equally effective on grayling as on trout. The E12 is normally fished on a dead drift. Cast two or three meters upstream of a rising fish, mend the line to avoid drag and float the fly through the fish's feeding window.

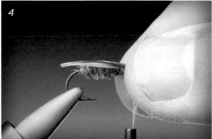

❶ Select and dress two hen mallard breast feathers as shown. Make sure that they are both the same size and correct length for your chosen hook size.

❷ Attach the tying thread to the hook and run it along the shank. Cut a length of yellow floss or heavy thread and tie this down until you come just to the hook bend, as shown.

❸ Wind on the dubbing; run it back to the hook bend and forward again. Once you've achieved the correct body shape, tie off the dubbing, leaving space behind the hook eye. Make four or five turns of yellow floss to form the rib. Tie off the floss and trim the excess.

❹ Place one of the two hen mallard feathers on top of the body, as shown. Secure the feather with a couple turns of thread. Now, holding the sides of the wing in position with your left hand, pull the shaft of the feather to the right with your right hand, until the wing is in the correct position and the right length.

❺ Do the same with the other hackle. You can now secure the wing with a few turns of tying thread, as shown. Make sure that you have enough room for the finishing hackle. Select two fine dryfly hackles, one brown and one grizzly. Tie in the hackles.

❻ Wind the hackles on one at a time; about four to five turns each should be enough. Whip-finish.

Hook: Mustad 94833, size 10 to 16
Thread: Dyneema (gel-spun poly)
Body: Fly-Rite #39 medium brown (dun variant)
Rib: Dark yellow tying thread or floss
Wing: Two hen mallard breast feathers
Hackle: Brown and grizzly cock, mixed

Streaking Caddis

The bullet-shaped aero- and aquady-namic form of the Streaking Caddis makes casting it a dream and allows for precise presentations; for me there is something magical from the moment my SC lands on the water with a distinctive "plop" that attracts attention. As the body is semi-submerged and the wing and head float high, I always follow the "plop" with a pause and let the fly rest on the surface for five to 10 seconds, allowing the leader time to sink and the fly to settle and hang. Then comes the retrieve. With your rod tip down close to the water and your line taut, start with short, jerky retrieves, streaking the fly a few inches at a time, creating a small wake. The sheer "fishability" of this pattern just has to be tried to be believed—particularly when adult caddis are streaking across the surface. In recent years, the Streaking Caddis has found its way into the fly boxes of sea-run-trout and salmon fishermen.

❶ Secure your hook in the vise. Run the tying thread along the hook shank, apply your chosen dubbing and dub the body of the fly. Run a little dubbing, but not too much, along the remaining hook shank to just behind the eye. This will help hold the deer hair in place and stop the wing and head from moving on the finished fly.

❷ Select your deer hair. The hair I use is from the European Roe deer that I shot myself on the last day of hunting (23ʳᵈ December) here in Norway. The colder the climate, the thicker and more buoyant the deer hair. The most common mistake in tying this popular pattern is to use too little deer hair. Remove all the underhair with a dubbing comb. Stack your deer hair in a hair stacker; measure the correct wing length.

❸ Holding the wing in place with your left hand, make not one, but two loose turns of tying thread around the deer hair as shown. These should be at the point where the clipped head goes over the wing.

❹ Now tighten the turns by pulling the tying thread upward. This is important; if you tighten by pulling down, the wing slips around the hook shank, and you need all this hair on top of the body.

❺ Continue adding hair for the head of the fly, as for any spun deer-hair pattern. Whip-finish, and cut the tying thread.

❻ Begin clipping the deer-head: Long, serrated scissors are best for clipping as they grip the hair and give a better cut. It also helps to clip from the back of the fly forward. The head should be cone-shaped, as shown.

❼ The next step is a good trick for all spun and clipped deer-hair patterns. Take a lighter, with the gas set on the lowest position, and carefully singe the clipped head. This seals the ends of the deer hair and makes a very even surface and a nice finished head. It will also tighten the hair and make the wing lie flat in the correct position. But take care not to burn the hair and tying thread.

❽ With an old toothbrush, remove all the soot from the head.

❾ The finished Streaking Caddis.

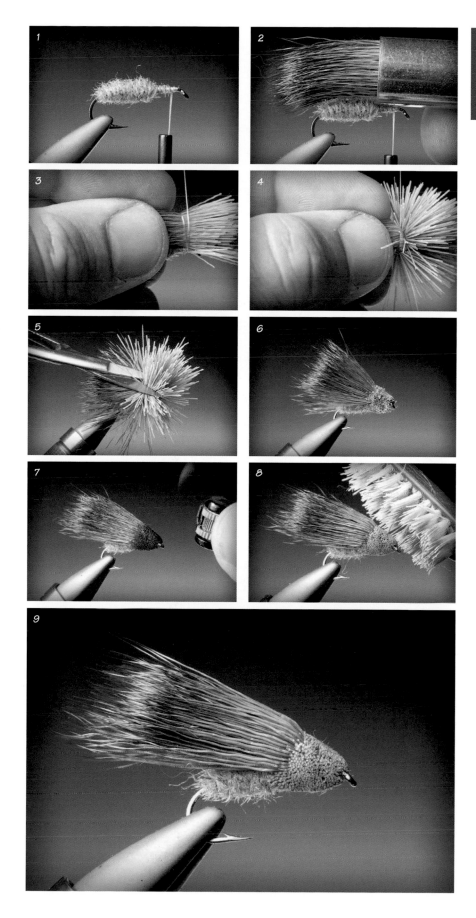

Hook: Mustad 94840, size 8
Thread: Dyneema (gel-spun poly)
Wing: Deer hair
Head: Spun and clipped deer hair

The Grouse & Flash

A modern style of wetfly tying

Nick Yardley
July/Oct 2004

Ever since I first cast a fly at the age of eight, the traditional wet fly has always been, for me, one of the most aesthetic and deadly flies to fish. Perhaps it's because much of my early fishing was done on the River Wharfe, in Yorkshire, England, the home turf of T.E. Pritt, one of the fathers of the North Country wet fly. Whatever the reason, these simple flies with slim bodies and flowing hackles have owned my soul ever since.

The Grouse & Orange and similar flies were the first artificials to come from my primitive vise. Even these first crude versions, tied more than 20 years ago, produced fish as well as wonderful memories for an inexperienced youngster.

I remember spending, at age 13, a day on the Bolton Abbey section of the Wharfe. The water was high, its usual tea color tinged with the honest chocolate brown of runoff from the surrounding fields. With a heavy heart and not much hope of hooking a fish, I headed to a large corner pool 100 yards upriver from the historic abbey. While still running high, the inside eddy provided some slower-moving water.

I unhooked my point fly from the cork handle of my rod and cast out a pair of size 12 flies, a Grouse & Orange on the point and a B&P Spider on the dropper. The point fly clipped the edge of the main current as I cast out, then the flies swung around into the slower current. I soon jumped to attention as a chocolate swirl and a dim flash of gold 30 feet out meant my point fly had disappeared into the hungry jaws of a brown. A few minutes later a beautiful, deep brown of 14 inches lay on the bank, sharp red and black spots radiating from its flank.

In the next two hours I fished the same honey hole, landing eight fish between 13 and 15 inches—big fish, both for me and for the river. I returned home that night soaked to the skin and grinning from ear to ear. From that point on, I was forever a wetfly addict.

Since moving to America, I've been exposed to a vast array of techniques and an uncountable number of weird and wonderful flies. A glutton for punishment, I've tried most of them and had fun doing so. Still, on my local rivers in the Northeast, I keep finding myself reverting back to a team of two wet flies. A couple of modern compromises have crept into my wetfly fishing, however—one being that in high or fast water, a beadhead Hare's Ear Nymph often replaces the point fly. But perhaps my most

significant leap into the modern world has been to replace more traditional wet flies with the Grouse & Flash series, which incorporates an abdomen constructed of artificial materials. As with many of the best flies, the Grouse & Flash series is more a style of tying than an actual fly.

Tied in varying colors and sizes, G&Fs can represent anything from emerging caddisflies and BWOs to—in a pinch, at least—small baitfish. Versatility is the name of the game here! I started tying and fishing the G&F four years ago, and today, I must confess, I rarely switch back to a truly traditional wet fly. The G&F is just too deadly for me to use much of anything else.

To date my most productive version has involved a base of white thread with a slim abdomen of pearl Krystal Flash wrapped around the shank on the rear two thirds of the hook. I finish with a small thorax of hare's ear (use a finer dubbing material on smaller sizes) and then a sparse hackle (two turns) of grouse. On smaller sizes, woodcock works well.

From the July/October 2004 issue

The combination of a translucent abdomen and "busy" thorax and legs really lends this series to a wide variety of emerging insects, from midges to caddis and mayflies. Just change colors and sizes to meet your needs. For deeper-fishing patterns, add a couple of wraps of lead under the thorax. In all sizes of Grouse & Flashes, I prefer a lean and mean appearance, sometimes opting for only a single wrap of hackle.

The use of Krystal Flash for the body of a traditional wet fly may not be as far removed from the thinking of the likes of Pritt as we may believe. In Pritt's time, a sparse dubbing of seal's fur the same color as the thread often would be used on traditional wet flies to produce a translucent effect. Today, though we opt for Krystal Flash, the tier's desire for translucency remains the same.

The body can be tied in a wide range of colors, either by varying the color of the Krystal Flash, or by changing the color of the underlying thread. Both options work, but the latter is my favorite.

Yes, the G&F can be fished with devastating effect in the traditional down-and-across method, but imagination is the only real limiting factor on how you fish this versatile series of flies. On my local river, the Winooski, I like to use an orange version, size 14, on the point and a pearl size 16 as a dropper. When I swing the flies down and across just below the surface, takes can often be seen as a strong swirl.

Fishing deeper, I often use a heavy beadhead nymph for a point fly and the G&F as a dropper about 24 inches above it. Add lead and a strike indicator and you can chuck and duck with the best of them.

If fished static in still water or dead-drifted in flowing water, the G&F, with its hard, slim abdomen and "busy" thorax, will hang in the surface film in a very realistic rendition of an emerging insect, be it a tiny BWO or succulent, fat caddis.

The Grouse & Flash

1, 2

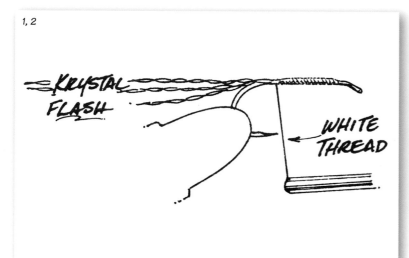

> **Hook:** Standard wet fly, size 10 to 22
> **Thread:** White for the abdominal underbody; black for the remainder of the fly
> **Abdomen:** Overbody made with four strands of Pearl Krystal Flash (size 12; fewer strands on smaller flies)
> **Thorax:** Hare's ear dubbing
> **Hackle:** Two turns of grouse hackle tied in by the tip

3

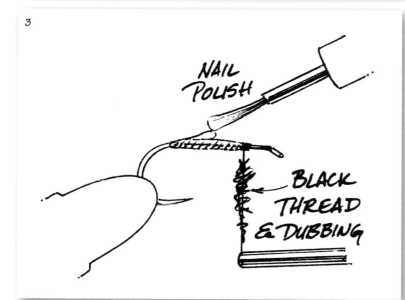

❶ Tie in white thread, and four strands of Krystal Flash, just behind the hook eye.

❷ Wrap thread to the rear of the shank in tight, touching turns, binding the Krystal Flash to the top of the shank. Stop just before the hook bend.

❸ Wrap the thread back forward to a point one-third of the shank-length behind the eye. Follow with flat, touching turns of Krystal Flash, maintaining a slim profile. Tie-off the Krystal Flash; half-hitch and trim the thread. Apply a thin coat of varnish or head cement to the body and allow it to dry (for efficiency, it makes sense to tie these bodies by the dozen).

4

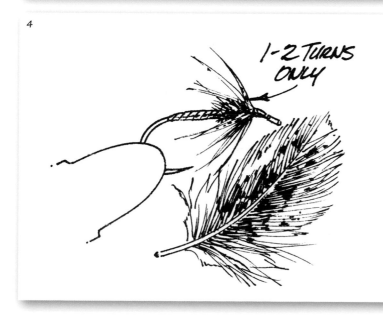

❹ Attach black thread in front of the abdomen and dub on a ¾" ball-like thorax of hare's ear dubbing (for flies 18 and smaller, use mole).

❺ Tie in a grouse hackle (it should be about hook length) by the tip, in front of the thorax. Take two turns of hackle, tie off, form a small head, whip-finish and apply cement.

D. L.'s No-Foul Rabbit Eel

A solution to a vexing problem

D.L. Goddard
May/June 2000

Bigmouth bass, striped bass, northern pike, cobia, speckled trout and tarpon are just a few of the fish that can be taken with regularity on an eel pattern. The eel fly—some refer to it as a worm or snake—has been around for a long time, with a number of variations. It has been tied with any number of different kinds of materials: rabbit skin, bucktail, tubing, cord, etc.

When tied with a weedguard and worked on the edge of a bed of lily pads, it's one of the deadliest patterns you can use for largemouth bass. Barry Reynolds' and John Berryman's *Pike on the Fly*, the definitive work on fly-fishing for northern pike, shows no fewer than seven variations of the eel. Fished in Southern salt water, around markers and buoys, or sight-fishing, it will produce cobia in respectable numbers.

Retrieve it deep and slow around jetties and submerged rocks along the Northeast coast and you'll get more than your share of large striped bass (brown, black, purple and olive are the colors of choice). Red, purple, chartreuse and black bring the slamming strikes of speckled trout from Chesapeake Bay south to Key West. An eel fly in crawfish orange will often catch you a backcountry tarpon when nothing else is working.

In order for this pattern to be effective it should be at least five to six inches long, and the tail should move in an enticing, undulating fashion. Herein lies the problem. Most eel patterns are tied in such a manner that the tail fouls on the hook on most of the casts. Once this happens, you are wasting your time and you soon change to another fly.

There are several ways to prevent the tail from fouling the hook; the most obvious is the addition of a weedguard. I almost always tie this pattern with a weedguard, since I often use it around weedbeds or in areas where seaweed has accumulated and becomes a problem. However, I also have another way to keep the tail where it belongs.

I simply take a piece of tubing two inches long and thread the tail through it with a piece of #2 leader wire that I have doubled and made into a sort of needle. I then tie this onto the top of the hook extending one inch beyond the bend. Encased in tubing, the tail can't wrap the hook bend, and you can even tie it without a weedguard if you like. The tubing requires an additional step or two in tying, but it's worth it. You can use any tubing you like as long as it is fairly stiff, and it should not unravel when you cut it.

I like to fish this fly on the slow side, with short, steady strips. When fishing around structure when there is a heavy current running I will drift the fly with the current, but you must keep in touch with it. A big striper will inhale the fly and it will just stop. If you allow slack in the line you will not detect this strike. Just pretend you're nymphing with a 6-inch fly. The real key to success with this pattern is a slow retrieve.

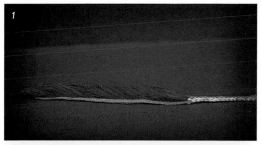

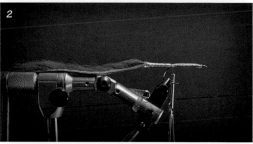

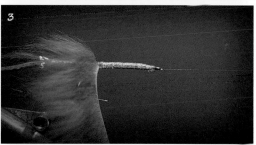

1 Double a piece of #2 leader wire. Feed it through the tubing, capture one end of the long strip of rabbit and pull it through.

2 Tie the tubing-encased rabbit strip on top of the hook; the tube should extend one inch beyond the hook bend. I like to saturate this tie-in with head cement, and I also put a drop or two at the back end of the tubing where the rabbit strip comes out. This helps to keep the tubing intact as you fish it. Run the thread to the back of the hook.

3 Tie in the strip of cross-cut rabbit hide at the bend of the hook. Run the thread back to the hook eye and lay it in a thread cradle.

4 Wrap the crosscut strip to the eye of the hook. Hold the hair of the crosscut strip back and tie off the strip. Wrap the thread back 1¼" to 1½" and tie off, but do not cut the thread. Cut the rabbit strip close to the thread wraps; catch the cut end with the thread and tie it down so there are no edges sticking out.

5 You can use 25- to 30-pound hard Mason leader material (1¼" long) for the weedguard, but I have switched to 30- to 45-pound Monel, or stainless twisted wire. They're much easier materials to use—you don't have to straighten them first—and pike and other toothy fish can't cut them off. To form the weedguard, insert the first ¹⁄₁₆" to ⅛" of the end into the jaws of a pair of pliers and squeeze the material flat. Flattening it like this keeps it from rolling under the thread torque when you tie it in. Then, still holding the tip in the pliers, push the long leg of the material against the pliers to form a permanent 60- to 90-degree bend. Remove the weedguard from the pliers, place the flattened tip against the bottom of the head of the fly, and tie it in.

6 Add your stick-on eyes and epoxy the head. You will find it much easier to apply the epoxy if you hold the rabbit hair back with the fingers of your free hand. This keeps the hair from falling into the wet epoxy. Let the epoxy dry and go fishing.

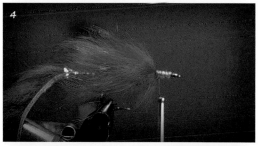

Hook: #2/0 Mustad 34007 or equivalent
Tail: 5" to 6" strip of straight-cut rabbit hide (a variety of colors will work)
Tubing: 2" piece of tubing
Body: Strip of crosscut rabbit hide
Thread: Fine, clear mono
Eyes: #2 black/silver stick-on
Epoxy: 5-minute Devcon or equivalent
Weedguard: 1¼" piece of 30-pound hard Mason or 45-pound nylon-covered twisted Monel or stainless wire leader

The Great Impostor

Tying the world's greatest brook-trout fly—the classic Hornberg—and a few of its variations

Mike Martinek
March 2006

In the gathering dusk of a perfect early July evening the boy made a rollcast into the pocket water across the stream. This was to be the last cast of the day. His father stood nearby and watched as the fly completed its swing. A solid strike and the bend of the rod signaled a fish on. A few moments later, a fat, 15-inch trout was landed, much to the joy and amazement of 11-year-old Paul Andrick, son of my best friend. His first fly-caught trout. The scene could have been of Paul's father, Steve, or myself, 40 years earlier. The fly pattern was a favorite of our New Hampshire summers past—the Hornberg.

The Hornberg, a "go-to" fly for many fishermen, and an absolute essential for the brook trout angler, is a multifunctional offering. Truly a "general imposter" that mimics trout food of several types (while not specific to any), it can be presented dry to represent the caddis-fly or the odd terrestrial, or fished subsurface as a small fry or struggling insect. It has worked its magic for me in New England and also in the Rockies, where a skeptical guide once watched, slack-jawed, as I used it to strip several trout from a tough section of a Wyoming stream.

The pattern was the concoction of Frank Hornberg, a Wisconsin conservation warden. The Weber Tackle Company, of Stevens Point, Wisconsin, helped tweak the fly design and began offering it as a commercial pattern. The earliest version was dressed in the late 1920s and the Weber entry was catalogued in the early '40s. The Hornberg's popularity can be attributed to a combination of Weber's expansive distribution and the fly's uncanny effectiveness.

In New England, the fly has a huge following and time-honored track record. It is fished in the North Country as a landlocked salmon and brook trout fly, but rainbow trout also fall to it with great frequency. In the smaller sizes, it may be cast upstream, allowed to drift dry and then twitched on the retrieve. In larger sizes I prefer it for subsurface fishing, letting it swim cross-stream, under banks, along seams and through pockets. Stripping a bunch of line out and letting it hang directly downstream can be extremely deadly, as can using a lively rod-tip retrieve in riffles and pocket water.

One day on the Moose River in northern Maine, I received a particularly powerful lesson on the Hornberg's effectiveness. I had thoroughly fished (or so I thought) every prime zone of a run and pool without success. Meanwhile, blackflies had begun attacking me without mercy, so I decided to move to shore for a cigar, and to regroup and plan my next move. As I made my way across stream, my fly line trailed behind me some 30 feet. Then, out of nowhere came a jolting strike, and I ended up playing and landing a heavy 17-inch brook trout. Just one more reason to trust in the Hornberg.

The original dressing for the Hornberg called for the mallard-flank wing to be stroked to a point. The yellow hackle points (the underwing) are sometimes replaced by a small bundle of calftail or marabou. The original hackle was wound on dryfly style in four or five turns. But, for a strictly subsurface dressing, a soft grizzly hen hackle can be wound on and pulled back with a few wraps of thread.

Hook: Light-wire streamer or long-shank nymph. No hard rule, but sizes 4 to 12 are favorites.

Head: Black

Body: Flat silver tinsel (can be coated with lacquer and allowed to dry before proceeding)

Underwing: Yellow hackle points, tied in on top of shank and extending slightly longer than hook (yellow hair or marabou can be substituted).

Wing: Two mallard breast feathers, lightly marked and tied in one on each side of shank. Once set, a small amount of cement can be worked into the tips of the wings, stroking them to a point (a variation using a wing of mallard flank tied in flat on top of the hook shank with yellow hair or marabou underneath is also effective). Allow room for hackle collar in front of wing.

Cheek: Jungle cock (somewhat long and narrow looks best). A very thin coating of cement may be applied to the back of the nail to adhere it to the wing.

Hackle: The original (wet) uses grizzly hen neck hackle, wound dryfly style. For a dry fly, use five to six turns of cock grizzly hackle in front of the wing, leaving room for a head. Hackle should be fairly wide ahead of the wing.

❶ Using black 6/0 thread, attach medium flat silver tinsel to the hook and cover ¾ of the shank with abutting wraps.

❷ Tie in two slender yellow hackle points, upright on the top of the shank, about ¼ of the way behind the hook eye.

❸ Place a mallard flank or breast feather on either side of the hackle points along the shank. Gently shape the ends to a point with head cement or dubbing wax.

❹ Add narrow jungle cock nails on each wing.

❺ **a** Hackle with good, stiff grizzly hackle, covering the forward ¼ of the shank with approximately 6 wraps.

❺ **b** For strictly wet fishing, use a softer grizzly hackle and tie back slightly at head.

Variations are endless and imaginative.
These are worth mentioning:
Teal wing: Strongly barred teal flank tied over yellow marabou
Wood duck flank wing: With yellow or orange hackle points or yellow marabou as inner wing, with front wound hackle of ginger
Conehead/beadhead: Styled and fished as a swimming or submerged insect or fry
Spun-deerhair head: Tied Muddler style. Good as a hopper imitation

Flies for the Salt

Tips & techniques for tying saltwater streamers

D.L. Goddard
March/April 1998

Early in my fishing education, some 50 years ago, my grandfather taught me something I never forgot: "Big fish eat little fish." This simple statement is the basis for the streamer fly, which has been used for at least a century in both fresh and salt water.

I am often asked what fly I like best for a particular location and/or species of fish. Since I am primarily a saltwater fisherman, perhaps 98 percent of the flies I use are streamers. Most saltwater fish (and I think freshwater fish as well) are very size-specific in their selection of baitfish. And the sizes they prefer will vary according to the season. In early spring the bait will start on the small side and will grow as the season progresses. Your flies should do the same.

When I set up my fly selection for a fishing trip I organize them in the following categories: Small, Medium and Large; Light and Dark. Then I fill in the various patterns to fit. That means doing a lot of tying. Following is a rambling selection of things to think about when you design or tie your own streamers (with illustrations where necessary or helpful):

When designing streamer flies, always try to include as many of the factors that trigger strikes as you can. For instance, eyes—we know that fish use the eye as a target, so the bigger the eye the more strikes you'll get. Motion is another strike trigger; the more action or motion a fly has the better it will fish. Silhouette and size are also items to be considered. And color needs to be factored into the equation.

A lot of tiers put too much material in their streamers. This prevents the fly from sinking properly, makes it difficult to cast and restricts its movement or action; it also makes the fly opaque. Very often, less is better.

In the past 10 years synthetic materials have come into their own. I find them a joy to work with, as they allow me to run rampant in my designs. The synthetics are more durable and less buoyant than many natural materials, and these last two factors are very important in saltwater fishing where the fish are often big, toothy and tough, and are likely to be found in deep water.

Some of the synthetic materials I use on a regular basis include five-minute epoxy, monofilament thread, Ultra-Hair, mylar

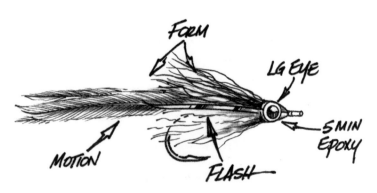

TOO MUCH

JUST RIGHT

tubing, Fly Fur, Krystal Flash, Sparkle-Flash and Fish Hair. But don't get me wrong here; I also use a lot of bucktail, peacock herl and hackle. Usually you will find me blending synthetics with natural materials to get the effect I want.

When tying saltwater streamers, I have found that by using fine monofilament thread I can apply a lot of thread pressure to tie in the materials very tightly. Mono thread also helps me avoid bulking up the head. If I want a different color head I can use a permanent marker or cover the mono with colored thread.

I never use head cement; I finish all my flies with a head of five-minute epoxy after I have stuck on a pair of the appropriate-size eyes. You will be able to finish five or six heads with the five-minute epoxy mix before it hardens. After coating the head with epoxy, I stick the fly in a rotating wheel and go on to the next one. It would take 10 to 15 coats of

head cement to achieve the same effects you get with the epoxy, and even then the first bluefish you hooked would bite through the 15 coats of head cement and your fly would fall apart.

Another technique I use, especially with bucktail streamers, is to tie the flash material in the center of the fly as opposed to on either side. By tying a flash material between two bucktail stacks you save time, and the flash material is protected by the bucktail and looks more natural; it allows the fly to appear almost translucent in the water.

Many patterns call for a side wing of hackle. How many times have you tried to tie in the hackle so that it rides alongside the body, only to have the feather turn out from the fly at a 60- to 90-degree angle? The hackle turns under thread pressure because the feather stem

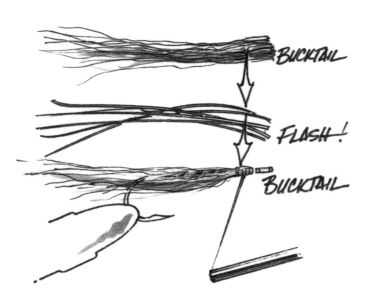

BUCKTAIL

FLASH!

BUCKTAIL

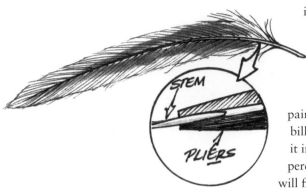

is oval rather than round. But you can easily overcome this problem by simply mashing the quill flat with a pair of smooth-jaw, duck-bill pliers prior to tying it in. This will work 95 percent of the time. You will find the odd renegade feather that insists on turning in the jaws of the pliers; instead of struggling, use these bad boys to clean out any epoxy you might get in the eye of the hook.

A trick passed on to me by one of my fly-tying students, Capt. Tim Tannis, of Ocean City, Maryland, consists of a practical way to use a rabbit-skin strip as the tail of a large saltwater streamer. The main problem in using rabbit-skin strips as tails has always been that they consistently fouled during the cast. Tim's solution was to take a piece of plastic tubing or the appropriate size, split it lengthwise for two-thirds of its length, then cut off one-half of the split. Now tie the half of the tubing in on top of the rabbit strip. Take a bobbin threader and reach through the remaining piece of whole tubing and pull the rabbit strip through. The tubing holds the rabbit-skin strip away from the bend of the hook so it doesn't foul. (This is much easier to do than it sounds.)

I tie a pattern that I call D.L.'s Epoxy Silverside. This is a full-body epoxy fly made with bucktail and Krystal Flash. The problem in tying this type of fly is in controlling the bucktail stack while you coat it with five-minute epoxy.

The easiest and quickest way I've found to do this, after I've tied the bucktail and Krystal Flash in place, is to make four or five wraps of .03" lead wire around the fly as tightly as I can, directly behind my thread wraps on the head of the fly. Then I slide the lead wraps to the rear of the hook, all the way to the beginning of the bend. The lead wire compresses and controls the bucktail and holds the Krystal Flash in place while I apply the five-minute epoxy to the body. I should mention here that when you cut your bucktail stacks—and prior to tying them in place—it is very important to knock out all the shorts and trash or they will begin to stick up out of the epoxy and your fly will look more like a porcupine than a minnow.

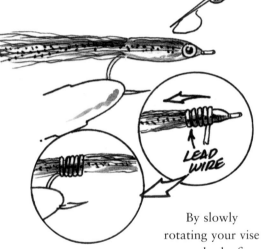

By slowly rotating your vise as you apply the five-minute epoxy you will end up with a very nice, full-bodied epoxy fly.

Another technique I have found very useful is to put feather tails on many of my streamer patterns. I start out by tying a 2" to 3" piece of small mylar tubing to the top of the hook shank. When you do this, be sure the rear of the mylar tubing does not unravel. Dip your bodkin into a head cement such as Dave's Flexament, and allow several drops to run up into the tubing. Just touch the end of the tubing with the bead of head cement on your bodkin and it will run right into the tube.

Now take an inexpensive black hackle and snip the quill with the point of a very sharp pair of scissors. Every time you do that a V-shaped tail feather will pop out. Take an appropriate-size V-shaped tail feather and at the point of the feather, on a 45-degree angle, cut back to the quill on each side. This forms what now looks like an arrowhead. Slide the arrowhead into the tubing and the head cement. Hang the hook up by the eye and allow the head cement to dry, then tie the fly around the mylar-feather tail. Be sure to tie the fly sparsely so that the mylar tubing is quite visible. The body of the fly gives it its profile, and the mylar tubing becomes its lateral line. You will want to stiffen the mylar tubing by either inserting a short piece of mono or by coating the tubing with a light application of head cement.

One of the main problems that I see on many improperly tied streamers is that they consistently foul when they are cast. This occurs when the tail material used is not properly stiffened or supported at the bend of the hook, allowing it to come forward and wrap itself around the hook bend (remember our rabbit strips?). There are many ways to overcome this problem.

Lefty's Deceiver is a good fly to use as an example in which, if tied properly, the long hackle used to form the tail will never foul. This is accomplished by tying in the hackles—from six to 10 or more—at the bend of the hook. Now surround them with a collar of bucktail that extends past the bend of the hook by ¼" to ½" or more. This prevents the hackle from wrapping around the hook.

When using hackle in a tail conFiguration, always be sure the quills are fairly stiff and that the feather will not droop if you hold it by the quill.

Another method to prevent fouling is to simply tie in a mono loop on top of the hook shank in the horizontal plane and then tie in your tail materials on top of the loop.

When you use natural materials such as bucktail, peacock herl and hackle you'll often find that, because the material was stored improperly, it has taken a set and is now very difficult to tie in the proper position. You will also find that your flies will take a set after sitting in a box for a while. Usually both of these problems can be quickly and easily solved by holding the affected material over a column of steam for a short time. A tea kettle makes an adequate steamer; just be careful of your fingers. Use a pair of pliers or forceps to hold the eye of your fly.

I once called a fly shop to introduce myself to the new fly-fishing manager and he quickly informed me that he only fished dry and that he didn't fish salt at all. After a lengthy conversation I finally convinced him not only to try the salt water, but also to carry a selection of streamers the next time he fished his favorite trout stream and to try them when the hatch was off. Several weeks later, I got a phone call from him and a very big order for a wide selection of my saltwater streamers. Fresh or salt, make sure you carry a selection of these fake baitfish, too.

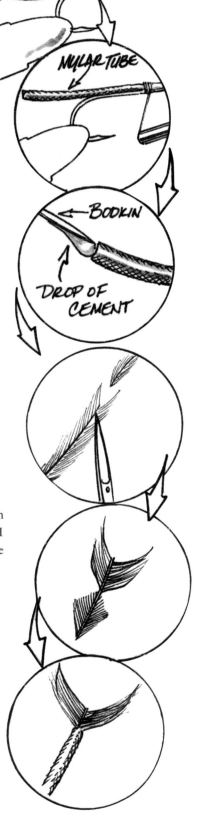

HACKLES TIED IN @ BEND

EXTEND COLLAR

OR

¼-1½"

MONO-LOOP

TOP VIEW

SIDE VIEW

The Gray Ghost
Tying the queen of the Eastern streamer flies

Darrel Martin
June 2001

Carrie Stevens (1882-1970), "the humble milliner of Maine," did not invent the feather-wing streamer. She did, however, significantly advance streamer design. By adding shoulders and cheeks, she made her Rangeley streamers imitate the swollen profile and the wiggle of baitfish. Her creations—such as the Gray Ghost and the Colonel Bates—are legendary. And that legend would, in time, enthrall contemporary fly tier Mike Martinek, of Massachusetts.

Though feather-wing smelt patterns were used by Herbert Welch as early as 1902, Ernest Schwiebert, in *Trout* (1978), stated, "the true feather-wing streamer is probably the work of Alonzo Stickney Bacon," a guide in the Grand Lake area of Maine. Legend has it that Bacon, shortly after the turn of the last century, grabbed a gob of saddle hackles protruding from a canoe cushion and crated an effective streamer. It was Stevens, however, who grabbed hackle and glued a legend.

In creating her fly, Stevens glued the cheek-shoulder-wing assembly together for later attachment to the rest of the fly. Mike Martinek, a nationally recognized streamer scholar and benevolent autocrat of the tying table, ascribes this glued assembly to her vocation as a milliner—building and gluing feather combinations for ladies' hats and hatbands. Her feather assemblies usually have rich or subtle color combinations.

Martinek considers the feather streamer to be the most hideously abused style in fly-tying today. He believes that, with today's superior tools and materials, the modern tier should be able to improve upon the past. A well-wrought Gray Ghost, he declares, is a "bouillabaisse of materials that melds into a harmonious whole." The Gray Ghost should have an attractive profile created by shoulder and wing, and a body subtly sheathed by translucent wings. For Martinek, it is a pattern for cold, gray days after ice-out, one to be fished a foot below the surface for large, aggressive fish—traditionally, brook trout or landlocked salmon.

Though Stevens left scant documentation of her craft, there are extant flies as well as cryptic notes sent to H. Wendell Folkins, who eventually bought Stevens' business. And, though we lack explicit tying information from her, we can learn something of the skill behind her mystique through Joseph Bates' *Streamer Fly Tying and Fishing* (Stackpole, 1966) and Graydon Hilyard's *Carrie Stevens: Maker of Rangeley Favorite Trout and Salmon Flies* (Stackpole, 2000). We can also evoke some of her talent through Mike Martinek.

While adding his personal touch, Martinek incorporates some of Stevens' method and theory, such as glued wing assemblies and wing positioning. But, before you wrap a legend, Martinek would like to remind you of some essential elements of tying a streamer:

● Begin with fine white thread. Replace the white thread with fine black thread when mounting the wing assemblies and whipping the head.

● Cement and assemble each wing-shoulder set prior to mounting. Martinek uses a thick nail polish—Sally Hansen's Mega Shine—that doesn't cavitate into the wraps or feather webbing. Before mounting materials, use this thick cement as a foundation. It secures and shapes the fly. Martinek considers streamer tying a malleable medium: He actually squeezes and forms the fly during tying and drying.

● When mounting materials, stagger mount points forward to minimize bulk. Wrap a slender, smooth body. Use materials sparingly, especially the underbelly hairs.

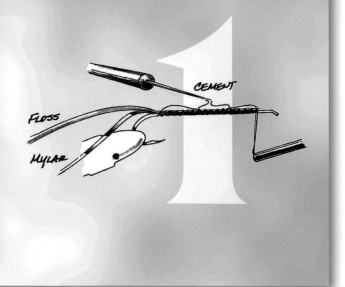

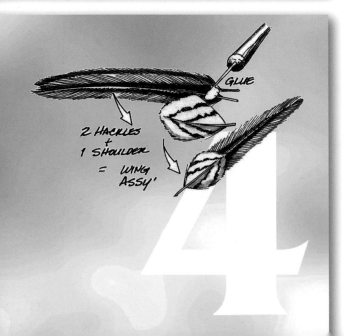

Tying the Gray Ghost (Martinek method)

Note: The part of the streamer denoted by the following terms may not have the same location or function as those on the traditional salmon fly. The "topping" is, as Martinek calls it, part of the "inner wing." It does not follow the outer perimeter of the wing as the traditional salmon-fly topping does. The streamer terms "throat" (the small bundles of schlappen barbs beneath and above the shank) and "beard" (the lower crest) are at best ambiguous. Consult the drawings for clarification.

Hook: The Mike Martinek Rangeley Streamer Hook, from Gaelic Supreme, size 6 or 8. This hook is based on the pre-war Allcock 1810 down-eye, Sproat streamer hook much preferred by Stevens. Martinek hooks have a long point and an attractive, finely-tapered, "half-down" ring eye
Thread: 6/0 white and 12/0 black
Tag: Flat silver tinsel
Body: Orange silk floss
Ribbing: Flat silver tinsel
Underbelly: White bucktail; rather straight, sparse hairs with tapered (not stacked) ends
Lateral line: Peacock-herl barbs
Beard: Golden pheasant crest
Throat: Stripped and bundled white hackle or schlappen barbs
Wings: Four fine-stemmed gray hackles. Martinek extends the wings about ⅜" to ½:" beyond the bend; much depends upon the hook and whether the streamer is cast or trolled. Wings may be longer for trolled patterns
Topping: Golden pheasant crest
Shoulders: Silver pheasant body feather, extends slightly short of mid-shank
Cheek: Jungle cock, mounted slightly cocked
Head: Black thread. As a trademark, Stevens added a narrow band of thread, often orange or gold, to the head

❶ Use 6/0 white tying thread for initial construction. Lay down a foundation of tying thread along the shank to keep parts in place. To avoid bulk, the tinsel may be laid total body length or mounted immediately behind the body on the hook shank. If you use the latter method, trim the end of medium mylar tinsel at 45 degrees and mount it with the silver side down. In Hilyard's book, the tinsel and the floss are mounted on the shank "one quarter of an inch forward of the hook point." Position the orange floss along shank spine and secure with tying thread. Floss should occupy body length or ¾ shank length. To hinder rust and rot, apply a coat of cement along the floss underbody. Let dry.

❷ Wrap a smooth, think silk floss body. Flare or widen the multi-strand floss when wrapping forward. As Martinek notes, wrapping the body is much like smoothly covering the shank with tape. Stop the body about ¾ shank length, then wrap a small, smooth head "bulb" at the front. This creates a foundation and "lock" for the wings and shoulders. Note that the body ends well forward.

❸ Stevens sometimes counter-wrapped the ribbing for greater strength. Take three turns back with the ribbing and three turns forward to form the tag. The rear of the tag should be directly above the rear of the barb. Stevens often varied the tag position: Some patterns have the tag mounted well forward of the hook point. Next, spiral the ribbing forward, leaving, according to Martinek, about a matchstick width between wraps. Martinek uses mylar because, unlike metallic tinsels, it stretches, and does not oxidize. Secure the tinsel and trim excess.

❹ With thick cement, join two hackle wing bases together for each wing assembly. Select a proportional shoulder feather and cement the stem base. Press the shoulder feather onto the base of a wing assembly and set aside to dry. Repeat this for opposite wing assembly. Note that each wing assembly will consist of two matched hackle wings and a shoulder feather. The outer edge of the shoulder feather should match, if possible, the profile of the hackle base. Remember, do not mount the wings to the body now.

❺ To make the underbelly, gather a small bundle of white bucktail. Martinek prefers fine, white bucktail from a young buck or doe. Select hairs that are moderately straight. Do not use a stacker to align the hairs. Instead, finger-stack to create a soft taper. Martinek believes a streamer can be delicate and graceful without being perfect. Mount the bundle beneath the shoulder section so that the tips extend about ⅜" (may be ½" to ¼") beyond the hook bend. Dampen the fingers and "romance"— lovingly persuade—the hairs into position. Add cement to the hair base.

❻ Mount a golden pheasant crest beard, about ½ shank length. Sometimes the lower crest is mounted in front of the "shingled" schlappen "spikes."

❼ Select four to six strands of peacock herl and mount on the shank top. The herl, without flare, should hug the hook shank. Apply thick cement to the herl mount. (Herl length matches wing length.) Compress and shape the herl mount section to receive the flat wings.

❽ Mount a golden pheasant crest, about wing length, on top. The crest should match, or nearly so, the wing length and lie along the spine on the shank. It should not arch above the wing like a salmon-fly topping.

❾ Attach short, white schlappen barb bundles as beard on bottom. Taper each bundle base before mounting, and stagger each bundle to erase the footprint of the previous bundle. Martinek points out that it is like "putting shingles down to cover up what came before." Use two or three tiers of barb bundles to create the baitfish profile and base for the wings.

❿ Match with another two or three tiers of schlappen "spikes" on top.

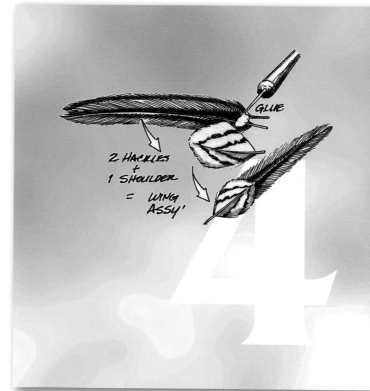

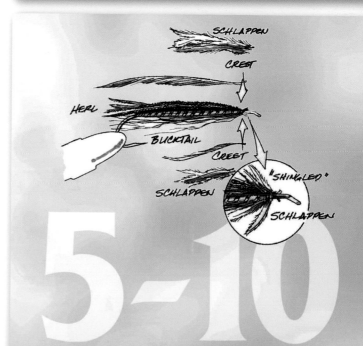

⓫ Whip off and remove the white tying thread. Martinek then mounts a 12/0 black Benecchi thread.

⓬ Place thick cement on the inside base of the left wing assembly. Position the wing assembly with three soft loops. Align the wing stem along the top of the hook shank and secure. Stevens recommended, in a letter to Folkins, that the hair and wings should extend about ⅜" beyond the hook bend. Martinek, following Stevens, rejects streamers that have a wing "like a half-opened jackknife." Such patterns do not resemble the sleek profile of a baitfish.

⓭ Repeat cementing and positioning for the right wing, making certain that wing tips match. When mounting the wings, a few thread wraps should "bite into the barbs" to keep the feathers flat. Martinek warns that positioning the wings is like being in De Beers' diamond cutting room, where "curse words are uttered and dreams and hopes are broken." According to Martinek, great flies are made by softly positioning the parts before anchoring them. Now, firmly compress the shoulder area to flatten and form the pattern.

⓮ Place a drop of thick cement on the back of the jungle cock. This makes the brittle and delicate jungle cock more durable. Attach the jungle cock feathers only after both wing assemblies are mounted. (Do not attach the jungle cock cheek prior to mounting the wing assembly, as then they cannot be "romanced" into position.) Position the left jungle cock with a slight upward cant. Repeat and match the jungle cock cheek on the right side.

⓯ Add a small "spike" of white schlappen barbs for a forward throat and a small spike on top for what Martinek terms a "reverse throat."

⓰ Finally, whip-finish with about five turns in the middle of the small head, clip tying thread and finish with a double coat of cement. Avoid copying Stevens' color band. As Carrie Stevens once wrote, "The narrow golden band tied in the head of my flies is sort of trademark with me—while it tends to beautify the fly, is also represents a fly of the highest quality in material and workmanship." Most headbands apparently were red, orange, yellow or gold. Modern tiers should instead seek their own design trademark.

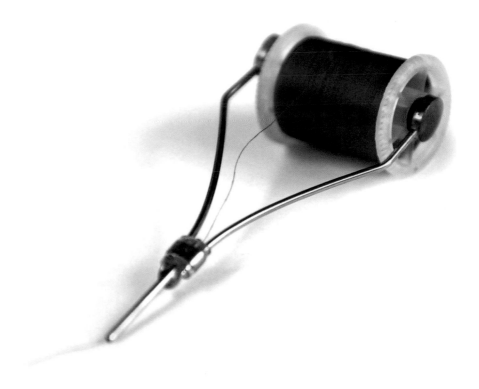

Though a classic, Stevens' Gray Ghost was not impervious to change. Apparently, she varied materials and methods when required or desired. Certainly material shortages during World War II contributed to some changes, as did the desires of her customers. Her wing hackles varied among grays tinged with brown, red or ginger. Stevens would, at times, mount the peacock herl under the shank with the underbelly, or on the shank with the wings. Sometimes she substituted translucent goat hair for the bucktail underbelly. At times, she even swapped the golden pheasant crest feather for durable, golden-dyed polar bear hairs.

According to Hilyard, Stevens' glue method, unlike the Eastern unglued method, produces a superior pattern. It keeps the shoulder in place and positions the wing so that it masks the hook point. Furthermore, Hilyard declares, the glued shoulder allowed a more realistic tail or "wing" wiggle. He notes that, "Carrie radically altered the profile by tying on material parallel to the side of the hook, sometimes slightly cocking the jungle cock eyes at an angle. This contributed to the slender baitfish profile characteristic of her work." The shoulders were the gill plates. The bucktail was the belly and the peacock herl, the lateral line.

Austin Hogan, artist and angling historian, was Mike Martinek's mentor. According to Hilyard, Hogan recognized Stevens' talents early and compiled what would eventually become the definitive record of her career. Though Martinek brings his own talent and techniques to that legend, that legend is also part of his talent and techniques.

In 1971, Martinek received a letter from Joseph Bates, in whose honor Stevens had created the Colonel Bates streamer. Bates sent Martinek an original Gray Ghost tied by Stevens, along with the fly card in her own handwriting. Bates added, "Of course very few of these still exist, but your reproductions of Carrie's technique are so exceptionally good that she seems to tell me that I should give this fly to you. I am pleased to enclose it because I know you will treasure it, and perhaps, frame it, in memory of her."

Tying outside the (Fly) Box

Experimentation leads to buggier flies . . . and more fish.

Darrel Martin
March 2004

> "I enjoy the quiet hours of discovery. I have never believed in speed tying; I have a different agenda – *I play with methods.*"

After all, most flies fish longer than it takes to tie them. Discovering new ideas and new combinations brings creative intensity to tying. Thinking outside the box produces, now and then, some remarkable methods and insights. Some discoveries are empty, but others are filled with promise.

Here is a body method from my vise, from those quiet, exploratory times of tying outside the box. It is certain that other tiers will take my method and improve it.

The Husk Body

This "husk" method creates a dubbing sack—a soft, wispy body for various patterns. The husk body has innumerable applications for ant, beetle, grasshopper and spider imitations. It may also be used for some tailed imitations as well. The husk or sheath may be constructed of yarn or any long-strand dubbing. For the underbody of ant patterns, I like to use a bulky, crinkly dubbing such as Master Bright.

Unlike a typical hook-shank body, with this method the hook hides directly beneath the husk body among the hackle or legs. This bulbous body does not decrease the hook gap. The hook, if color-matched, blends with the parachute hackle. The "naked" hook encourages penetration. Furthermore, the husk body is not stiff and straight; it is soft, arched and realistic. Sometimes a unique or odd tie, such as a husk body, takes trout when tradition (and every other fly) fails.

The Single- and Double-Husk Body
(Antron or polypropylene husk)

❶ Mount a slender needle in the vise.

❷ Select polypropylene or Antron yarn about three times the required body length. Match the diameter of the poly yarn to the fly size. For example, a size 12 hook requires about only 2-ply of a 3-ply poly yarn. Because the fibers are often twisted together, it may be best to separate them with a comb prior to mounting. This widens the husk and allows it to encircle the needle. The husk, which should completely encircle the needle, need not completely encircle the body when folded forward; interesting effects are possible if the husk just covers the back or sides of the body. Mount the yarn at the needle point and then wrap the thread back to the rear of the body space. Remember that the yarn foundation should completely encircle the needle. Whip-finish at the rear of the body.

❸ Dub a full "wispy" body and position thread at body front.

❹ Next, fold "husk" forward to encircle or sheathe the body, overwrap and whip-finish for a single husk body. With a quick tug, remove the body from the needle.

❺ For a double-husk body (photos), keep the first body on the needle and continue to overwrap the poly to create a slender midsection, the willowy "waist" of many insects.

To add another body segment (such as a thorax), merely push the husk back, advance the thread and then dub another body segment.

❻ Fold the husk forward, capture the husk and whip-finish. Finally, with a quick tug, remove the bodies from the needle. For a secure finish, add a drop of superglue to the final whip wraps. Once dry, the "lip" (which ultimately forms the head) may be trimmed short.

If required, several body sections of varying sizes may be dubbed and enclosed in this manner. Interesting effects result from contrasting body dubbing and husk colors. Other long-strand fibers, such as the dubbing itself, may be used in place of the poly or Antron husk. Strand length should be about three times body length. Any dubbing that is long enough may serve as the husk. Master Bright Dubbing, for example, is as long as eight inches. Even Nature's Spirit Fine Natural Dubbing has strands about six inches long. Small bug bodies, even on a size 20 hook, may be made in this manner. Brief finger stacking aligns most fibers prior to mounting. Again, make certain that the husk completely, though sparsely, encircles the needle. Allow the body to show through the filmy husk. Follow the procedure for a single or double body.

The body or bodies may now be mounted in any manner (the photos at right show a Husk Ant), detached or extended, on a hook shank. Add other requirements such as legs, hackle and wings to complete the pattern. Following are several single- and double-bodied husk patterns.

✖ **Caution:** Remember to wear adequate eye protection when tying with an exposed needle.

The Husk Pupa
(Single-husk body)

This is a remarkable, simple introduction to the single-husk body.

> **Hook:** Daiichi 1100 or 1180; Tiemco 100 or 5210; or similar dryfly hook, size 12 to 20
> **Thread:** 3/0 bark brown or black
> **Husk:** Antron or polypropylene yarn
> **Thorax**: Nature's Spirit Dubbing, dark brown, or similar
> **Hackle:** Brown or cree

❶ Mount a single-husk body at mid-shank

❷ Dub a dark thorax over the body mount and fore-shank.

❸ Mount and wrap hackle. Whip-finish head.

The Husk Caddis Pupa
(Single-husk body)

This realistic caddis pupa—complete with antennae, legs and wing pads—may be weighted with a bead hidden within the husk or body. Though this pattern has antennae and emergent wings, simpler and more practical patterns may omit these. The Antron husk covers the bright underbody with a silver sheen, much like the natural. Unable to find appropriate emerger wings, I size and shape my own with a wing burner. Select "patterned" hen patch feathers for the wings. "Drape mount" the wings to slant back beneath the body.

> **Hook:** Daiichi 1560 nymph hook; Tiemco 3761; size 12 to 14
> **Thread:** 3/0 bark brown
> **Husk:** Antron yarn, fluorescent white
> **Body:** Rusty orange Master Bright dubbing
> **Antennae:** Two pheasant tail barbs
> **Legs:** Two or four pheasant tail barb tips
> **Thorax:** Hareline STS Trilobal Dub, brown or brown stone

❶ First, make a single-husk body, approximately shank length.

❷ Mount the body so that the rear of the body is about even with the hook bend.

❸ Add a pinch of thorax dubbing before mounting the legs and wings. Add another pinch of dubbing before mounting the antennae.

❹ Complete with dubbing and whip-finish the head.

❺ Brush thoracic dubbing aft with a dubbing teaser.

The Husk Ant
(Double-husk body)

The following ant pattern is one of the buggiest imitations that I have developed or encountered. Though I have called this an ant pattern, perhaps the term "Spant" (spider/ant) may be more descriptive. A dark body and dappled legs create remarkable realism.

> **Hook:** Daichi 1100 or 1180; Tiemco 100 or 5210; or similar dryfly hook, size 12
> **Thread:** 3/0 bark brown or black
> **Husk:** Three-ply polypropylene yarn
> **Body Dubbing:** Rusty orange Master Bright dubbing
> **Hackle:** Hen cape hackle with contrasting marks

❶ Make a double-husk body with slender waist as illustrated. The thorax segment should be about the size of the abdominal segment. Mount the body assembly with three or more firm thread wraps immediately behind the thorax (the front body segment). Select a hen hackle and remove barbs from one side. Attach hackle by the tip and secure firmly at body mount point.

❷ Wrap the parachute hackle—no more than once or twice—around the thread junction that secures the double body to the hook shank. Pass the stem under the thorax in front and secure it with thread wraps. Trim excess stem.

❸ Capture the front "lip" of the first segment and wrap down for a head. Whip-finish the head. Bend the leg barbs for realism. For a different Husk Ant color scheme, see previous spread.

Fly Tying

by Darrel Martin

Retired from his position teaching
English literature, philosphy and writing
at Washington State, Darrel Martin
has nothing short of an encyclopedic
knowledge of fly-tying. He's the author
of a healthy handful of books on the
subject of wrapping natural and synthetic
materials on a hook; his Fly-Tying column
debuted in *Fly Rod & Reel* in 1991.

Terrestrials, Part I
Trout cannot live by aquatics alone

Darrel Martin
April 1996

Terrestrials—ants, grasshoppers, beetles, bees and countless other creatures born on land—have a lengthy and illustrious lineage in fly-tying. They are, in fact, some of the earliest recorded artificials.

The Treatyse of Fysshynge with an Angle, dated 1496, included a "waspe flye" with "a body of blacke wull & lappid abowte wt yellow threde: the winges of the bosarde." This "waspe," however, is still enigmatic; W.H. Lawrie believes that it may have been, in fact, a cranefly rather than a wasp. In the 1676 edition of *The Compleat Angler*, Charles Cotton wrote about the Ant Fly and the Palmer-Worm. The Palmer, which imitated a caterpillar, would eventually evolve into our Woolly Worm and Woolly Bugger, patterns that imitate a variety of creatures, including the stonefly, the dragonfly and the leech.

Alfred Ronalds (1836) gives an ant dressing—peacock herl tied with red-brown silk, starling wing and red hackle. G.P.R. Pulman (1841), though he cared little for the lowly ant, still felt obligated to give a dressing "for the sake of a good variety": copper-colored peacock herl, red hackle, dark red silk and jay wing. Though Pulman claimed that he was "indifferent" to ants, he did, curiously enough, insist that the wings had to lie flat along the body like the natural.

Michael Theakston (1853), writing with more reverence and respect for the humble ant, recommended peacock-herl body, amber thread, reddish-brown mohair legs and snipe or starling wings. In these wet dressings, peacock herl was the staple. Although iridescent, it hardly matches the lustrous ebony or amber and apparent hardness of the actual insect body. F.M. Halford, in *The Dry-Fly Man's Handbook* (1913), while bestowing only an abrupt and brief paragraph on the ant, does list it as one of the six insect families exploited by the dryfly fisherman. Halford's red ant was tied with a honey dun hackle, copper-colored peacock herl and orange tying silk, with or without starling wings. Halford notes that it was "one of the best patterns" during hot weather and "one which is too often neglected by dry-fly fishermen." G.E.M. Skues, that sage of the sunken fly, offers a red ant made from chestnut colored wool in *Silk, Fur and Feather*. He also advocates a blob of thread and varnish for smaller, wet patterns similar to those illustrated here.

J.W. Dunne's *Sunshine and the Dry Fly* presents perhaps the most ingenious ant pattern devised. Dressed with a synthetic "cellulite silk" on a white-painted hook, the pattern had hackle-point wings and a honey dun hackle. When soaked in colorless paraffin, the hook shank disappeared and the body darkened to a deep, ruddy, translucent chestnut. The radiant beauty of the ant confirmed his theory of "translucent tying": "The ball-like abdomen of the brown ant is fairly transparent, so that it constitutes really a sort of spherical lens, in some part of which you will nearly always see a beautiful gleam of red, transmitted light." Dunne, who wanted to capture that gleam of transmitted light, goes on to say that the pattern is not often needed. But when needed, it is truly needed.

Vincent Marinaro, in *A Modern Dry-Fly Code*, observed that only the red ant glows "as though lighted by some inner fire," while the black ant is "absolutely opaque." Marinaro's red ant incorporated transparent horsehair or nylon dyed golden brown to realize some transparency. No matter; even translucent insects, such as fragile spinners, fail to glow if lighting conditions are not suitable.

Most anglers know the McMurray Ant and the succulent Whitlock Hopper. Other traditional and innovative terrestrials include the Coch-y-bondhhu (the Bracken Clock), Welshman's Button (the beetle, not the caddis), the Letort Cricket, Marinaro's Jassid, Marinaro's Pontoon Hopper, the Michigan Hopper, the daddy long legs (the Harvester), the wasp, the foam ant, the foam beetle, the green oak worm, the common ground beetle, the soldier beetle, the Palmer (the caterpillar), and Calcatera Ant, the Calcatera Beetle and other exotics.

Some novel terrestrial ties, fashioned from balsa and cork, come from Swedish tier Rolf Ahlkvist. Ahlkvist shapes a stylized balsa body, glues it to the hook and then delicately paints it. His Wasp (*Getingen*) is a popular Scandinavian pattern. According to Robert Lai, a Swedish tier, the Wasp also imitates the caddis pupa during night fishing

for trout and sea-trout. It has a low, sharp silhouette and floats forever. To tie the fly, cover the threaded shank with epoxy before embedding it in the shaped body. Overwrap body and shank with thread five or six times before whipping off. Paint the body light brown, adding black stripes. Finish with a dry grizzly hackle.

The Stink Bug (*Barfisen*), topped with a fluorescent indicator dot, imitates the insect frequently found in the water in late summer and early fall. Ahlkvist's Hopper (*Grashoppan*), an enchantingly stylized fly, matches the color of various hoppers. Eyes, legs and hackle are usually done in contrasting colors. Mount the legs—merely two closely trimmed hackle stems—with a thread "band" after the body has dried. Then cover the thread band with paint and add the contrasting eyes and dry hackle. Such petite, "plug-like" dry bugs made from balsa or cork were popular in America at the turn of the last century. Though we may dispute they "dryfly" legitimacy, no one should argue their history and artistry.

Following are tying instructions for the Nirihuao Hopper. Opportunistic trout favor such morsels throughout the year, not just during the warm and windy days of late summer. Many terrestrial patterns are simple, pleasurable ties. And, as the past proclaims, most "complete" anglers carry a few land-borns.

The Nirihauo Hopper

There are several effective grasshopper patterns. The Nirihuao (nee-ree-wow) Hopper, named after the graceful Chilean meadow stream and its hopper hordes, is an excellent balance between attractor and imitator. If the trout has no preference, the legs may be omitted. Without legs, the pattern becomes the Fluttering Nirihuao. The underwing imitates the radiant yellow or orange hindwings of many short-horned grasshoppers.

Hook: Tiemco 200R in appropriate size
Thread: Pale yellow (imitates abdominal sutures)
Body: Dyed gold, pale yellow or orange deer hair to match
Underwing: Orange Krystal Flash
Overwing: Dark deer hair. Color should match the hatch
Hackle: Dun, cree or grizzly
Legs (optional): Knotted pheasant-tail fibers, trimmed hackles or emu. Durable legs may be made from coarse hackle feathers

1 Mount gold, orange or natural deer hair body as shown. For greater durability, coat the underbdody with Dave's Flexament before folding overbody forward.

2 Fold body hairs forward, forming a plump abdomen. Pass tying thread through body hairs and spiral forward.

3 Mount and spread Krystal Flash fibers. Trim to overwing length, slightly beyond the hook. Make certain to push Krystal Flash fibers down along the sides. Add deerhair overwing and wrap securely.

4 Mount matched legs along the sides. Select hackle feathers (or emu feathers) with wiry stems. Bend the feather and trim as illustrated, creating a slender tibia and wide femur. For realistic legs, paint the femur purple with permanent markers and add black bands. Apply Dave's Flexament to knee and tibia. Legs may also be fashioned from knotted pheasant-tail fibers.

5 Finally, mount and wrap dry hackle. For greater attraction, wrap the hackle area with orange or yellow thread and space the hackle wraps to reveal the contrasting under-color.

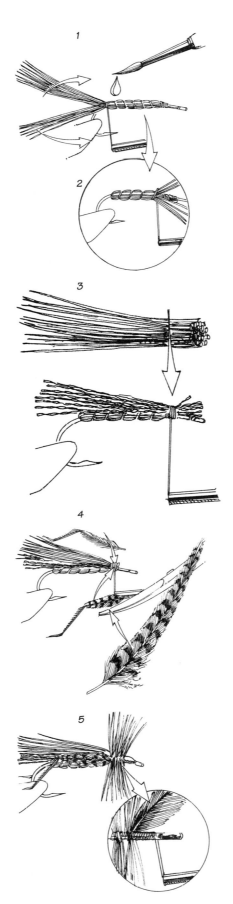

Terrestrials, Part II
And more recipes for cooking them up

Darrel Martin
May/June 1996

Tying terrestrials seems to encourage radical methods and materials. Perhaps the bizarre body profiles provoke creativity. There are even beetles made from floating fungus and seed pods. And Lee Wulff created his looped-hackle hopper by looping feathers on each side of the fly. The leg feathers—badger hackles with the dominant black cores—were mounted at the head and anchored either back at the head or at the tail. Wulff believed that the open-loop feathers mimicked the prominent legs, camouflaged the hook bend and increased flotation. Furthermore, when the pattern was twitched, the legs quivered with life. This became the first of his looped-wing patterns.

Here I offer more methods and patterns for common land-born creatures—the Winged Ant and the Sack Spider. The directions for the Sack Spider include similar methods for tying beetles, ants and wasps.

Terrestrial as well as aquatic spiders sometimes fall prey to trout. But not all spiders are spiders. W.C. Stewart's short and slender "spiders" imitate various nymphs and emergers rather than actual spiders. His spiders perhaps take their name from their arachnid-like legs (the long, radiating barbs) rather than from their object of imitation.

But actual spiders ballooning through the air on strands of their own silk may fall upon water. Other spiders, such as the semiaquatic fishing spider and the wolf spider, live near water and hunt small insects and fish; true aquatic spiders spend most of their lives under water. Even if trout are not taking spiders, often a novel pattern like a spider or beetle will take trout when "traditionals" fail.

Small wet spider imitations may be tied much like Skues' wet ant—with thread and colored cement. The Sack Spider, however, requires a small nylon sack and float ball. Spiders come in various body shapes and sizes. Permanent markers provide many body colors and designs.

The Winged Ant

The ubiquitous ant, in its various sizes and dress, is perhaps the most common angler's terrestrial. The larger versions are usually fished wet; the smaller ones, dry. Small, dry black ants may be fashioned with two whorls of peacock herl and a hackle. Hackle and wings help them float. Realistic wet ants (like this one) are simply fabricated from thread and colored cement.

> **Hook:** Daiichi 1190, size 12 to 16
> **Body:** Red, black or amber tying thread, sized to wrap a body quickly
> **Cement overcoat:** Red, black, brown or cinnamon gloss cement (Loon Outdoors Hard Head or gloss nail polish)
> **Wings:** Two white hackle tips or cul de canard feathers, tied delta (V-shaped)
> **Hackle:** Ginger, black or brown, sparsely wrapped

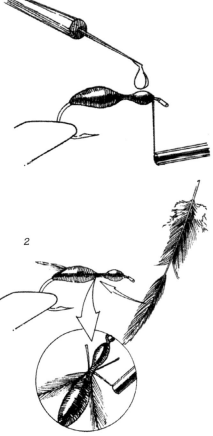

❶ Wrap two body whorls—a tapered thread abdomen and a narrow waist—and finish with the thread at the head. Apply two or more cement coats. After the first coat, rotate the shank so that the cement gathers and hardens on top of the hook shank.

❷ After drying, add tying thread at waist. Now mount two white matched hackle-tip wings (or use cul de canard feathers). Wings should be delta tied: flat and slightly spread.

❸ Finish with a sparse hackle and a drop of cement at the waist.

To make the Winged Ant drift in the surface film, replace the thorax thread with a full dry hackle. Add flotant to the hackle prior to fishing.

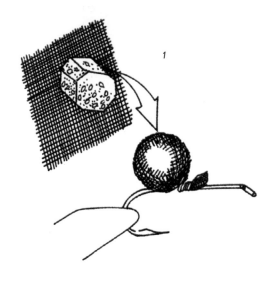

2-3

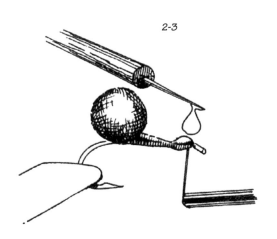

1

3

Hook: Daiichi 1190, size 12 to 14
Thread: 6/0, color to match the spider
Body: Small foam float ball and a swatch of a nylon stocking. White or cream nylon are best. Float balls may be shaped from Evazote (Dry Fly Foam) or any similar closed-cell foam
Legs: Emu feather, pheasant-tail barbs or soft-hackle, with the stiff barbs of an emu feather best. Cut off the wiry barbs from one side of the feather. Sparsely wrap the emu and, when completed, bend the barbs for realism
Head: Thread and Loon Outdoors Hard Head Cement

The Sack Spider

❶ For a single mount point, enclose the foam ball completely in a nylon square about 2" wide. Twist all four ends together into a small mounting tag.

❷ After mounting the abdominal ball, form thorax and head with thread wraps. The single-ball method creates the narrow, extended thorax (cephalothorax) common to many spiders.

❸ Coat the head and thorax with colored cement. After drying the head and thorax, add sparse legs made from an emu feather, pheasant-tail barbs or soft-hackle. If you use a soft-hackle, merely wrap hackle two times to imitate the legs. Although most spiders are predominantly black, gray or brown, some are adorned with gaudy blotches and baroque patterns.

The Sack Spider method accommodates a menagerie of other terrestrials. The nylon sack (after enveloping one or two float balls) may be single or double mounted for different terrestrial profiles. The ladybug, for example, may be made by double mounting (fore and aft) a single float ball. Loop thread over the back to divide the split wing case.

You can tie beetles in a similar manner, with two float balls. A brace of artificial beetles appears in Francis Francis' *A Book on Angling* (1876, fourth edition). One beetle is made with black gut legs and a peacock- or ostrich herl body overlaid with a brown or mottled feather case. Lead strips add weight and tight laps of thread divide the abdomen from the thorax. Francis claims that the wet artificial beetle is "very useful at times" but that it does demand "much skill and quickness" when fishing. One reason, perhaps, why there is no common beetle pattern may lie in the fact that the 30,000 species vary significantly in size, shape and coloration. Usually, a medium-size, dark, generic imitation serves as surrogate for all.

Wasps and bees are best imitated using two float balls; the double-mount method pulls the body down along the shank. Throughout angling history there have been many bee and wasp patterns. However Alfred Ronalds, in *The Fly Fisherman's Entomology* (1844), brusquely concluded that trout never take wasps or hive bees and only rarely do they take the larger "humble bee." Despite Ronalds' condemnation, Francis Francis illustrated a charmingly plump black-and-yellow bumble bee in *A Book on Angling*. Ronalds may have been unduly narrowed by his native waters.

The flies we've covered in our discussions of terrestrials—the Winged Ant, Nirihuao Hopper and Sack Spider—and their variations on a theme yield many other landborn patterns. Enough, perhaps, to match most crawling creatures. Remember that trout selectivity is not confined to aquatic insects. Matching the hatch with terrestrials can be as difficult as matching duns and spinners. Lee Wulff, in *Lee Wulff on Flies* (1980), describes terrestrial selectivity: "A profusion of terrestrials coming down the stream can sometimes be even more confusing than a difficult hatch. There may be some insects hatching out and trout rising furiously but refusing to take any of the hatching aquatic insects." Instead, the trout are intent on tiny drifting beetles trapped in the scum or flying ants adrift like spentwing spinners. Terrestrials are more than late-season condiments.

There were days when I believed that authentic tying was only about mayflies and caddis. But even a mere glance at the literature reveals that anglers have tied and tossed terrestrials for more than 500 years. And they tie and toss them for a simple reason: Trout take them. One warm English summer, while I was fishing the River Kennet, hordes of ladybugs blanketed everything. After increasing their population by one small artificial, I tossed it near two cruising trout. Sure enough, one swung over for a take. Truly, the juicy, crisp grasshopper, the tart ant and the peppery jassid all add spice to the trout's table and, more important, to our tying bench.

Imitative Tying and the BWO
New options for an old standard

Darrel Martin
May/June 1997

What tier has not modified or created flies? Modifying a traditional pattern or developing a new one comes naturally. Today's "standard" Adams is far from the archetypal Adams. Leonard Halladay's original, according to William Blades, had a gray wool body, golden-pheasant-tippet tail and advanced, semi-spent wings. Later, with a touch of color, Mrs. Adams (or should it be Eve?) was born. We all believe we can make a pattern better or a better pattern. And often we can, especially for the particular waters that we fish.

Creating a fly is usually not an arbitrary exercise. As early as 1850, G.P.R. Pulman noted that imitative tying (an unfortunate phrase) was impossible. We cannot imitate every part and appendage of an insect. At best a tier can only suggest reality with materials. No insect wears a conspicuous and unnatural hook and tippet. And no tier can match the subtle color, delicate form and gentle buoyancy of the natural.

Yet most tiers do believe that imitative tying is possible. After all, Frederic M. Halford said so. At the turn of the 19th Century Halford was the headmaster of the school of exact imitation and the modern tier is, essentially, still a pupil in that school. Though mislabeled a realist by modern standards, Halford did emphasize the crucial elements of imitation: size, form and color.

Modern tiers accept this Halfordian trinity of tying. Within acknowledged limitations, size, form and color should match the natural.

But beyond these three there are other concerns. For example, the pattern should suit the particular water (the angling conditions) and the trout (the degree of selectivity). Finally, both tying materials and methods should fit the size and design of the fly. Imitative tying is not merely covering a hook with material; it is a creative process of reasoning, inventing and selecting. Most of all, tying is the art of making small discoveries. Not all tiers will go through the same thought processes or realize the same solutions in the same way. But all tiers, unless they are merely mindlessly replicating patterns, evaluate and select both materials and methods. Here then is that evaluation and selection process for one fly, the Blue-Wing Olive.

The first consideration is the insect. These small, ubiquitous mayflies—both Baetis and *Ephemerella*—seem to create selective trout. I have always needed an effective imitation of the small Olives for clear, quiet spring creeks.

In such waters the fly doesn't need heavy hackling, but it does require: 1) a clean profile that preserves the form; 2) a realistic dun wing; and 3) minimal

hackling. This fly must seem authentic while afloat—the trout in these slow, clear waters have fastidious taste. Olives have either two tails (like many Baetis) or three tails (like many *Ephemerella*). My natural Olive Dun, about a size 18 or 16, has three tails, a slate-gray wing and a medium olive-brown body.

A stripped peacock-quill body has proven extremely effective at times for Olive patterns, but such a body requires some time and skill. Evidently, the stripped peacock quill suggests the distinct abdominal segments of the insect. They don't call some Blue-Wing Olives "Little Quills" without reason. I can, of course, always tie just a few quill bodies for any super-selective trout. I will, however, get far better flotation and translucency from a lightly dubbed body.

The insect's olive-brown body argues a blend. Therefore, I use an olive-brown dubbing blend to achieve the appropriate color. Both my dubbing blends, impregnated with preen gland oil, have superb buoyancy. Even with minimal hackle I still get good flotation.

I have used hen-hackle dun wings for several seasons. But finding broad-tip dun hackles and mounting them properly always proves a problem. I need something simpler.

I could also make the shoulder hackle from CDC barbs spun in a dubbing loop.

This, however, is another problem I wish to avoid. I find that the solution for this pattern is the panel wing, which produces a flattened wing and an extended hackle at the same time; like any good technique, it produces more with less effort.

The panel wing has other merits. It provides a degree of realism, especially with the slanted, flattened wing. Additionally, the fly has a clean silhouette without the shrouding standard hackle. Contrary to the Halford manifesto, some early writers claim that color may not be too important for a dry fly. But matching the basic color seems simple enough. At the least, color allows me to identify the pattern. All is compromise. With these thoughts in mind, we now turn to the vise.

Hook: Daichii 1220; Tiemco 101; or similar, size 16 to 18
Thread: Uni-Thread, 6/0 or 8/0 olive-dun
Tails: Nutria guard hairs, hackle barbs or Micro-fibetts (tan or olive)
Dubbing: Nature's Spirit Fine Natural Dubbing, Brown Olive #8 and Blue-Wing Olive #3, blended in equal amounts
Panel or Thorax Feathers: Two types of feathers make the panels: either short, fine-stemmed CDC feathers or the nipple plumes that cap the preen gland. Mount either variety, dark or medium gray, by their natural tips. Nature's Spirit sells medium and dark-dun nipple plumes under the label Tufts of CDC. These make excellent panel feathers; there is no stem to remove
Wing: Two or three CDC feathers stacked, stripped, rolled and flattened

❶ Mount and splay the tail fibers. Notice that the tail is slightly lengthened—approximately 1½ times shank length—for better flotation. The buoyant nutria guard hairs are wide and long, making excellent dryfly tails. When spread apart, the guard hairs have a tendency to stay open, thus increasing buoyancy. A more realistic pattern may use just three guard hairs.

❷ Coat the tying thread with a fine film of high-tack wax. Then dice the dubbing into one-millimeter bits and, while spinning the thread between your fingers, apply the dubbing. Do not compress the dubbing on the thread. The finely minced dubbing creates a spiky, hazy, translucent body.

❸ Dub the body forward about ⅘ of the shank length. The panel wing requires minimal shank length for the extended barb legs.

❹ Mount two small, fine-stem CDC feathers (or nipple plumes) at the front of the body. Secure by the natural tips so that the stem bases (or nipples) point aft. In one experiment, I tried to form the side panels by folding forward some of the CDC barbs from the rear of the wing; it was difficult to keep the barbs together. The attached stem or nipple consolidates the feathers during tying. After completing the pattern trim the central stem or nipple, creating the CDC barb hackle.

❺ Match two CDC feathers and strip the barbs. Roll the barbs into a bundle and trim the stripped ends. Tie in the wing bundle, ramping toward the rear, by the base with the natural tips tilted aft. Remember to use only two or three CDC feathers; try to suggest a wing with just a few barbs.

❻ Fold the panel feathers forward on each side of the wing base. This flattens and splays the wing. Secure the panel feathers on top of the shank, immediately in front of the wing.

❼ Spread the panel feathers to each side and add a touch of dubbing in front of the "hackle" before whip-finishing the head. The wing-base panels on each side suggest the swelled thorax of the BWO mayfly. For nipple plumes, merely prune the stubby nipples, allowing the barbs to fan and create the hackle. The stemmed CDC feathers require a different finish. After whip-finishing cut the thick stem from the barbs with a single-edge razor blade and remove it.

❽ Finally, shape the BWO's elongated-oval dun wing. If the hackle is too long, merely fold the fibers down and scrape off the excess between a scissor blade and thumb. This creates curled, natural ends.

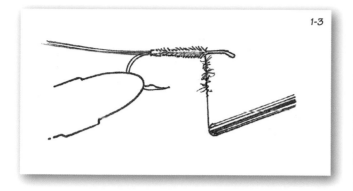

1-3

4

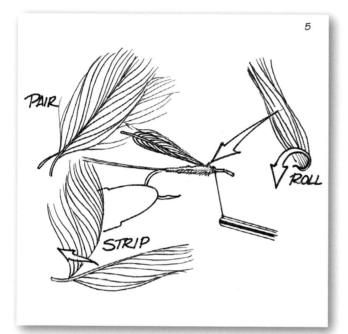

5

PAIR

ROLL

STRIP

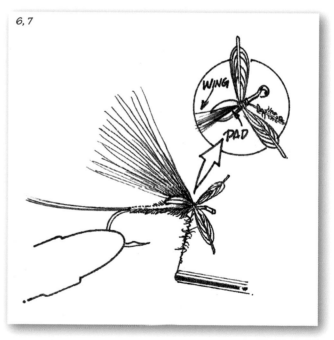

6, 7

WING

PAD

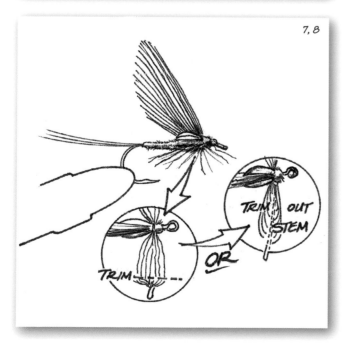

7, 8

TRIM OUT STEM

OR

TRIM ....

A Supernatural Art
Two guys who try to tie the hairs on a honeybee

Darrel Martin
July/Aug 1997

In a recent column I asserted that imitative tying was impossible. We cannot imitate every part and appendage of an insect. No tier can match the subtle color, delicate form and gentle buoyancy of the natural. But, as with all generalizations, there are anomalies. Some tiers push the tying envelope to achieve startling realism that goes far beyond size, form and color. These tiers create the supernaturals, the super-realistic patterns. Bob Mead and Bill Logan are two such tiers.

Realistic patterns appear early in tying literature. J. C. Mottram and Leonard West toyed with ultra-realisim in the 1910s. In the '50s William Blades created individual legs, antennae and lifelike extended bodies. His mayfly even had brown enamel eyes. More recently, Ted Niemeyer startled tiers with his famous stripped-quill stonefly nymphs.

Supernatural patterns are not fishing flies—they are museum art. These stiff and still patterns may not fish well, but they do comprise an artistic genre of their own. Collectors throughout the world buy and display them. These artificials, trapped in glass or miniature dioramas, represent hours of meticulous tying for the sake of tying. Though tying such flies is akin to model-making, both Bob Mead and

Bill Logan incorporate as much natural material as possible; they use synthetics only when absolutely necessary.

Note that supernatural patterns in general often include fewer synthetics than many flies, especially modern epoxy saltwater flies. Bob Mead, like most supernaturalists, believes that tying with synthetics is akin to cheating. Nevertheless, underbodies and wings often demand man-made materials. The real challenge lies in finding materials and creating methods for making these flies. As we shall find, even the basic stuff of fly-tying—feathers, hackles, feather stems and biots—can create startling realism. For Bob Mead and Bill Logan, there are materials and methods unique to their individual talents. And all tiers, even casual wrappers, can appreciate this awesome artistry.

Bill Logan's Gallatin River Salmonfly Nymph

Bill Logan was born into fly-tying. He grew up in Colorado where, for 23 years, his father was an outdoor writer for the *Rocky Mountain News*. Logan was about five when his father taught him to tie. But the supernaturals did not really hatch for him until he attended Southern Illinois University. For Logan, Illinois was "flat country with muddy rivers." He began realistic fly-tying as a proxy for fly-fishing.

With a Masters in Fine Arts, Logan is a sculptor and has done illustrations for *Life*, *The Saturday Review* and *Forbes* Magazine, among others. His flies are works of art, more like sculpted models than fly patterns. The 150 hours of intense, detailed tying Logan needs to produce a single stonefly is brief compared to the amount of time he's often invested in other types of art projects. As Logan says, "I've been off in the bushes tying more for my own giggles, stress and satisfaction than for anything else."

Bill Logan creates startling taxonomic detail and realistic morphology. His tying tools are not unique, but Logan does rely upon the highly maneuverable Renzetti vise to position the fly during tying. There is as much tying to be done under as on top of the fly.

Logan approaches tying as an artist. "Every time I tie a new bug, I often experiment with new methods and materials. For this reason, I keep a 'bench book' on each fly I tie to record the new methods and new materials. Generally each bug takes me between 125 to 150 hours to make. I usually try to do most of the tying in a single block of time because it is very intense. I lose my train of thought too easily if I were to putter, now and then, on a bug."

Logan's tying is complex. First, an intricately shaped and slotted brass shim, stiffened with piano wire, forms the foundation. The shim notches correspond to the design and thread layout. Once the shim is lashed onto the hook, an underbody, molded from polymer clay, is baked on. The tails are porcupine quills. Notice that Logan's "signature" is a broken appendage, such as a tail segment, for increased realism.

The abdomen segments are wild turkey primary biots, mounted on top and bottom. Some proprietary techniques, such as the leg spines and hairs, merely involve embedding ostrich herl in the femur sections. Logan tries to assemble the legs in the same structural manner in which they grow. The first two leg sections, the femur and tibia, use straight pins

as a foundation. Twisted thread creates the tarsal segments and claw. The wing case is a speckled hen body feather, impregnated with epoxy. Plastic sheets, which reject the polymer, help form the transparent texture of the wing pads. The cure time must be carefully calculated to produce a leathery, transparent wing. Further shaping and texturing takes place while it is still soft.

Epoxy sheets also form the prothorax, mesothorax and the head. Twisted thread creates the mouth parts; dots of epoxy, the eyes. The antennae are Hungarian partridge feather stems—steamed, flattened, twisted and then coated with Pliobond cement. A small cylinder of porcupine quill slips over the antennae, creating the swollen base. A needle makes a hole in the epoxy sheet to accept the gill tufts of Hungarian Partridge fluff; a loop of thread pulls these through to secure them. A water-base acrylic paint finishes the pattern.

Logan acknowledges that his creations are intricate. "I spend more time developing techniques for the realism than the time required to tie them.

"Great things elude me, however. My Holy Grail is a grasshopper. I'd also like to learn how to do the severely tapered bodies of bees and wasps. And truly triangular mayfly wings and the sparse and directional hairs on a honeybee."

Bob Mead's Damselfly

When Mead was about eight years old, Jim Schmidt, a distant cousin and renowned knife maker, showed him how to tie a fly. After that, wrapping feathers captured his imagination. For a few years he collected feathers from reluctant birds on his grandparents' farm, while relatives brought him hunting results—partridge feathers and deer

hair. These materials, however, captured with sewing thread, never produced an attractive fly. Later, one Christmas, an inexpensive tying kit offered the greatest gift, a booklet that unraveled the mystery of tying. Here at last were better flies. Mead fished the local streams, believing that the bubbling pocket water hid all his tying mistakes.

Once, during a long walk to the river, he stopped to rest. While resting, some twigs fell onto his waders. Surely, he thought, this was an omen. He had always felt susceptible to omens, claiming, as he does, Mohawk blood from his great grandfather. He never made it to the stream that day. Instead, he stopped at the house of an uncle who was a cabinet-maker by vocation and a gambler by avocation. Soon Mead became a heavy gambler. It took guts, Mead recalls, to step up to the betting office and place $200 on the counter. Then the worst thing happened—he won.

In time, Mead married on the condition that he get a good job. Working at the telephone company gave him little free time, but he found enough for bets and bookies. At the track one day, Mead was sitting on the back benches when he looked down and saw a twig on his trousers. He bent over to brush it off. But this twig moved; it was a walking stick insect. Here, finally, was a challenge more seductive than betting. In his fascination, Mead tied, with passion and purpose, his first supernatural. He would often stay up all night, struggling to imitate the insect with exacting detail. Through supernatural tying, Mead rediscovered himself and gave direction to his life.

He found the ultimate challenge in creating the more neglected insects: water scorpions, crickets, grasshoppers, wolf spiders, praying mantises and mosquitoes. Bob Mead, though now known principally for his realistic praying mantis, ties more than 40 different patterns, each fly requiring 60 to 70 hours to complete and selling for about $125. One of the most fascinating patterns is his damselfly.

Mead's damsel comes from creative thinking. The blue sheath stripped from 26- or 28-gauge wire forms the damsel's underbody. After stripping, the claspers are cut and blackened on the ends. Goose biots, tied for body segments, fold to hug and encase the underbody. Tweezers position the biots for cementing and tying.

Adhesive strips reinforce the trimmed cellophane wings. The thorax, a creased corner section from a bubble pack, accepts the base of the wings. Ostrich herl covers the thorax, duplicating the fine, dense cilia. The leg strand—a thread covered with drops of glue—is crimped for feet and knees. Mead favors legs made from hair. For example, he makes his mosquito legs from porcupine hairs (not the thicker, larger quill). He darkens the hair with permanent marker, then crimps the joints. A smear of cement along the extremities, particularly the tibia and tarsus, suggests the joints, spurs and setae of the lower leg. The waxy, oily hair surface causes the cement to bead, creating the minute projections. This method, which Mead discovered by accident, creates lifelike insect legs. Biots form the wider femur.

"For me, realistic tying is psychic," Mead muses. "I hope that I have carried it a little forward. So many tiers are doing amazing things today." Though Mead has caught bass on his supernatural crickets, the time and consummate skill required for these flies would be wasted on fish. They belong in museums.

For Bob Mead and Bill Logan, strange methods and materials merge to make an exquisite whole. When I gaze on their creative work, I am reminded of another insect, the Snap-dragon fly, in Lewis Carroll's *Through the Looking Glass*: "Its body is made of plum pudding, its wings of holly leaves, and its head is a raisin burning in brandy." Carroll would certainly understand living twigs and the quest for honeybee hair.

From the July/August 2007 issue

The Neglected Shrimp
So effective even Skues overcame his qualms

Darrel Martin
Jan/Feb 1998

In *Minor Tactics of the Chalk Stream* (1910), G.E.M. Skues offers an attitude about an early shrimp pattern. "I was at one time greatly interested in an attempt to imitate the freshwater shrimp, and I tied a variety of patterns, including several with backs of quill of some small bird dyed greenish-olive, and ribbed firmly while wet and impressionable with silk or gold wire; but somehow I never used or attempted to use any one of them." Skues had "felt qualms" when he caught fish on an artificial alderfly larva and was "conscience-stricken" when he had "mad success" with a caddis larva pattern. He was not certain as to the sporting propriety of imitating these insect stages. It seems that he also had some misgivings about the modest shrimp. He never did cast his shrimp fly; instead, he gave it to a colleague who promptly lost it to a large fish. That should have told him something.

The freshwater shrimp fly is curiously young. Early shrimp patterns were tied for salmon, but it would be some time before the trout variety was developed and accepted. It has been claimed that The Shell fly, in the *Treatysse*, is a shrimp imitation. Though now generally considered a caddis, the green wool body, peacock herl rib and bustard wing might suggest a shrimp. The name, perhaps, suggests shrimp more than the fly does.

Eric Taverner, as early as 1933, thought that traditional wet flies (such as the Partridge and Orange) and nymphs (the ubiquitous Gold-Ribbed Hare's Ear, for instance) might imitate freshwater shrimp. Traditional slip-wing wets may be shrimp surrogates. Perhaps the arched gray wings suggest the carapace or shell-back. Even the familiar Zug Bug might proxy for shrimp. William Blades, in *Fishing Flies and Fly Tying* (1951), offers a shrimp pattern. Tied on a straight-shank hook, it is made with goose or swan fibers coated with cement. There are also Mike Tucker's modern scud patterns, the bodies wrapped with a tubular material filled with vegetable oil (!).

Al Troth's Olive Shrimp has an olive elkhair carapace and palmer hackle. Gil Nyerges created his Nyerges Nymph to imitate the shrimp in the shallow alkaline lakes of the Northwest. The Nyerges Nymph has a chenille body and trimmed palmer hackle. George Herter, who had potent opinions about most things, was never satisfied with his shrimp patterns. Although Herter made shrimp imitations for "a great many years," he "never felt that they were really what they ought to be."

They were "difficult to imitate because of their unusual actions." Evidently, Herter found the erratic, flicking darts of the shrimp impossible to imitate by design alone.

The natural

A few tiers, like J. Edson Leonard in *Flies* (1950), make a distinction between the shrimp (*Gammarus*) and the smaller scuds (*Hyalella*). In tying and trouting, however, there is no notable difference. Shrimp are laterally flattened and have a distinct shellback or carapace. Although competent swimmers, most spend their time among plants or on the bottom. General shrimp flies may also imitate the stalk-eye and cylindrical fairy shrimp (Anostraca) as well as the horizontally flattened aquatic sowbugs (Asellidae).

The unusual shape and structure of the shrimp has sired some curious imitations. International fly fishing competitions affirm the effectiveness of modern mid-European shrimp flies. These, including the woven Polish nymphs, are usually heavily weighted on curved hooks, often with several colors in a single fly for a sense of life.

Indeed, some of the strangest and most innovative shrimp flies come from Europe. Neil Patterson's Red-Spot Shrimp, a popular English pattern, has a touch of fluorescent red wool to represent developing eggs. Ljubo Pinter, a Slovene, ties a *Gammarus* pattern made with dormouse fur and an eelskin carapace. Ivo Kajnik, another Slovene, creates remarkably realistic

hand-painted flies. Hans Nischkauer, of Austria, uses catfish skin treated with picric acid to form the shellback. And T. Preskawiec, of France, has a Gamma pattern made with a gray palmer hackle and two colored pike scales.

Despite these strange ties, shrimp patterns are extremely simple—a weighted hook, a dubbed underbody and a synthetic carapace or canopy ribbed with wire. Though many patterns call for a round or circular-bend hook, swimming shrimp are usually elongated. If desired, it is possible to suggest a body curve, rather than to tie on one. All hooks may be tied slightly down the bend to suggest a curved body while preserving a wide gap.

Another factor may recommend the straight shank: Some circular or rounded hooks may be reluctant hookers. Recently, while fishing a spring creek, I met heavy rises. My Adams tempted nothing on the surface. So I tossed a round-hook shrimp pattern that was immediately taken by an athletic trout. After a twist and turn he was off. The problem may be more the angler than the hook, but I have always been wary of circular irons.

Gary Borger, in *Naturals*, notes, "During

body. A fine black netting, seen through a transparent carapace strip, creates the etched dorsal plates of the shrimp. The netting, an ultra-fine mesh tulle, is available at most fabric stores. (White tulle is easy to color with permanent marking pens.) Select a net color that contrasts with the body dubbing, and use a dubbing loop to flare the fibers. Also mix and vary the dubbing colors along the loop. A pinch of red or amber at midpoint, suggesting the viscera or an eggsack, adds a flash of life. The spiky dubbing, which emulates the body and bushy swim-legs, should be long enough to touch the hook point. Wapsi markets Sow-Scud dubbing expressly for shrimp and aquatic sowbug patterns. Available in 18 colors, it's a blend of opossum, Super-brite and Antron. Also, Wapsi's Thin Skin provides an excellent flexible carapace in 15 colors, including clear, and eight printed colors. These transparent sheets, with matte and gloss sides, have appropriate stretch for shrimp backs. Ribbing is often done with fine gold wire or clear monofilament. The following pattern, a variation of the Czech Shrimp, is tied with fine tulle netting.

swimming the thoracic legs are pointed to the rear and the body is held straight. For this reason, scud patterns should not be tied humpbacked, but with a straight body." Some shrimp even swim on their sides; thus there is no need to provide a "keel" with weight. Weight, however, is often required to quickly sink the fly to the trout. I often use Skues' preferred bend, the Limerick. Shrimp hooks include the Partridge J1A (Limerick Wet Fly Hook) and the K12ST (caddis hook); the Tiemco 2302 (nymph hook) and the 2457 (round bend); the Daiichi 1530 (round hook), the 1150 (heavy) and the 1480 (Limerick fine-wire). Most medium-wire, straight-shank hooks work well. An adequate gap is necessary as much of the tie is beneath the hook shank.

The Czech Shrimp, perfected by Jan Siman, of the Czech Republic, is a simple and effective pattern. It achieves maximum realism with minimal tying. A spun-wire dubbing brush or a dubbing loop usually makes the

Twenty years after his first shrimp search, Skues found his fly. In the 1931 *Field* Magazine, Skues tells us of an acceptable freshwater shrimp pattern. He dubbed paleorange and olive seal's fur on a size 16 downeye Limerick hook, wrapping down into the bend to suggest the shrimp's curve. He then palmered on a pale red hackle, added fine gold-wire ribbing and trimmed the barbs off the back. Skues' shrimp has an adequate gap, a suggested curve, a dappled body and trimmed hackle. With triumphant epilogue Skues' shrimp, no longer a fugitive of his flytying, took two good fish, both heavy with natural shrimp.

Thread: 6/0 Uni-Thread, color matching dominant dubbing color
Hook: Partridge J1A or K12ST; Tiemco 2302 or 2457; Daiichi 1530, 1150 or 1480
Underbody: Wapsi Sow-Scud in various colors
Shellback or carapace: Black, fine-mesh tulle-net strip, and Wapsi's Thin Skin, color and print matching the natural
Rib: Fine gold wire or clear mono

❶ Mount the hook, and weight it if required. For weight, mount two or three wire strands on top of the shank. This increases sink and preserves the hook gap.

❷ Mount the wire rib, Thin Skin carapace and net strip. When folded over—after dubbing—the carapace should be wide enough to pull down the dubbing fibers beneath the shank. Shrimp patterns look best when the fibers flare and fold beneath the body.

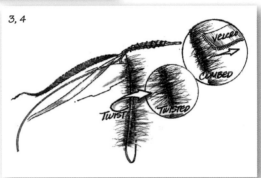

❸ Select a multicolored dubbing, such as amber, olive, brown and gray. Mount the short, spiky dubbing at right angles to the dubbing loop.

❹ Spin the loop tightly. Hold the dubbed loop firmly and then comb out the dubbing with a Velcro hook patch to extend and align the fibers before wrapping the dubbing along the shank. The Velcro hook patch, merely a 2" strip of hook Velcro, aligns the fibers prior to wrapping.

❺ When wrapping the dubbing on the shank, pull the fibers back to avoid their being trapped by subsequent wraps. The dubbing should extend far enough to screen the hook point.

❻ Fold the net strip forward and secure at the head. Then fold forward the carapace strip and secure at the head.

❼ Spiral ribbing forward and tie off at the head. Whip-finish. Darken head and carapace, if required, with a permanent marker.

The Humpy Hatch
Variations on the fastest (selling) fly in the West

Darrel Martin
Nov/Dec 1999

I was asked, several years ago, the perennial question: "If you could fish only one fly, what would it be?" At the time, I answered with conviction, "The Humpy." But, because the Humpy was not a hatch, my answer only gathered frowns and censure. Obviously I was an angler with much to learn.

In the West, the Humpy and its variations can constitute more than 30 percent of the total patterns sold by a shop in a single season. A Western angler who has not cast a Humpy is usually an angler without experience. I thought then as I do now that the inquisitor did not realize the creative possibilities of the Humpy.

There are, of course, the standard variations such as the Double Humpy and the Royal Humpy. Even the traditional Humpy appears with various tails, hairs, underbellies and hackles. This buoyant, "insectile" pattern works well in fast and still waters. And with minor variations on the Humpy's bodywing lap, a horde of delicate, practical flies hatch.

According to Jack Dennis, the term "Humpy," descriptive of its distinctly humped body, may have originated near Jackson Hole, Wyoming. Montana's Dan Bailey popularized the name "Goofus," a term sometimes given to a Humpy with mixed brown and grizzly hackles. True, the Humpy is effective because it imitates anything that the trout wants it to imitate, especially caddis and terrestrials.

The following variations use the Humpy's "body-wing lap method" with materials other than the traditional deer hair. Despite the name, these pattern are almost humpless. They have, instead, a delicate, easily tied two-tone body. These variations may be more effectual imitations of mayflies. Here then are some variations on the Humpy hatch.

When tying any Humpy, proportions—especially body-wing length—are the key. If proportions are wrong, the pattern is awkward. Even a small error in proportions significantly distorts the pattern. However, these four patterns eliminate most proportion problems and create a slender, subtle fly. A Humpy hook must have adequate shank and

gap space for body and hackle. Avoid short-shank hooks. For simplicity, the tying thread creates the underbody color.

The body-wing material must account for the underbody, overbody and the wing length. Using long, soft fibers (poly yarn, CDC barbs, wood duck barbs and pheasant tail barbs) makes all these patterns simple. Bulky body-wing materials, such as the traditional deer hair, require more length due to the wider body and wing bends. These new body-wing materials require less length. If the tail and wing equals shank length, then the body-wing materials will be slightly more than twice the shank length. The following illustration reveals that the total body-wing length is 2¼ shank lengths. A body-wing length of slightly more than twice the shank length including the hook eye usually is adequate. This may be measured directly on the tailed hook and easily adjusted for the proper proportions.

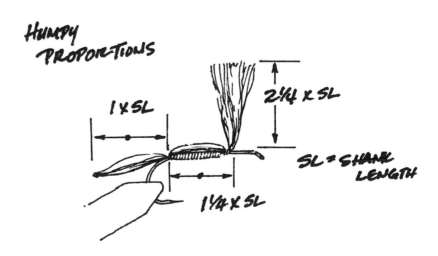

HUMPY PROPORTIONS

1 X SL

2¼ X SL

1¼ X SL

SL = SHANK LENGTH

The Shucking Poly-Humpy
Hook: Daiichi 1222, 1220; Tiemco 100, 102, 5210; Mustad 94840
Thread: 6/0 Uni-Thread, pale yellow
Shuck: Cream, yellow or white polypropylene yarn
Body-Wing: Polypropylene yarn
Hackle: Quality dry hackle to match the hatch

❶ Polypropylene yarn makes an excellent shuck; it is buoyant and available in a variety of colors. The durable poly shuck readily expels water during the cast. Here are two quick, simple methods for making a poly-shuck. Tie an overhand knot in a few fibers of white or pale yellow poly yarn. This creates a "capsule" shuck. Seal the end of the poly shuck by flame or gel. Then:
Flame method: Trim the excess poly yarn and melt the knot tip with a butane lighter or match. Melt only the extreme end of the knot, not the entire knot.
Gel method: Apply a small drop of Duro Quick Gel non-run superglue to the knot. When completely dry, cut the knot in the middle to create two shucks, one on each side of the severed knot.

❷ Mount the shuck at the tail position. Shuck length should equal body length.

❸ Take a length of poly yarn, about three inches long, and mount the tip at mid-shank (see illustration). Three-ply poly yarn may be thinned for the smaller flies. Two-ply or a ply-and-a-half may also be used for smaller flies. Overwrap the mounted butt smoothly with tying thread to create the underbody color.

❹ Fold the yarn forward as illustrated and wrap so that the yarn extends to the forward ¼ shank point.

❺ Select and mount a hackle. For a clean head, strip the hackle tip first so that when whipping off, the thread captures only the hackle stem. This avoids close trimming captured hackle barbs. Wrap the hackle as many times behind the wing as in front. Note that the hackle fills the front half of the shank. Tie off hackle.

❻ For a standard shank-length wing, trim the wing equal to the rear extremity of the hook. Extend the poly wing to rear of hook as illustrated and trim to length. Because the wing extends from wing mount point to the rear of the bend, the wing will equal the shank length when trimmed. Take care not to cut tail or shuck.

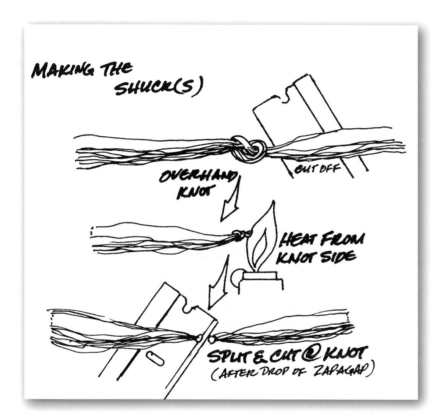

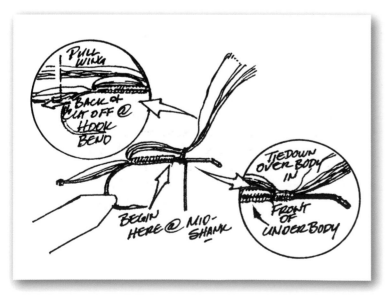

❶ For a standard dry tail, stack and mount a bundle of stiff hackle barbs.

❷ For the body-wing, select and overlap two CDC feathers with fine stems and long, fluffy barbs. Trim the butts and mount them at mid-shank. Overwrap with tying thread to create the underbody color. Although CDC wings may be trimmed to length, it is best to proportion the body-wing to avoid trimming.

❸ Fold the overbody forward and whip down.

❹ Add CDC barbs to a dubbing loop, trim barb base to length and spin, creating a faux-hackle. Or use a dry hackle instead.

❺ Mount and wrap the CDC "hackle" equal turns behind and in front of the wing. Whip off. If the wing requires trimming to proper length, extend wing back and trim length equal to rear of bend. However, try to mount and proportion the body-wing to avoid trimming the wing tips.

All these Humpy variants are heirs of the body-wing lap method. With creative, lateral thinking, various materials (polypropylene yarn, CDC feathers, wood duck flank feathers and pheasant-tail barbs) create delicate and effective Humpies. Moreover, these patterns are simple and seductive. From sizes 12 to 20, my Humpy variants have taken cutthroat in Montana, marble trout in Slovenia, and wild browns in England and Finland. Perhaps there is a new perennial question: Which insect does a variant Humpy *not* match?

The CDC Humpy

Hook: Daiichi 1220 or 1222; Tiemco 100 or 102; size 16 to 18
Thread: 6/0 Uni-Thread, pale yellow
Tail: Stiff feather barbs
Optional shuck: Furled CDC barbs or nipple plume. For the emerger, furl a few strands of long CDC goose barbs or mount a small nipple plume (also known as a CDC tuft) for a trailing shuck. The nipple plume may be tied in by the base bud, or the open ends, or gather and mount for a shuck "capsule"
Body-wing: CDC feathers (duck). Alternately, bundled CDC goose barbs may be used. Strip off long goose CDC barbs, trim the butt for alignment and mount at mid-shank
Hackle: Standard dry hackle or CDC barbs (dubbing-loop method)

The Wood Humpy

Hook: Daiichi 1220 or 1222; Tiemco 100BL; various sizes
Thread: 6/0 Uni-Thread, pale yellow
Tail: Stiff hackle barbs
Body-wing: Bundled wood duck barbs
Hackle: Dry hackle

Mounted and folded in the same manner as other variant body-wings, the lemon-brown flank feather of the wood duck provides a delicately mottled body and wing. Since the days of the Quill Gordon, the wood duck flank feather has furnished some of the most attractive fly wings possible.

The PT Humpy

Hook: Daiichi 1220 or 1222; Tiemco 100BL, various sizes
Thread: 6/0 Uni-Thread, pale yellow
Tail: Stiff hackle barbs
Body-wing: Bundled pheasant-tail barbs
Hackle: Dry hackle

Pheasant tail feather barbs make a durable and attractive body-wing. Merely cut a small barb bundle off the stem. Finger-stack to align the tips. Trim to the appropriate length. Mount and fold in the traditional manner.

The Body Beautiful
The foundation of all our flies

Darrel Martin
May/June 1998

Bodies offer the greatest creative scope in fly-tying. There are more materials and methods for tying bodies than for wings, tails and hackles combined, and the curious and creative tier will want to do plenty of experimenting. Though the insect body consists of the head, thorax and abdomen, it is the abdomen, often dramatically segmented and distinctly colored, that is the most conspicuous to trout. For the tier, the abdomen is the body. Surely, it deserves close and careful imitation. Here, then, are a few observations and methods for creating that body beautiful.

The insect body

An insect's abdomen, typically the longest of the three body sections, is made up of dorsal plates (tergites) and ventral plates (sternites) bounded or connected by membranous channels or lines (sutures). The abdomen, typically dark on top with a pale underbelly, consists of from eight to 11 segments separated by sutures.

Some patterns duplicate only the underbelly, as the darker top is less visible to trout. Most modern imitations usually ignore a differing color in the thorax. Saltwater and streamer patterns may have head colors that imitate the naturals. Some insects have prominent and colorful eyes, and a few early tiers believed that the thread color should match that eye color. The suture bands are roughly imitated with ribbing, though ribbing spirals forward and creates fewer "bands." In the insect world, all legs are located on the thorax. If we were tying "truth," only six hackle barbs would form the legs and eight or nine, non-spiraling ribbing bands would duplicate the sutures. But tying is not truth; it is impressionism.

When approaching the insect body, a tier must weigh several factors: buoyancy, transparency, color and color contrast, texture, durability, weight, texture and simplicity of construction. Early tiers used a variety of materials, such as cork, balsa, quill, raffia, mohair, gut, feather barbs, clipped hackle, hackle stems, stripped or flued peacock herl, horsehair, India rubber, silk, wool, chenille, fur and hair; modern tiers still use some of them.

Perhaps the most unusual bodies appear in William Blacker's rare and beautiful *The Art of Fly-making* (1855). "Gold-beater's skin rolled over flat tinsel" sheathes one body. His "winged larvae" body is made from the shriveled sack found at the end of raw silk gut. Golden pheasant tippet barbs whipped to the sack created tails. The "larvae" were mounted, detached fashion, immediately behind the hackle. Blacker noted that "There is nothing can exceed the beauty of these flies . . . ." This curious, attractive imitation, however, must have been rather fragile.

David Foster, in *The Scientific Angler* (1882) offers one of the earliest and most comprehensive analyses of the fly body: "To distinguish the correct colour of a fly as presented to the fish, we know of no better method than to place it in a clear glass of water, and hold it between the eye and the light in such a position as to be able to see underneath the insect." Seen from the trout's point of view, the precise body color and translucency is apparent. But the dead opacity of most body materials defeats any attempts at proper color and translucency. After Foster, the quest for the perfect body expanded. Even so-called imitationists—such as Halford—wished, within the confine of their chosen materials and methods, to imitate only a few features of the insect's body—color and size.

The tinsel body

Often an unsightly lump occurs when you tie tinsel in at the rear and then wrap forward. To avoid this, first mount the thread at the shoulder. Do not lay down a thread foundation. With three thread laps anchor the end of the tinsel and—with smooth, taut turns—wrap the tinsel to the tail and then return to the shoulder, near the mounting point. When wrapping, slightly overlap each turn and then, with added tension, force the tinsel to slip over the edge of the previous wrap and "click" into place. This produces tight, touching wraps. After wrapping forward, hold the tinsel end and carefully undo the initial three thread wraps. Next, capturing both tinsel ends with the thread, rewrap three times over both ends. This creates a remarkably smooth, slender, taut tinsel body held with only three wraps.

For fine control, select a narrower tinsel than recommended for the pattern. Narrow mylar tinsel is more elastic and more maneuverable than wide tinsel, and makes neater flies and cleaner turns, especially when reversing the wraps or when wrapping into hook bends.

Stripped peacock herl

First, check to see that the selected herl has a contrasting dark edge. These are found within the eye of the peacock tail. The eyed herls show a larger proportion of the pale ground and a finer, darker edge strip. Check peacock eyes by turning the eye over and pressing the eye herls flat against a surface. The paler the herls, the darker the edges. There are various methods for removing the "metallic" flue, from hot-wax baths to eraser scrubbing. The best method, however, is simple and speedy. First, I select a soft and high-tack tying wax. I then lay the tip of the herl across the wax and draw the herl, from tip to base (opposite flue-growth direction), along the wax. I do this

edge should face aft, creating a finished body edge. To strengthen a stripped-herl body, counterwrap with fine wire and/or coat with lacquer.

The clipped-hackle body

In *Fly-tying Principles & Practice* (1945), Sir Gerald Burrard advocates the clipped-hackle body for dry flies. First, select a hackle of the proper length. Stroke the barbs toward the base to erect them, and then, with long, sharp scissors, trim the barbs, leaving only short stubble on both sides. Mount the hackle by the point and wrap on as body. Despite the conventional wisdom that clipped barbs absorb water, the resulting barb stubble, when saturated with flotant, will float the pattern well. Burrard tenuously asserts that the clipped hackle is not appropriate for small flies. Perhaps he thought that the short stubble would not support a small fly. However, as the dense barb stubble traps flotant, it's fine for small and large flies. Fine ribbing will increase durability. Multicolored hackles, such as Cree and grizzly, create mottled translucent effects. Clipped-hackle bodies are attractive on shaggy sedges and rough nymphs. The singular advantage of the clipped hackle is that larger hackles may be used for smaller applications. The modern, ultra-narrow saddle hackles, however, might depose the clipped-hackle body.

The hackle-stem body

Stripped hackle stems are more durable and colorful than stripped herls. The natural taper produces a shaped body. The most famous hackle-stem pattern is Lunn's Particular, developed in 1917. The body is the stripped stem from a Rhode Island Red hackle. Multicolored hackles, such as grizzly, produce a mottled body. When removing the barbs from the stem, pull the barbs toward the base. Mount the stem by the tip and overwrap with fine, flat thread. Then, spiral the stem forward with touching wraps. Some tiers flatten the stem with pliers prior to mounting. A protective coat of lacquer over the body creates an attractive gloss.

two or three times and then, with my fingernail moving in the same direction, scrape the flue off. The result is a clean, waxed stripped herl. I label and set aside a super-soft, high-tack wax, expressly for this purpose.

To wrap a stripped-herl body, snap off the tender herl tip. Pulling, rather than cutting, breaks the tip at the naturally weak point. Then, lay the herl along the shank, extending about to the shoulder. Mount the narrow tip to use the natural taper of the herl. Overlap with fine, flat thread to secure. When wrapping the herl forward, the dark

The married-thread body

Try tying thread alone for very small flies. Waxed tying thread comes in various diameters and colors. Bodies are simply wrapped as well as shaped with a single thread. If you require a change of color, you can add another colored thread. And permanent markers make white tying thread any color at any time. It's easy, for example, to build and color match the swell of a Trico's thorax with thread.

Another technique, not much seen today, is the married-thread body. Various colored waxed threads "marry" to produce a single, flat "ribbon" thread. Traditionally, the choice strands are the ultra-fine flosses or Pearsall's Gossamer silks. On small flies, 3/0 tying thread may be used. When wrapped, the married threads create a vibrant, multicolored body. Normally the threads are kept flat so they do not entwine. Spun married threads create swirled, dazzling bodies, often kaleidoscopic. Different degrees of spin create different body patterns.

To make traditional married threads, apply a smooth coat of clear high-tack wax to two or three contrasting colored threads. The wax waterproofs and, more important, fuses the thread strands. Mount and wrap the married threads as a single body strand. To preserve the color intensity, spin unwaxed threads.

Attractive multicolored bodies, such as those for mosquitoes and some duns, may be fashioned in this manner. Also, spun bodies can mimic hackle colors: Combine and spin red (ginger), black (gray) and cream (white) threads for a Cree body. These bodies may suggest the iridescence or opalescence observed in some insects.

Depending upon the materials and methods, most bodies are tied with a slight taper increase. For a smooth, neat body, the base materials, such as ribbing tags or tail butts, should extend the complete length of the body. This avoids cracks and knobs in the overbody. Tinsel, herl, hackle and thread all make attractive and effective bodies.

Like many tiers, I enjoy past methods. Though few, if any, tiers will wrap William Blacker's winged larvae, I believe that most tiers find it fascinating. Early materials may no longer be available, but this, for a modern tier, is no limitation. The range of modern materials and methods would stagger early tiers. Yet, the past offers something more than material. It offers creative imagination. Modern tiers should substitute available materials and modify these methods for their own delight. A thoughtful and creative tier limits neither knowledge nor skill. Tying is perpetual discovery, and a tier who does not experiment never grows. Tying history, if properly approached, is still remarkably inventive.

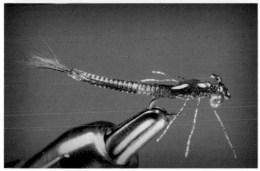

Leech Patterns, Part I
Even the wariest trout will fall for these juicy suckers

Darrel Martin
March 2002

Yes, leeches do suck. That is how they anchor and feed. Dark, slimy, slithery, sucking leeches also inspire effective fly patterns. But while trout and bass give closer attention to leeches than most anglers do, leech patterns are one of the major seducers of large fish.

According to Dave Whitlock's *Aquatic Trout Foods* (1982), leeches are best known "among fly fishermen who specialize in lake fishing and large trout," though most modern patterns are only "crudely suggestive of the real thing." For most anglers, a dark Woolly Bugger is close enough, and more exact patterns are not commonly found in tying books or fly boxes. Some leech patterns, however, are remarkably attractive morsels.

Leeches (class Hirudinea) are segmented worms, or annelids. Unlike other worms, however, leeches have suckers at each end—anterior ones for feeding and larger, posterior ones for anchoring. Their muscular bodies have multiple segments, or rings. They inhabit shallow ponds, lakes, marshes and sloughs. Though freshwater leeches prefer still or slow waters, some species may be found in fast-flowing waters. Most leeches feed on snails, worms, insect nymphs and larvae. They can survive for several months on a single meal. Though lacking conspicuous eyes, they do have acute senses of touch and smell. The jawed leeches (family Hirudidae) attack warm-blooded animals and inflict a painless bite from a toothed sucking plate. Most leeches, however, are not human parasites.

Leeches explore their surroundings by extending and waving the body and head; when swimming, their bodies stretch to about twice the relaxed length. Aquatic leeches swim with fluid, vertical undulations in open water. They elongate when swimming and contract when at rest on the bottom. Consequently, swimming-leech patterns should mimic their distinct flat "spindle" body, movement and elongation.

Patterns

In the beginning there was bait. Francis Francis, in *A Book on Angling* (fourth edition, 1876) noted "Leeches form an excellent bait for trout, and may be used with advantage at times." Specific leech patterns, however, are notably modern. Most modern ties call for soft fur or feather to imitate the leech's mobile body. An early "Leech Streamer" had several hackle feathers—such as black, maroon and brown—tied flat on top of the hook. Some patterns use soft marabou strands for their rhythmic, undulating swim. In *Naturals* (1980), Gary Borger advocates leech "strip patterns." Borger uses a tanned fur strip ($\frac{1}{16}$" to $\frac{3}{16}$" wide depending upon hook size) to create body movement. The fur strips should be cut so that the fur line—the direction of fur growth—runs down the length of the strip. Such patterns are often tied Matuka-style, i.e., the fur hide-side mounts flat against the top of the hook shank, and the ribbing spirals through the fur to secure it. The fur strip is vertical on the hook shank. Sometimes, Borger completes the pattern with "a soft, body-feather" hackle.

A rather realistic leech pattern, as well as leech habits and fishing instructions, appears in Dave Whitlock's *Guide to Aquatic Trout Foods*. This pattern uses soft chamois leather for a supple, flat body. The weighted hook sinks the fly and a retrieve ripples and undulates the extended body. An open Duncan loop to attach the fly to the tippet promotes full and realistic movement. Typical of Whitlock's tying mastery, the pattern is simple, yet realistic. His basic leech-fly colors are black, olive and gold, as well as mixed brown, olive, black and gold.

The Whitlock Chamois Swimming Leech

Though leeches may appear black, there is always a subtle color sheen or overcast of another color. Most leeches are camouflaged to blend with their bottom environment: They wear muddy background colors, especially browns, olives, tans and grays. These colors are often streaked, stripped, stippled, brindled and dappled with gold, orange, red or black. A paler color usually covers the underside. Though many leeches are dull and dark, some are pale gold and many have gold and red spattering. In any case, it may be best to brighten part of the fly to attract fish, especially in deep and dark waters. This is the rationale behind bright beads

or brilliant mottling. But brighten just enough to seduce, not scare.

The Leather Leech

As with Whitlock's leech pattern, leather forms the body. Soft-tanned elk leather is remarkably soft and durable, while being only 50 percent thicker than commercial chamois. It offers more form and substance, and when wet has a slimy, slithery, "leechy" texture. This unusual pattern incorporates a gold or tungsten head for weight and a closed-cell "buoyant" patch. The small buoyant patch significantly accelerates the swim action. The closed-cell patch, of course, may be mounted on most "strip" or extended-body patterns. The patch raises the rear of the fly, creating a tail wag during the retrieve. The patch also prevents the tail from wrapping around the hook bend.

Proportion is important in an extended-body leech fly. If the body is too long, the strike might not engage the hook. Furthermore, an overly long body encourages bend wrap. Conversely, an overly short body restricts the "swim action." Most patterns work best with the hook bend near the middle. For pronounced swim action, the strip should extend a hook-length or more beyond the bend.

To create the undulating leech swim, use a leisurely, pulsating retrieve—slowly retrieve the fly with short strips. The sink-head and the buoyant butt create exaggerated undulations when retrieved. This action alone may attract fish—both bass and trout—and encourage strikes.

The Whitlock Chamois Swimming Leech

Hook: Whitlock recommends the new Tiemco 765TC, sizes 2 to 8. Size 4 seems the most effective. The pattern was originally tied on Mustad's Limerick bend 3658-B

Thread: Nylon floss or Monocord; match color of leech body

Weight: Bead chain or "hourglass" eyes

Tail/Body: Chamois strip, dyed to base color, cut to shape and mottled with waterproof marking pens

Head: Dubbing same color as body

The Leather Leech

Hook: Daiichi 1560 or 1550, or Tiemco 947BL, size 6 to 10

Thread: 3/0 tying thread. Also used for ribbing. Color-match body

Weight: Tungsten or brass bead. Use bright enamel beads for color

Body: Soft-tanned elk hide. Chuck Furimsky's Bugskin may be used, especially the Speckled Leech material. All other Bugskins may be dyed and marked

Tying the Leather Leech

❶ Mount bead on hook shank, small hole toward hook eye.

❷ Mount the tip of the shaped body as illustrated. Note that the long, narrow extension mounts first.

❸ Dub a slender body from the front to the rear.

❹ Overlap the body extended along the hook shank.

❺ Spiral the tying thread forward to create segments and whip off directly behind the bead.

❻ Cut out a closed-cell patch. Use a gel superglue or Pacer's Zap-a-Gap (for leather, rubber and plastics) on the patch. Follow all directions when using superglue. Use a long pin to hold the patch when applying the glue and aligning the patch on the underside tip of the body.

❼ Finally, mottle and brindle the fly with permanent marking pens.

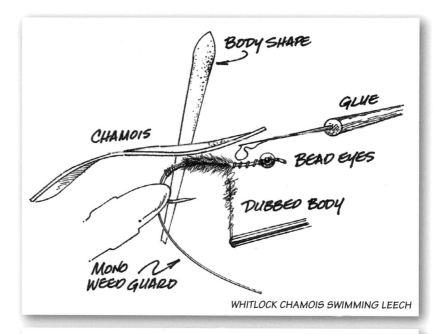

WHITLOCK CHAMOIS SWIMMING LEECH

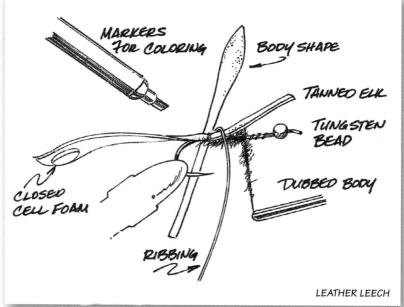

LEATHER LEECH

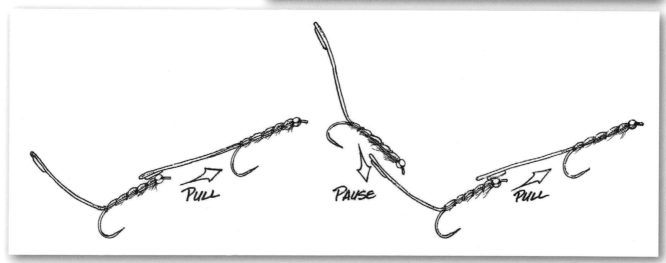

Leech Patterns, Part II
Three more flies to imitate those juicy suckers

Darrel Martin
April 2002

Here are three more leech flies to choose from the next time you're trying to seduce one of those very large trout that seems to have slight interest in smaller imitations. Following the patterns and recipes are sources for the leech-tying materials I have mentioned.

The Bunny Leech

McLean's bar-dyed rabbit pelts (in yellow-black, gray-black and olive-black) make an excellent, variegated leech pattern. After attaching a bead, mount the fur strip immediately behind it. A spun fur-loop covers the thread base. For a realistic leech, reproduce the shape, illustrated above, on the hide side of the fur. Then cut out the leech body with an X-acto knife. Avoid cutting the attached hair.

This "strip" leech requires few materials—a hook, a bead and a fur strip. To decrease body bulk, select pelts with short hair. The various color bands create attractive patterns.

The Bloody Leech

In dark waters, a brighter fly may work best. The Bloody Leech incorporates a colored bead and red thread for increased attraction. The body is made from soft, fine llama hair.

The Llama Leech

Soft and supple llama fur makes excellent extended-body leech patterns. Llamas commonly have two coats—a long, coarse overcoat and a fine, soft undercoat. The crimp and crinkle of the hair create volume. When retrieved, the llama hairs expand and contract like a leech. Use two different fur colors (one for back and one for belly) to produce contrast and attraction.

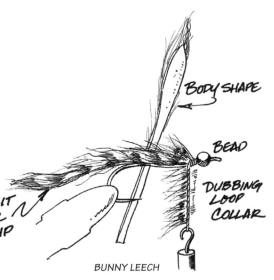

BUNNY LEECH

154

The Bloody Leech

Hook: Daiichi 1710 2X long, size 10; Tiemco 2302, 2X long, size 10; Daiichi 1273, 3X long, curved shank; Tiemco 200RBL, 3X long, curved shank

Thread: Crimson or orange-red 3/0 or 6/0

Body: Long, soft llama underfur, dyed black or dark brown. Soft arctic foxtail fur may be used for smaller flies

Weight: Tungsten or gold bead, 3mm to 3.5mm, double drilled

The Llama Leech

Hook: Mustad 3399, wet nymph hook; Daiichi 1550, standard wetfly; or Daiichi 1560, 2X long, 1X strong nymph hook

Thread: Color-match body

Underbody: Pale llama fur, gold, gray or dull orange

Overbody: Dark llama fur, black, gray, dark-brown, dirty gold or olive

Bead: Black tungsten bead, size 3/16"

❶ Slide bead onto hook with small hole toward hook eye.

❷ For tail, mount llama fur (sans guard-hairs) approximately twice hook length.

❸ Mount approximately four or five fur tufts along top of hook shank. Finger-stack each tuft to casually align hair tips. The body should be slender and some-what flat. Avoid a bulky body and tail. Crimson tying thread should be visible from the sides.

❹ Immediately behind the bead form a dubbing loop of fur. Spin and wrap a short fur collar. Whip-finish and remove tying thread.

❺ Consolidate and flatten the tail tip with a touch of adhesive tying wax.

❶ Slide tungsten bead onto hook.

❷ Select long, pale llama fur for underbody. Remove all guard hairs. The underbody should be approximately twice hook length. Before mounting, finger-stack to form a "spindle body."

❸ Form and mount a black or dark-brown "spindle" overbody.

❹ Immediately behind the bead, wrap a fur collar (formed by a dubbing loop and spun) to cover the base wraps of both body spindles.

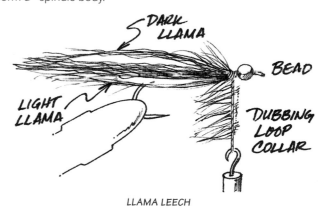

LLAMA LEECH

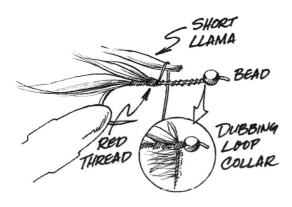

BLOODY LEECH

Once I proudly showed Sandra, my wife, a newly tied leech fly. She shrank back, shuddering. "Keep it away. It's ugly," she said. When that happened, I knew it might be successful. While anglers (and wives) usually shun this murky, slithery shape-changer, trout, especially larger ones, seldom ignore the undulating waterdance of the leech.

Midges, Part I
Chironomid larvae and the CDC Mirage Midge Pupa

Darrel Martin
July/Oct 2002

You know them. The small, dark ones on the surface. The red strands whipping themselves in the shallows. The tiny husks hatching winged specks. Though the term "midge" has been used by anglers to designate any small insect, the term properly refers to the ubiquitous Dipterans, the chironomids.

Chironomids are the most prolific and widespread of all aquatic insects and, for that reason alone, deserve tying attention. Curiously enough, it is claimed that a tier can base the larval pattern color on habitat alone. In general, olive and brown larvae are most common in alkaline and moderately to highly oxygenated waters, whereas red and purple larvae are usually in highly acidic and poorly oxygenated waters. The reds, sometimes called "blood worms," live in lake mud, oxygen-poor bogs or the depths of lakes, as well as rivers and streams.

Dense patches of midge larvae attract feeding trout to the shallow, weedy margins of lakes and streams. In *The Biology of Freshwater Chironomidae*, L.C. Pindar notes that "Fish that feed on chironomids show a high degree of selectivity," and, "Such selectivity is likely to be caused, at least in part, by differences in behavior that make certain species or life stages more or less available. Sometimes, however, it also appears to be related to size of larvae." One English study claims that up to 80 percent of the insects found in trout stomachs may be midge larvae and pupae.

If adults are on the water, then pupae and larvae are active in the water column. Some species, such as the tube dwellers, periodically leave their tubes and swim about with a whipping action, often going to the surface. Such ramblings are probably due to low oxygen. The angler, with draw and sink retrieves, imitates this active ascent-descent behavior. Typical hook size of larvae ranges from about 16 to 20, though some species may be longer.

The San Juan Worm has a spotted reputation; some tiers accept its simplicity, others doubt its legitimacy, its "pattern paternity." It is, after all, merely a length of yarn whipped to a hook. Though it has proven effective, it demands little from a tier and offers only slender satisfaction. I enjoy thoughtful patterns as well as thoughtful trout. Nevertheless, I should not denigrate simplicity, and the San Juan Worm does take trout in waters with heavy angling traffic.

The San Juan Worm claims lineage, according to various writers, from a common reddish-brown aquatic annelid, a threadlike tubifex worm or, tied in an appropriate size, a midge larva. A typical tying method covers the hook shank with thread. Then a length of Ultra-Chenille is spot mounted fore and aft with a whip-finish. Thread and cement sometimes secure the Ultra-Chenille along the shank top. The body is trimmed to length; the ends are then tapered with a flame. Such a tie, however, creates a rather stiff worm. In any case, two modifications—the Twisted Worm and the Bead Worm—present some variations on the "blood worm." A tier can also change the size and color of the Ultra-Chenille to imitate the broad range of midge larvae.

Be sure to select curved (Tiemco 2457, Daiichi 1150) or straight-shank (Tiemco 3769 and Daiichi 1550, 1530) hooks. Traditional wet hooks may also be used. Match a 6/0 thread color to the Ultra-Chenille. For a bloodworm, the micro Ultra-Chenille body is red, crimson or reddish orange; however, other colors such as green, burgundy or tan may be used for other midge larva colors.

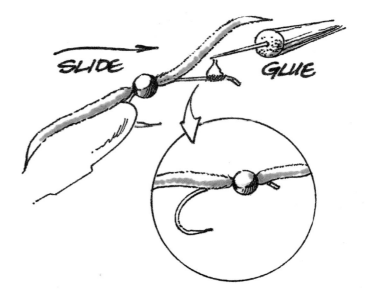

The Twisted Worm

To create a skewed body loop, tightly spot-mount the Ultra-Chenille at the rear with a whip-finisher. For fantastic shapes, mount the Ultra-Chenille on the outer hook bend, then firmly twist the Ultra-Chenille body prior to mounting forward. This skewed loop creates more "visual volume" and encourages pattern flutter during the retrieve—two factors that may entice a take.

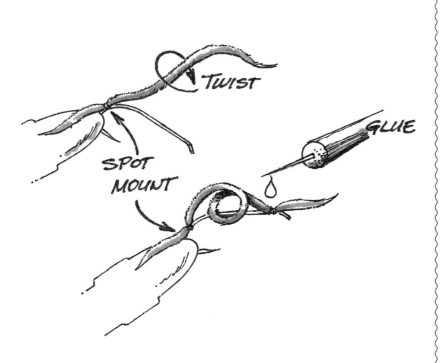

The Bead Worm

The Ultra-Chenille may be attached (single or double beads) to the hook shank with metal or glass beads. This adds weight and a spot of sparkle. First, taper one end of the Ultra-Chenille with a flame. To avoid burning the chenille, pass it rapidly back and forth through a flame. Once the end is tapered, slide the bead onto the Ultra-Chenille. Then whip-finish a spot of thread on the hook shank where you wish to attach the bead. Slide the hook through the bead previously attached to the Ultra-Chenille. Then place a drop of superglue gel on the thread spot and slide the bead and Ultra-Chenille into place. Finally, trim the Ultra-Chenille body to size and flame taper both ends.

The CDC Mirage Midge Pupa

The emerging chironomid, the midge pupa, is perhaps the most common stage of tying imitation. The genus *Chironomus* is most important for the angler. The insects often loiter near the surface prior to hatching free. Some remain hanging stationary with their head filaments just touching the surface; others wiggle about, periodically diving toward the bottom. Still others swim horizontally, searching for a weak spot in the surface film. Many pupae adopt a horizontal attitude.

For a tier, the imitative characteristics of the pupa include 1) a distinctly segmented body; 2) an enlarged thorax; 3) wing pads; and 4) pale head filaments. These characteristics appear in most imitations.

While working on *The Trout and the Fly* (1980), John Goddard and Brian Clark developed, with the help of Neil Patterson, the Suspender Midge Pupa. This pattern, inspired by Charles Brooks' Natant Nylon Nymph, incorporated a small ball of closed-cell Ethafoam in a patch of nylon stocking mesh. The Suspender Midge Pupa has become, over the years, a popular stillwater pattern. Today, however, flotation may be achieved with an adequate bundle of CDC (cul de canard) barbs. These white barbs imitate the pupa's respiratory head tufts, which absorb dissolved oxygen. Though the pattern will eventually drown, a few brisk false casts usually dry the tuft and collar for continued flotation. If desired, a few CDC tail barbs can even create the horizontal "hatching" posture. Furthermore, the white CDC respiratory tufts create good visibility for angler and trout. A spark of color (in abdomen or thorax) may grant additional attraction.

Flashabou Mirage, pink or red strands, forms the abdomen. These strands have a bright, chameleonlike, color-shifting iridescence that proves attractive to trout. The reflective strands suggest the trapped gas that hoists the hatching insect to the surface. Use orange or red 6/0 thread and Daiichi 1220 (bronze) or 1222 (silver) hooks, size 14 to 18. These hooks have a unique raised foreshank that opens the gap. If desired, mount black tying thread for ribbing or CDC tail barbs for a horizontal float. A CDC float collar forms the thorax. A CDC barb bundle, the respiratory head tufts and CDC collar float the pupa pattern.

❶ Mount black tying thread for ribbing (optional) and Flashabou Mirage strands. Flashabou strands may separate during wrapping. Select only a few strands (3 or 4) and secure the laps with a finger as you wrap the body. Body length should be about ¾ shank length. If present, spiral ribbing forward for strength and segmentation.

❷ Stack three or more white CDC feathers and remove barbs. Mount the barb bundle—sufficient to float the fly—immediately behind hook eye. I often mount a long, full head tuft that can be trimmed and thinned to match various water conditions.

❸ Load a dubbing loop with CDC barbs for a float collar. Use a contrasting color—such as pink, orange, red, rose or black. Wrap the float collar directly over the base of the white tuft. Trim excess; pass thread to the front and whip-finish a small head.

1, 2

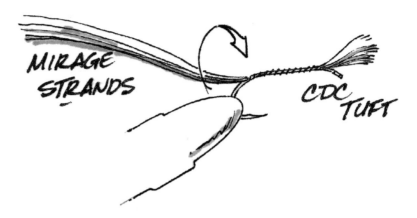

3

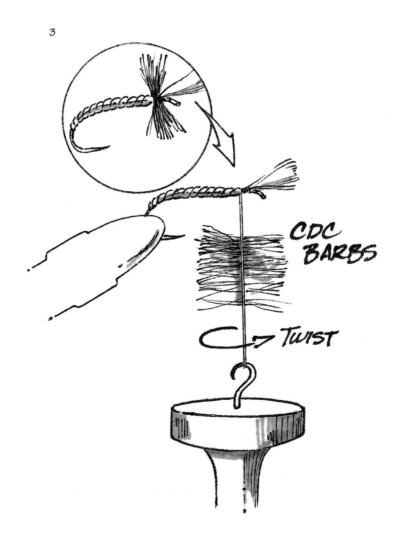

Midges, Part II
The pupa and emerger

Darrel Martin
Nov/Dec 2002

H.C. Cutcliffe, in *The Art of Trout Fishing* (1863), advocated that fly patterns should have a harmonious blending of tints and shades of color. Patterns should avoid, he asserted, "anything approaching a contrast of colours." Though generally valid, this theory may not apply to micropatterns that require something to announce their presence. Micropatterns, in particular, should entail an element of attraction, some enhancement, exaggeration or overstatement that draws attention: flash, color, movement or contrast. Something, such as a pinch of bright color, should set the pattern apart from all the surface drift that passes over a trout. This enhancement should attract just as realism should seduce.

As a midge emerges, the abdomen fills with gas and the insect partially withdraws from the nymphal shuck. J.R. Harris, in *An Angler's Entomology* (1973), describes the emergence: "The tail end of the hatching nymph then immediately assumes a much greater luster, and in fact it strongly resembles a section of glass tube which has been filled with mercury. This effect is even more noticeable in the pupae of those long-legged midges, the chironomids, when they are hatching at the surface of open water of lakes, and I think that it explains the added attraction which a flat tag of gold or silver gives to many artificial flies." An emergent midge pattern should probably incorporate a bright or highly reflective shuck, wing or body section. Not only does it duplicate emergence, it also flashes its presence to feeding fish.

Though the following patterns have conventional wraps for body or hackle, there are some unusual tying techniques for wings and float pods. Standard dry bodies may be made from dubbing or stripped peacock herl. Body colors include mahogany, cream, olive, orange, red and yellow.

The spun-strand body

A fine, slender midge body can be made by finger spinning a strand of teased-out dubbing. Mounted by the tip, the tightly spun strand is then wrapped like yarn. Nature's Spirit preen-oil-processed, natural dubbing works well for spun-strand bodies; it has fine, soft, crinkly, long fibers, about three to four inches or more. Most soft, long-strand dubbing may be spun and "corded" in this manner. Continue to spin the strand tightly as you wrap the body forward. For a remarkably slender body, form a strand with only a few wispy fibers. A tightly corded strand, in fact, can create a fine, segmented body for various midge patterns.

The Puff Pupa

The search for a float system for flies has spanned the years. J.C. Mottram, in *Fly-Fishing: Some New Arts and Mysteries* (1915), used small, wedge-shape cork strips (Fig. 1), blackened with ink, to float larva (cork wedge over the hook bend) and pupa (cork wedge over the hook eye) midges. The Puff Pupa is yet another CDC variation for an emerging midge.

Standard looped CDC feathers often close or crush easily. It is important that the loop stay open in order to trap air for flotation. This unique, circular tying method promotes a permanent open loop for long, effective drifts. A single back cast dries the fly for another long float.

Thread: 6/0 tying thread
Hook: Wide-gap, straight-eye hooks, Daiichi 1110 and Tiemco 101, size 16 to 22
Float puff: Two CDC hackles, white or dun
Body: Nature's Spirit Dubbing, mahogany
Ribbing: One or two strands of pearl Mirage

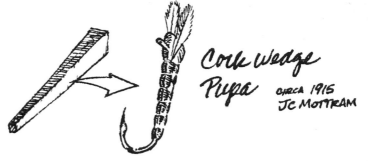

Cork Wedge Pupa CIRCA 1915 JC MOTTRAM

FIG. 1

❶ Stack and mount two fine-stemmed CDC feathers concave side up (Fig. 2). This ensures that the loop conforms to the natural curve of the feather. Gather and compress the barbs at the tip before mounting. To capture all the barbs, trim the fragile tip. When mounted, the feather bases should point aft. Secure both CDC feather tips at the head (Fig. 3). Use a small plastic tube (or dowel), about 2" to 2½" long, to form the loop. The tube keeps the loop open during mounting and ensures uniform loops. Most hobby shops offer various diameters of plastic tubes. Match the tube diameter, which determines the size of the finished float puff, to the hook size. Below you will find a general tube guide for standard dry hooks. Using different tube diameters can help you calibrate the float according to hook weight, tying materials, proportions and water type.

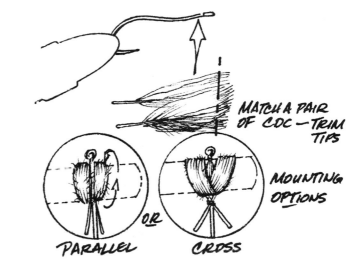

MATCH A PAIR OF CDC — TRIM TIPS

MOUNTING OPTIONS

PARALLEL

OR

CROSS

FIG. 2

❷ After mounting, loop both CDC feathers forward and around the tube. The stems should circle around on their respective sides to mount on top of the shank close to the puff base. For a wider, fuller float puff, cross the stems above the shank before securing them (Fig. 2, inset). After securing both stems, remove the tube (Fig. 3) and trim stem excess. Finally, complete the fly.

Long, stemless CDC barbs, such as goose, may be mounted, divided and looped more than once, creating a large puff. In this method, trap the looped barbs with thread at each revolution. For most small patterns, however, a single loop of two CDC feathers is sufficient.

For greater flotation, attach a CDC barb collar at the puff base. The puff creates an excellent platform for parachute hackles, especially a split-thread CDC parachute hackle. This combination—a CDC puff and a CDC parachute—creates various patterns with exceptional flotation.

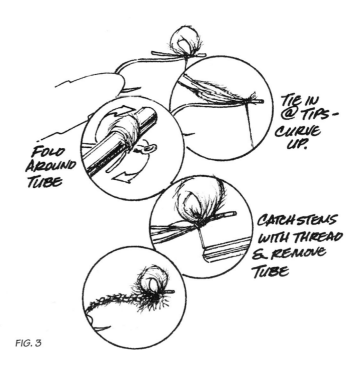

FOLD AROUND TUBE

TIE IN @ TIPS — CURVE UP.

CATCH STEMS WITH THREAD & REMOVE TUBE

FIG. 3

The Pop Pupa

Most CDC patterns, when pulled under, trap air. After a brief pause, they pop to the surface, imitating, perhaps, the struggle and emergence of an insect. Chironomids are usually active emergers, periodically testing the surface tension or, after hatching, "buzzing" and whirling on the surface. The term "buzzer," a name given to the midge by the English, may describe its circular surface dance prior to flight. Thus, a gentle "pull and pop" suggests these actions—actions that imitate the insect and attract fish. The stump may suggest the partially emerged body and the forewing, the expanding wings and legs.

To take advantage of the sink-and-pop action, CDC fibers should be mounted in a particular manner (Fig. 4). The Pop Pupa, which exploits the properties of CDC, is a mild modification of the CDC Magic that appears in Gerhard Laible's *CDC Flies* (1993). Unlike the original pattern though, the rear stump is merely the upturned base of the forewing. The stump keeps the forewing flared over the body during the retrieve. During the pull, the trapped bubbles created by the flare encourage the pattern to rise or pop to the surface.

The Puff and Pop pupae utilize the properties of CDC for float and function. Furthermore, these simple, effective patterns add tactics and techniques to all tying. What is learned from one pattern becomes a skill to apply to others. Our methods should number like midges on water.

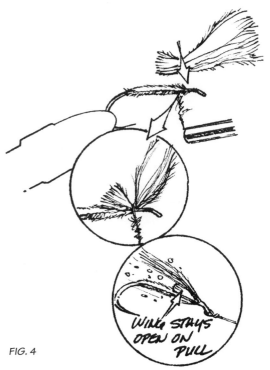

FIG. 4

Thread: 6/0 tying thread
Hook: Daiichi 1110 or Tiemco 101, sizes 14 to 18
Body: For increased buoyancy, use CDC dubbing. In addition, an excellent segmented body may be made from stripped peacock herl
Stump/forewing: Dun CDC barbs, or color-match the CDC barbs to the local hatch. Total length of the forewing should extend to or slightly beyond the hook bend. When pulled under, the long, sparse forewing should fold back, trapping air

HOOK SIZE	TUBE SIZE (Outer Diameter)
12	3/16 " (4.8 mm)
14	5/32 " (4.0 mm)
16	1/8 " (3.2 mm)
18	3/32 " (2.4 mm)
20	1/16 " (1.6 mm)

Midges, Part III
The adult midge: winging it

Darrel Martin
Jan/Feb 2003

An intense fascination comes from tossing midges to large, sipping trout. It also comes from tying the midge. Though trout apparently feed more often upon the larvae and the pupae, the adult midge can be extremely productive, especially when presented to close, stationary trout. In other words, don't go gnatless; the tiny, ubiquitous adult midges always attract trout.

Like all Dipterans, the adults have two flat wings. The slender abdomen extends beyond the transparent wings. The legs are long and the colors of the adult body, like those of the larval body, can be black, brown, tan, olive, amber, mahogany, green or cream. Lake species are often larger than their river relatives. Most patterns are tied on hook sizes 12 to 18 (lakes) and 16 to 24 (rivers). Generally, the insect becomes progressively smaller at each successive stage, from larva to pupa to adult. The adult midge is, in fact, the smallest fly pattern in your box.

Winging a midge is often considered a classical tying problem. Charles Edward Walker, in *Old Flies in New Dresses* (1898), notes that " . . . it is extremely difficult to put wings on these flies, hackle patterns may be tried, but the winged patterns are the best." Though winging gnats may challenge tiers, there are solutions. Furthermore, wings can serve several functions; they can add flash and float to a pattern. Here then are some variations on winging midges. And I've also included a wingless pattern that apparently mimics the adult midge effectively.

The panel wing

For years, I have used a folded wing for the adult midge. The fold keeps the wing flat over the back. Originally tied with feather vanes or "quill slips" from a duck-wing feather, the wing is best imitated with a panel of turkey flat (they lack the thick, coarse base of a duck-wing feather, minimizing splitting during mounting). Select either white—the most visible—or gray feathers. The key to tying a flat wing is an aligned feather panel.

First, caress the barbs so that they are straight and parallel. Then lightly mist both sides of the feather with Grumbacher's Tuffilm Final Fixative (matte). Once dry, cut the base and remove an appropriately sized panel from the feather. Depending upon the hook used, wing width should be about ¾ gap width to one gap width. Mount the thin panel tip along the top of the shank. Then mount and wrap the body. The body may be made from standard dry dubbing, peacock tail barbs or chopped CDC dubbing. With a straight metal edge, fold the wing forward. The wing should extend slightly beyond the hook bend. Secure the wing forward with a few tight thread wraps. Mount and wrap a variegated hackle, such as cree or grizzly, over the forward wing mount.

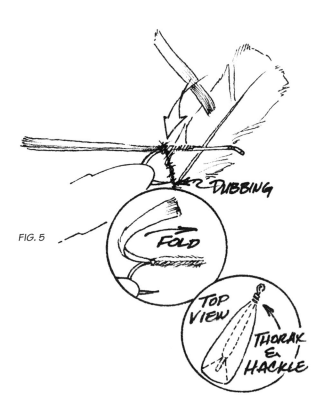

FIG. 5

DUBBING

FOLD

TOP VIEW

THORAX & HACKLE

Thread: 6/0; pale oranges and dusty reds work well
Hook: Daiichi 1110 or Tiemco 101, sizes 16 to 20
Body: Dubbing, pheasant tail barb, stripped peacock quill or other. Boldly segmented bodies usually work best
Wing: The wing panel comes from a turkey wing flat. Caress the barbs so that the panel is straight
Hackle: Preferably a variegated hackle, such as the tricolor cree or bicolor grizzly, dyed in subtle shades of yellow, orange or tan

The film wing

Though I usually avoid the weight of most synthetic wings, they are excellent for small, dry midges. Because the wings are so minute, they can add little weight, and yet great spark. Moreover, some synthetic sheets or films have a remarkable transparent sheen and flash. One of the best wing sheets is Spinner Wing Film, a Scintilla product. This tough, iridescent film reflects silver, green, red and blue highlights, making it visible to both fish and angler. Furthermore, the crinkle surface suggests the reflective crumple of an insect wing. The wings may be cut or burned to shape. Some instructions come with each wing pack:

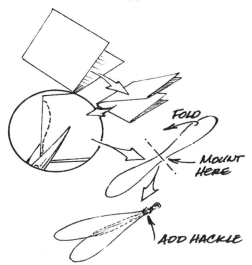

Thread: 6/0 tying thread
Hook: Daiichi 1110 or Tiemco 101, sizes 16 to 20
Body: Fine dubbing, spun strand mounted
Wings: Scintilla Spinner Wing Film
Hackle: Cree, grizzly or other

The CDC delta wing

Floating flush in the surface, the CDC delta midge has the swollen thorax and paired wings of an adult midge. Color contrast comes from the wings (white or dun) and the body (mahogany, orange, yellow or black).

First, dub a fine body approximately ¾ of the way up the shank. Then mount a small bundle of CDC barbs pointing aft. Select two short, fine-stem CDC feathers (white or dun) and cross-mount the stems with two or three thread wraps. Adjust the wing length by pulling each CDC feather forward. When positioned, secure both wings. Finally, fold the thorax (the CDC barb bundle) forward to the head position and secure with a whip-finish.

You can use CDC tufts (nipple plume) for wings instead of standard CDC feathers. CDC tufts are dense and lack a central stem. Due to the barb density and short stem, the tuft barbs may be divided and mounted as wings. Mount the tuft close to the stem. Merely pull the short stem forward to create the proper wing length. Secure and trim stem excess. Finally, fold the thorax forward and whip-finish. Though the CDC tuft makes delicate wings, the standard CDC feathers create flatter wings. Keep in mind that while the midge habitually folds its wings above the back, a delta-wing spread promotes flotation.

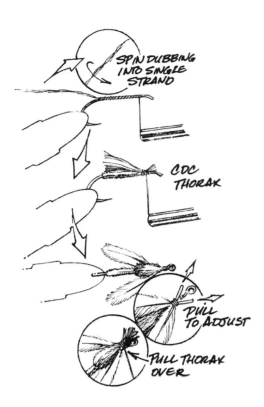

The CDC wing

This pattern, tied in various color combinations, aligns the wings midge-fashion. For superior floats, stack two CDC tips for wings. The imprint of the CDC hackle and wings imitates the dimpled surface impression made by many insects. In any case, the pattern may be tied to size 20 or smaller. It floats in the surface film like a spent gnat.

First, dub a fine body approximately ¾ shank length. After gathering the barbs along the stem, firmly mount one or two CDC feather tips for wings. Next, insert one or two CDC feathers with stems attached into a "split-thread" loop. The stems properly space the barbs in the thread split. Remove the stem or stems and spin the thread and captured barbs, creating a CDC hackle. Avoid trapping the barbs when mounting the hackle. Free, extended barbs increase flotation. Finally, secure the CDC hackle and whip-finish the head. For natural breaks, prune long barbs with hackle pliers or fingernails. Do not cut them.

Thread: 6/0; pale oranges and dusty reds work well
Hook: Daiichi 1110 or Tiemco 101, sizes 14 to 20
Body: Fine, dry dubbing, such as Nature's Spirit Dubbing. Again, try for a boldly segmented body
Wing: Two small CDC feathers or one CDC tuft
Hackle (optional): Variegated hackle or a modest CDC collar may be added for extra flotation

Thread: 6/0; pale oranges and dusty reds work well
Hook: Mustad AC 80000BR; Tiemco 101 and 900BL; Daiichi 1110 and 1100; sizes 16 to 24
Body: Fine, dry dubbing, such as Nature's Spirit Dubbing. Stripped peacock herl for segmented bodies
Wing: One or two small CDC feather tips
Hackle: CDC feather mounted in split thread loop

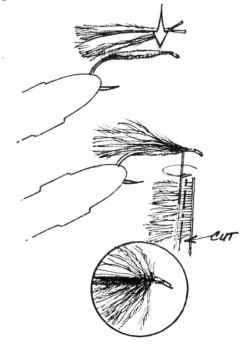

The dub wing

You can tie this on the smallest hooks. The wing is merely fine, long-strand dubbing trapped by thread and trimmed to length. An excellent wing is made from fine-denier Antron dubbing. In sunlight, the bright Antron shines and sparkles. A dubbed body and split-thread CDC hackle enhance flotation.

The Tagged Palmer

Though lacking wings, the Tagged Palmer (or Tagged Gray Palmer) might suggest a stillborn adult midge or an adult midge awash in the surface scum. The Tagged Palmer is kith and kin to Gray Palmers, Red Tags, Zulus and Griffith's Gnats. If a young Red Tag marries an elderly Gray Palmer, the offspring is a grizzled palmer with a scarlet spot. Though the Tagged Palmer lacks the adult midge wings and silhouette, it apparently has the surface imprint that attracts "midging" trout. The traditional Gray Palmer lacks both tag and ribbing. A bright tag, however, might entice a take. Variants of the Gray Palmer, also known as Griffith's Gnat, are palmered with dark hackles—hackles that may be difficult to track during a drift. The original George Griffith dressing had a peacock herl body and a palmered grizzly hackle. The standard Red Tag wore a shoulder hackle and a scarlet tag.

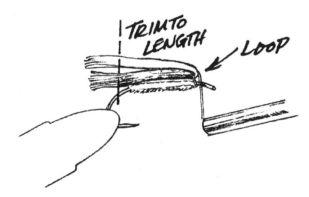

Thread: 6/0; pale oranges, yellows and dusty reds
Hook: Mustad AC 80000BR; Tiemco 101 and 900BL; Daiichi 1110 and 1100; sizes 16 to 24
Body: Fine, dry dubbing, such as Nature's Spirit Dubbing
Wing: A fine strand of Antron dubbing locked in a thread wrap
Hackle: CDC feather mounted in split thread loop

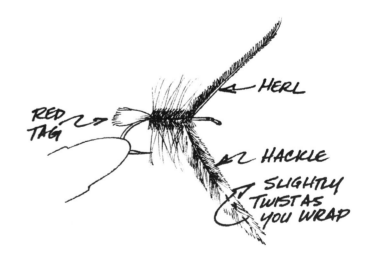

The tag was a short strip of red wool or scarlet ibis. Scarlet CDC or polypropylene, however, enhances flotation. For hooks size 20 and smaller, use the fine, long herls from the base of the peacock sword. These herls, below the "spatter herls" at the tip, are less than 1 millimeter wide and more than 20 centimeters long. Sword herls are generally finer than most eyed herls.

Wrap the hackle concave-side forward, by slightly twisting the stem during palmering. Theoretically, the forward-cupping barbs provide better flotation. Today we have perfect palmer hackles: fine, long-stemmed saddle hackles. In fact, the modern stiff-barb saddle hackle may be so rigid that it hinders the take. In this case, merely open the gap by snipping the barbs beneath the fly.

Thread: 6/0 black, gray or orange
Hook: Mustad AC 80000BR; Tiemco 101 and 900BL; Daiichi 1110 and 1100; sizes 18 to 24
Tag: Scarlet CDC feathers or polypropylene yarn, trimmed short
Hackle: Saddle grizzly with strong contrast

Wrapping midges does require some special materials and methods. Midge hooks should be strong, the materials soft and suggestive and the methods, simple. These midge methods may be used for other, larger patterns as well. The small midges are often called curses—a curse to tie and a curse to fish. Perhaps these wing methods abolish some of the curse. No tier should strain at gnats.

From:
July/October 2002
November/December 2002
January/February 2003

Parachute Patterns, Part I
Tying the radical radials

Darrel Martin
March 2003

Leaves twirled down from the branches in the mild autumn light. My parachute Adams matched their slow descent and drift. It floated long and flush in the surface until a trout took—and left a ring in exchange. October always hatches size 18 parachutes. The Adams was small, subtle and, due to the design, seductive.

A parachute pattern has a hackle that radiates horizontally from a vertical stem, such as a wing base, supporting the pattern on the water surface. According to Paul Schullery's *American Fly Fishing* (1987), parachute patterns go back at least to the late 1920s.

In 1950, J. Edson Leonard called the parachute pattern "a radical among dry flies." Leonard lists the attributes of the parachute design: 1) parachutes provide maximum surface area with minimal barbs. All the barbs lend support; therefore, few turns are required; 2) parachutes float the fly flat on the surface rather than above it, thus eliminating the arching monofilament—that reflecting alarm—near the fly; 3) parachutes imitate the "straddle-legged" appearance of natural insects; 4) the horizontal hackle settles the hook softly upon the surface "as delicately as a lazy snowflake."

There are several other aspects of the horizontal hackle. Parachute barbs may be shorter than conventional hackle barbs.

William Blades, in *Fishing Flies and Fly Tying* (1951), notes that heavy hooks require long and dense parachute barbs. When wrapping parachutes, Blades also strokes the barbs down so they are at right angles to the stem. This allows each barb complete exposure. I often strip one side of the hackle for a neat pattern; merely increase the number of wraps for adequate buoyancy.

Parachutes create a unique light pattern and imprint on the surface that is perhaps more suggestive of natural insects. Stance and imprint upon the water and the resulting light pattern produce certain signals that provoke rises. Conventional hackling, which punctures the surface film, restricts the barbs to a comparatively small area beneath the wings. In contrast, parachute barbs radiate on the surface. A parachute design cocks the pattern well and permits full view of the wings.

Curiously enough, C.F. Walker, in *Fly-*

tying as an Art (1957), opines that the parachute hackle, with the front (forward) barb arc trimmed . . . semi-circle barbs cut away, could only imitate spent spinners. Walker found no advantage in the parachute. But in the '50s the parachute became popular. T. R. Henn, in *Practical Fly-Tying* (1950), notes that the "hackle setting [of the parachute pattern] shows up the full values of the body colour; and many fishermen consider this to be the most important component of the fly."

Not all have been enamored of the parachute. Frank Elder, in *The Book of the Hackle* (1979), proclaims that the parachute and other variations are supposed, by their inventor, to be a step forward in the evolution of the dry fly. "They are, of course, nothing of the sort, all that they are attempting to do is to produce an alternative to the proper dry-fly. The dun sits on the surface of the water, so the imitation must do the same." He adds that "A parachute fly . . . is not a representation of a newly hatched dun. It is simply a production which is easily seen and will float for a long period before becoming waterlogged. The fact that it will catch fish and indeed at certain times may be more effective than a really good dry-fly is not the point."

Elder acknowledges that the parachute may be taken by trout for an emerging or trapped dun. At such times, he then concedes that a parachute may be used. "But," he concludes, "we should clearly realize that we are representing a dun in a special condition, we are not representing a dun as it sails down the stream waiting for the wings to dry." Thus, the undignified parachute emerger, according to Elder, loses to "the proper dry-fly." Such attitudes are not prevalent today.

A parachute pattern is usually less durable than a traditional tie. Furthermore, the parachute presents a tying problem: The hackle tip must be secured beneath a tangle of barbs. Some of the following methods appear exacting and difficult. Practice and patience solve most problems. Besides, some of the solutions are delightfully curious. Here then are some tactics to solve those problems with parachutes.

From: March 2003 and April 2003

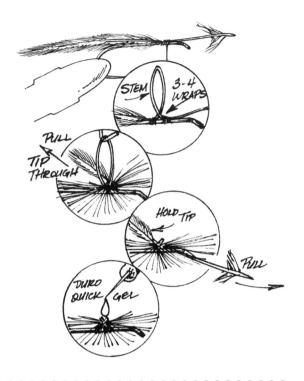

The Barlow gallows (stem-loop) **method**

I would be remiss to leave out the original stem-loop method. Besides, I love the magic of it. Years ago Bob Barlow, an English engineer at the Woomera research station in Australia, stepped into the Veniard Fly Shop in England. The collaboration of John Veniard and Bob Barlow created the gallows tool, a simple wire scaffold with a hanging hook. John Veniard described the meeting and the Barlow method in *Fly-Tying Development and Progress* (1972). The idea is simple: A light spring tension holds a stripped and looped hackle stem. The hackle then wraps around its own stem and locks to create a knotted parachute hackle.

❶ Strip the hackle base of barbs and fluff. For grip, I leave a small webbing tuft at the extreme base. Mount the hackle concave side down with a few firm wraps.

❷ Loop the stem as illustrated. Use no more than four wraps, held by bobbin weight, to secure the loop. This is important because the stem must be able to slide under these wraps during the knotting process.

❸ Connect the tension hook to the stem loop. Next, wrap the hackle at the base of the loop several times while the loop is held in tension. After sufficient hackle turns, use fine-tipped tweezers or hackle pliers to draw the hackle tip through the stem loop.

❹ Remove the tension hook from the loop and gently hold the hackle tip and pull the stem base to knot the hackle. When knotted, trim the stem and hackle tip, leaving about 1 millimeter of excess ends for security. For complete security, place a drop of no-run super-glue, such as Duro Quick Gel, in the hackle hub.

The self parachute

If the parachute remains in position on the hook, then mount the hackle firmly. However, the Barlow method also permits creating parachute disks that may be mounted in any position on a hook. The mounting thread does not form the parachute; the stem knot does. To create a removable parachute, mount the hackle (with few wraps) on a needle. (When working with needles, always use protective eyewear.) Form the stem loop and continue as explained.

After tying the hackle in a knot, merely cut the bottom threads with a razor blade and remove the "self-parachute." Place a drop of Duro Quick Gel Glue in the hackle hub and press the parachute between glass sheets for several hours. These flat parachute disks (looking like circular saw blades) may then be sewn on a hook with tying thread, like buttons, in any desired position.

Veniard's *Fly-Tying Development and Progress* illustrates how the tips of two hackles, wrapped and knotted in this manner, form wings and how the long base stems form a foundation for an extended body. Practice may be required to achieve proper wing length.

The Parachute Emerger (the Barlow method)

This generic pattern uses the Barlow, or stem-loop, method to tie emerger and "suspender" patterns. Match the hatch for size and color. A dark thorax and a pale yellow abdomen serve well for various emergers and drifting pupae. Note that the parachute is mounted in the final position. This method is simpler and faster than appears. Position hook 45 degrees down during tying.

1 Mount, with a dubbed thread, the stripped stem hackle, concave side down, as illustrated. Place dubbing over the wraps.

2 Create a stem loop and secure with three dubbed-thread wraps. Once you've formed the parachute hub, you'll find it difficult to place dubbing beneath it.

3 Wrap the hackle around the base of the loop.

4 After sufficient wraps, pass the hackle tip through the stem loop. Then, while holding the hackle tip, gently pull the hackle stem (pull the "cord" of the parachute) to knot the hackle.

5 After knotting the hackle, trim the hackle tip. Then trim and secure the stem end along the hook shank. Add tails if required, dub the thorax and the abdomen. Finally, whip-finish the head.

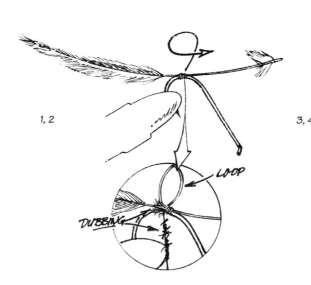

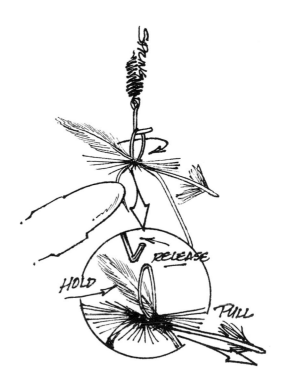

Parachutes, Part II
More on tying the radical radials

Darrel Martin
April 2003

Unlike the Barlow method mentioned earlier, most parachute ties require supporting posts. These posts can be made from yarns, feather fibers, animal hairs, hackle stems and wires.

Parachute proportions and density vary among tiers. The water usually determines the hackling. To imitate insect legs, hackles may be short and sparse. To float over fast or broken water, the hackles may be thick and long. Unlike the traditional dry fly, parachutes require few hackle wraps. The traditional fly pokes its barbs into the water; a parachute's barbs sit gently on the surface. For this reason, parachute hackling can be short and sparse. For increased buoyancy, barb length may be the standard ¾ shank length or longer. Datus Proper, in *What the Trout Said* (1982), advocates mounting the parachutes thoracic style (hackle mounted at mid-shank or slightly forward) for better balance.

To offer the trout contrast and sheen, Proper wraps the hackle shiny side down. Flotation may be improved, however, by mounting the hackle concave (dull) side down. For hackles with prominent concavity, this pushes the barbs down for support.

The Parachute Pupa

This is a simple and effective fly. Polypropylene yarn, with a specific gravity slightly lighter than water, forms the parachute post and wing case.

❶ Mount a length of poly yarn as illustrated and attach the yarn to a tension hook. Mount the hackle securely and dub the thorax.

❷ Wrap the hackle several times around the base of the yarn. Capture the hackle tip with thread and secure.

❸ Pass the poly yarn down between the barbs to form a swollen thorax and secure. Add the abdominal dubbing and whip-finish.

Mounting and wrapping the standard parachute

One can mount and wrap parachute hackle in various ways. This method, which I consider one of the best, solves many problems. The classic challenge with parachutes is the finishing wraps. The hackle tip, which must be secured, is usually hidden beneath a logjam of splayed barbs. This method produces a rather neat finish, devoid of ornery barbs.

❶ First, carefully prepare the hackle. Caress the hackle so that barbs stand out at right angles to the stem. Strip the barbs from the stem base to the proper barb length. In some cases it may be appropriate to remove the inside barbs from one side of the prepared hackle. In any case, clip hackle pliers to the hackle tip and strip both sides of the smaller, top barbs by pulling them toward the base, opposite the growth direction. Strip all barbs that are not the proper length.

❷ Next, attach the hackle vertically along the post with firm wraps. The post may be held in tension with a gallows clip. Note the illustrated angular L-shape stem lock.

❸ With touching wraps, spiral the hackle down over the post wraps. When the hackle stem arrives at the hook shank, pull the stripped stem down. Push the front parachute barbs back and capture the stem with a few firm wraps. If desired, dub the foreshank. Whip-finish to complete the pattern. The stem, sans barbs, allows a small, neat finish for any type of parachute post.

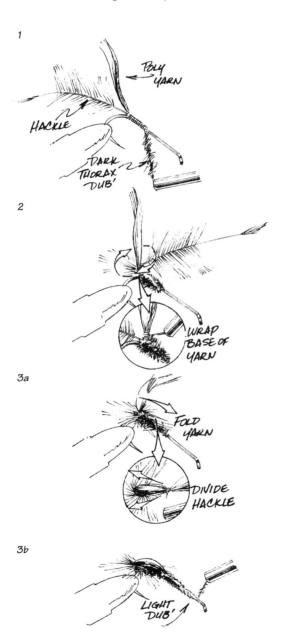

1

POLY YARN

HACKLE

DARK THORAX DUB'

2

WRAP BASE OF YARN

3a

FOLD YARN

DIVIDE HACKLE

3b

LIGHT DUB'

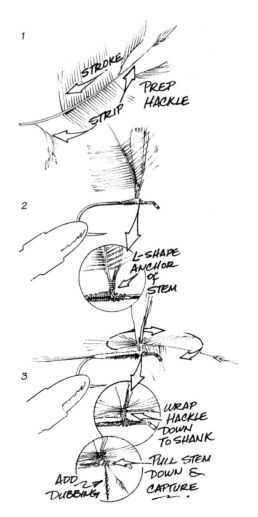

1

STROKE

PREP HACKLE

STRIP

2

L-SHAPE ANCHOR OF STEM

3

WRAP HACKLE DOWN TO SHANK

PULL STEM DOWN & CAPTURE

ADD DUBBING

flytying

The Lemhi parachute method

The small, bright Lemhi River slides past ranches, loiters along valley pastures and weaves through willow, "clump" birch and quaking aspen. It is a lovely high-mountain river that traces the Lewis and Clark Trail on Idaho's Continental Divide. From the Lemhi comes Karl Amonson's parachute post method.

Amonson is the president of Lemhi Valley Expedition Inc., and a contract pattern developer for Scientific Anglers. His simple, durable and attractive post uses any cape hackle. Though softer hackles with high contrast make excellent wings, stiff dryfly hackle also may be used.

1 For a proper length wing, select a hackle with the barbs that equal the hook shank. Though long wings may be trimmed, natural barb tips make an attractive wing. Mount and wrap the hackle forward as a dry hackle. Secure and trim excess.

2 Trim underbarbs, or gather them as part of the wing.

3 Gather and hold the barbs erect.

4 Wrap the barb base (the post) with the thread maneuver as illustrated. Note how the thread passes around the barb base and pulls it slightly toward the tier.

5,**6** Continue the thread path to wrap around the base and pull it away from the tier. These two, simple maneuvers erect the wing.

7 Keeping the barb wing erect, wrap the thread back near the center of the hackle. Then, pass the thread behind the wing and wrap forward to create a small wing post. If required, make more than one wrap around the barb base. For double wings, merely Figure-eight to divide.

8 Mount the parachute hackle on the side and wrap it around the base. Pull the forward parachute barbs back and secure the hackle tip in front of the wings. Finally, trim excess, dub foreshank and whip-finish.

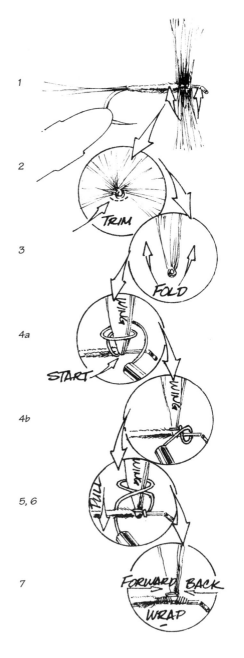

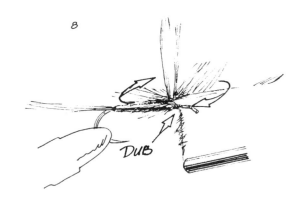

The posted hook method
(The single Wire Post)

By attaching a small wire post, any hook becomes a parachute hook. Use .020" wire (or finer), available in hobby stores. To decrease the added weight, keep wire length short. (For safety, wear protective eyewear when shaping and cutting wire.) Bend wire before trimming to length. After mounting the post, add a drop of superglue to the wraps. Mount the tail and body after connecting the post. Mount, wrap and secure the hackle before dubbing the front. Pliable post wires may be crimped down, usually by bending them back after the pattern is tied. Although the process approaches "fussy," it can create some unusual patterns.

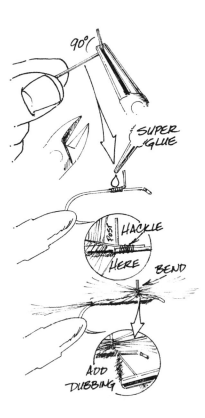

The expanded parachute:
The Double Post Method

For increased flotation, expand a parachute hackle with two posts. This technique works well for terrestrials such as ants and spiders. After hackling, fold down the soft wire posts.

An All-Purpose Nymph

Dave Whitlock's versatile Red Fox Squirrel Hair Nymph

Darrel Martin
June 2002

When I want humility, I merely watch Dave Whitlock tie. What attracts me most is not the remarkable grace of a Whitlock pattern, but rather the thoughtful touches. Whitlock flies have a distinctive charm and character, and they appeal as much to trout as they do to anglers. Whitlock is a native Oklahoman who resigned from his job as a research chemist to devote his many talents to fly-fishing. He shares these talents in numerous ways through videos, words, teaching and art. Some of that talent appears in his Red Fox Squirrel Hair Nymph.

The Red Fox Squirrel Hair Nymph is actually a series of patterns, because variations in hook and hackle mimic a remarkable range of fish foods. Extra-short shanks create scuds, sow bugs and midges. On these smaller patterns, spiky dubbing often serves as hackle. Standard, 2X-long hooks produce mayfly nymphs, caddis larvae and stonefly nymphs. Longer shanks with narrow bodies suggest

damselfly nymphs; thicker bodies, burrowing mayfly nymphs. Curved shanks and long hackles imitate emerging caddis. Bead heads and rubber legs spawn bass patterns. And there are variations for steelhead and Atlantic salmon patterns. Tied "in-the-round" on size 2 to 20 hooks, the Red Fox Squirrel Hair Nymph truly is a fly for all seasons.

Before whip-finishing the head, Whitlock "wets" a short length of the tying thread with Dave's Flexament. This cements the head without clogging the hook eye. Though Whitlock uses a monofilament loop as a whip-finisher, cementing the thread prior to whipping may be done with most conventional whip-finishers.

The effectiveness of the pattern may lie in its colors—a foxy orange-tan abdomen, a dark speckled thorax and a barred tail. The materials are carefully selected for quality and color of imitation: Many immature insects have a pale abdomen and a dark, mottled thorax. Close examination of the squirrel pelt reveals several hair bars. The rusty, flecked back hair has cream tips above a black bar. An orange-tan bar separates the black bar from a gray-dun base bar next to the hide. The belly is an orange-tan. These mottled, rich colors can suggest a variety of fish foods.

The pattern also incorporates some thoughtful, unusual tying details. Here then are the small, discerning maneuvers that create a Whitlock original:

Hook: Tiemco 5262, size 8 (standard & bead-head); Tiemco 2313 or 2302 (caddis emerger)
Thread: Danville 6/0 orange or black; for hooks smaller than size 14, use 8/0 Uni-Thread, orange-brown
Cements: Dave's Flexament and Zap-a-Gap. These cements create a durable fly
Tail: Red fox squirrel back hair. Tail length equals approximately ⅓ to ½ hook-shank length
Weight: Lead-free wire or bead head
Ribbing: Flashabou #6967 Pearl-Gold
Abdomen: Red Fox Squirrel belly hair and "Squirrel Belly" Antron. Abdomen equals approximately ⅔ hook-shank length
Thorax/head: Red fox squirrel back hair and "Squirrel Back" Antron. Thorax and head equal approximately ⅓ hook-shank length
Legs: Brown, speckled game-hen hackle

❶ Before mounting the hook in the vise, Whitlock roughens the shank with a fine file. I often debarb a hook by clamping the point in the vise jaws. Whitlock, however, debarbs the hook by placing it within the vise jaws (generally adjusted to be only slightly wider than the hook wire) and by turning the hook to depress the barb (Fig. 1b). This is quick and simple. He then mounts the hook to the vise with minimal pressure—just enough to hold the hook. During tying, the hook may be pushed up or down (actually manipulated in the vise) for greater access. This is especially useful when mounting and wrapping materials beneath the hook shank or bend. Furthermore, minimal vise pressure averts hook damage.

❷ Because the file removed the hook finish, Whitlock covers the hook shank with a fine smear of Zap-a-Gap. This prevents corrosion and creates a tacky foundation for thread and wire. Unlike standard superglue, Zap-a-Gap dries rather slowly and does not penetrate thread and materials quickly.

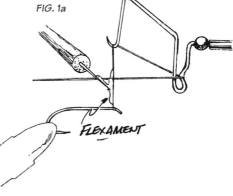

FIG. 1a

FLEXAMENT

FIG. 1b

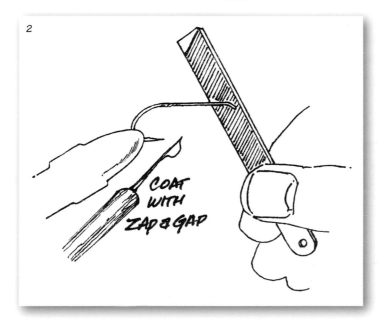

2

COAT WITH ZAP & GAP

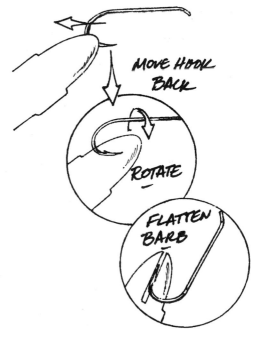

MOVE HOOK BACK

ROTATE

FLATTEN BARB

3, 4

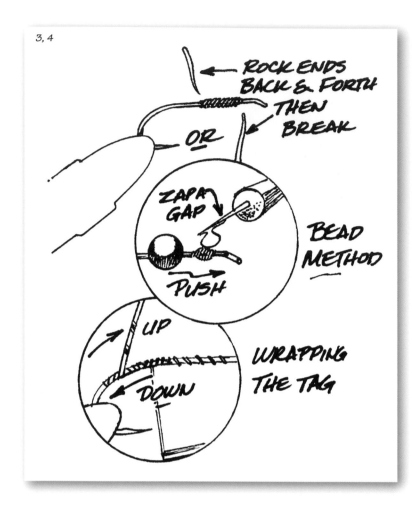

ROCK ENDS BACK & FORTH THEN BREAK

OR

ZAP-A GAP

PUSH

BEAD METHOD

UP

DOWN

WRAPPING THE TAG

❸ Mount the thread and then add 8 to 10 wraps of wire for weight. After wrapping, Whitlock merely rocks the excess lead wire back and forth, then pulls and pinches it off. This creates tapered ends and, consequently, a neater body. Non-lead wires, of course, may be more difficult to break in this manner. Whitlock matches the wire diameter to the hook diameter. Incidentally, the hook-wire diameter traditionally matches the inner diameter of the hook eye. If the end of the wire fills the eye then it closely matches the hook-wire diameter.

You may prefer a bead head instead of wire wraps. For a bead foundation, Whitlock wraps a small bundle of thread secured only with Zap-a-Gap. For a snug fit, adjust the thread bundle diameter by sliding the bead over it.

❹ Spiral the thread back to the bend and mount a strand of Flashabou. Wrap an extended tag down the bend to add sparkle and realism. Trim excess. Without the tag, Whitlock believes the hook is merely "a dark object hanging down."

❺ Wrap the thread to the rear and mount the tail. The tail comes from the fine squirrel back, not the squirrel tail. The hair is banded with several bars of color. The base gray bar is tied in so that the attached tail color continues the color of the fly body. Next, add a length of pearl-gold Flashabou for ribbing.

❻ Coat the hook shank with Dave's Flexament to prevent the wire from discoloring the overlaid dubbing. Flexament also remains tacky during dubbing, thereby offering a solid foundation for the body.

❼ Whitlock's dubbing method is unique. The abdomen and thorax dubbings come from red fox squirrel belly and back hairs. Whitlock increases the appeal by mixing equal amounts of Antron with the abdomen and thorax dubbing. This is quickly done in a small, inexpensive coffee grinder. The dubbing fibers should be cut about an inch long. If the hair is too long, it will tend to "cord," creating body segments rather than the attractive spiky bush.

5

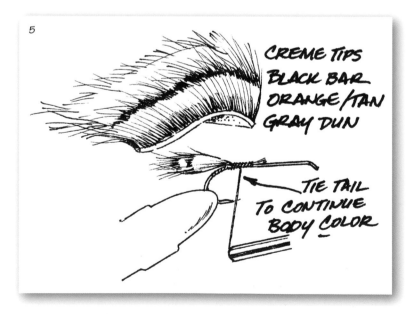

CREME TIPS
BLACK BAR
ORANGE/TAN
GRAY DUN

TIE TAIL TO CONTINUE BODY COLOR

Whitlock tests the dubbing by merely hand spinning a noodle. When twisted, the noodle should continue to elongate without cording. To dub, select about 1½ times the amount of dubbing required. Pull some dubbing out for an attachment point. Connect this short point or "starter length" to the thread. With the right thumb and index finger roll this point back and forth, encircling the thread. Slide the dubbing bundle to the shank. As the dubbing orbits the shank, it locks on and slowly feeds onto the thread to form a tapered body. Continue to twist the dubbing strand on its own axis as you wrap forward. By pushing the dubbing up the thread toward the shank, Whitlock increases the amount of dubbing spun on. By pulling the dubbing down the thread, he lessens the amount of dubbing applied to the shank. To finish the dubbing, merely pull down on the dubbing bundle to make it thin and then secure with a thread. This method creates a shaggy, spiky body—a body that shimmers and "halos" in sunlight.

8 Wrap the abdomen ¾ shank length. Then spiral the Flashabou forward in open wraps. Whitlock is not trying to create body segments with the ribbing; rather he wishes to bed the "flicker and flash" within the body. When tied on curved shanks this imitates the gas bubbles trapped within the shuck of an emerging caddis. Such sparkle bubbles may give all emergers greater realism.

9 Next, add darker dubbing for the thorax and wrap to the front. Now, add a speckled soft hen hackle. Select the barbs to be mounted and trim excess. Place a bead of Zap-a-Gap on the tag end and mount in place. After mounting, remove the offside barbs for a sparse wrap.

10 After wrapping one or two times, secure the stem and trim excess. Now, add a small skein of dubbing in front of the hackle to create a more realistic fly. Finally, whip-finish.

In this single pattern, there are more than a dozen tiny techniques that make the fly extraordinary. Tying talent is in the detail, and it is this detail that gives life and character to the fly. Behind Dave Whitlock's soft Oklahoma accent is a remarkable treasure of tying. His tiny touches come from years of thoughtful wrapping. Izaak Walton once remarked that angling promotes humility. Well, so do the creative skills of Dave Whitlock. We should remember, though, to create our own small touches that make our own tying more creative and more personal.

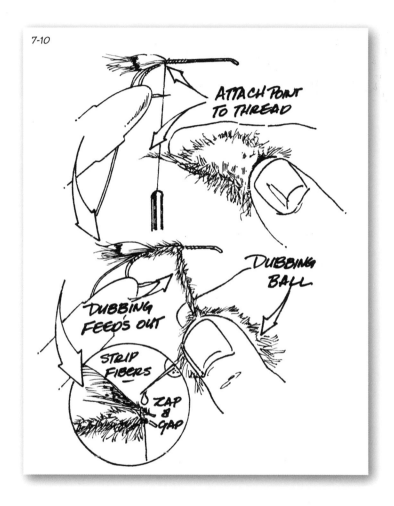

7-10

To increase your humility you may wish to watch the excellent video: *Dave Whitlock Originals: Red Fox Squirrel Hair Nymphs* (Volume 3). For this and other videos, books, flies and artwork, visit www.davewhitlock.com. Whitlock patterns and videos are available from many fly shops that carry Umpqua Feather Merchant products.

Tying the Tracer
A streamer that casts like a burning bullet

Darrel Martin
May/June 2000

The high humidity matched the temperature. Pushing a large baitfish fly through the heavy air was exhausting. Sometimes, however, the exhaustion was rewarded with a ravenous strike that sliced through the water. The Amazon challenged both casting and tying.

Clearly, I needed a large, light fly that would cast and swim well. This, of course, is a basic tying conundrum when creating bulky baitfish patterns for large, aggressive gamefish. After returning home, I sought a solution. I admire Bob Popovics' Spread Fly, on which epoxy creates a wide, flat body of Superhair. The Spread Fly, though, has a single dimension; I wanted width as well as height. I wanted a pattern that was castable, yet one that created disturbance during the retrieve. I also like Big Fly Fiber for tying large flies. However, I wanted that same wispiness for all synthetic strands, including the Holographic and Mirage Flashabous. I wanted intense flash in a large pattern.

Though the problem was simple, the solution was not. I tried to curl various strand materials with heating curlers and clothes irons. Nothing really worked. When my wife, Sandra, saw me using her clothes iron on tying material, she offered me a solution—use boiling water. But I had to make a tool that would form the curl before it was heated. After several prototypes, I designed a curling rod that created the "frizzled" strands I sought. And when the bright strands became a fly, it cast like a burning bullet, a tracer. And so it was christened.

The Tracer method produces a boundless variety of large fresh- and saltwater patterns. Curled synthetics offer an illusion of bulk while creating a smooth, slick fly that collapses during the cast to achieve minimal wind resistance. Frizzled synthetics create "empty," airy patterns that have size, form and flash. Even a full, fine-strand body can capture water, making the fly difficult to pick up and cast. Curled bodies, however, need few strands for bulk. Depending upon the materials, even 4/0 and 5/0 flies cast easily.

I wanted to imitate brightly-colored, generic baitfish. Many large gamefish, such as the so-called "peacock bass" (Tucanare), specialize in eating various large, brightly colored baitfish of a pound or more. I wanted an imitation that was about five to six inches long and about one inch in diameter at the head. Some prey fish, in fact, are nearly transparent, much like the wispy Tracer pattern itself. My fly needed a number of characteristics:

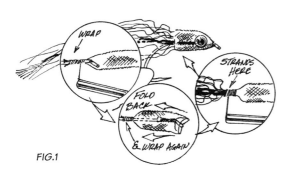

FIG.1

The wide eye

Eyes add color and contrast and, perhaps, betray the alarmed look of a frightened and fleeing baitfish. I often use Spirit River's 3-D Molded Eye inserts, in gold or red, in the appropriate Real Eye or Deep Sea Eyes. For ultralight patterns, I can avoid excess weight by using large doll eyes or prismatic tape eyes. The large tape eyes have the added benefit of trapping the fibers for a secure hold.

One can make a light bait head with E-Z Body tubing (Fig.1). The curled body strands completely fill the tubing. Prismatic tape eyes can then be added. To make the E-Z Body head, mount the tubing over the hook eye, then fold it back for a tie-down. Merely push the tubing back to invert itself, creating a head. Follow the drawings to create a simple bait head.

The flash back

What sequence should I follow in mounting materials? First of all, I want some highly reflective materials on top. In the thick Amazonian waters, the sun penetrates the rivers and streams to ignite the backs of baitfish. This bright back is then reflected in the surface mirror (the surface underside), broadcasting the presence of baitfish to predators. A bright, shimmering topping might be an enticement to hungry fish. There are several appropriate flash materials for the topping, such as Flashabou or Holographic Flashabou. However, I like the bright, iridescent color-shift in Hedron's opal Flashabou Mirage. These highly reflective strands should prove attractive.

The painted heart

Many Amazonian baitfish are brightly colored. They often flush colors when pursued by predators. I wanted that vivid panic in the eye and body of the fly. I wanted the colors—bright red, orange or yellow—to give a sense of life and flash, to make contrast with the bright body and the dark water. The new Mirage Flashabou is excellent for this kaleidoscopic shimmering blush, the iridescent color shift in each fiber.

The bend wrap

To prevent tail strands from wrapping around the bend, you can mount stiffer strands on top of the hook shank. Dangly strands may be controlled with epoxy, silicone or Softex. For example, epoxy may occupy ½ the shank length of the pattern. Stiffer strands may require only ½ body-length epoxy. As the epoxy moves aft, the strands become less likely to tangle with the bend during casting. If necessary, apply epoxy, Softex (Icon Products) or Hard Head (Loon Outdoors). To maximize movement, minimize the epoxy area. Tying "tarpon style," in which the body is mounted at the extreme rear of the hook shank, also minimizes bend wrap. There are, in fact, some "beaked" baitfish, such as the Characin, that the tarpon style might imitate.

I wanted, however, to explore other solutions to the bend-wrap problem. Many years ago, I received a steelhead fly from Frank Matarelli. It had a spun-wire loop that elevated the tail of the fly. This idea suggested another possible solution to prevent tail wrap: the hook harness. The harness, made from fine, stiff stainless-steel wire (.0140" in diameter), holds the long body away from the bend during the cast and retrieve. A 14-gauge stainless-steel electric guitar string works well (Fig. 2). Fold

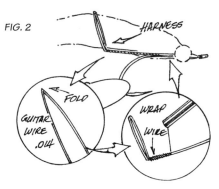

FIG. 2

HARNESS

FOLD

GUITAR WIRE .014

WRAP WIRE

the wire and then wrap with tying thread as illustrated above. Secure the wraps with a drop of superglue. Then bend the wire loop up to support the fly body.

Mount this harness on the hook before adding any materials. Notice that, for long patterns, the harness loop may project beyond the bend. After completing the fly, pull the body through the harness loop with a monofilament noose. Unlike hard and heavy epoxy, a harness adds little weight and allows the material expansion and freedom.

It will be interesting to see how effective this might be for large gamefish. Though bent during the strike and struggle, a harness should be able to be readily reformed.

Making curls

I wanted a fly that had the shape of a fish, that was easily cast, yet pushed water on the retrieve. I wanted it on a 2/0 or 3/0 hook. To achieve bulk at the head, I decided to make synthetic ringlets for volume. This technique, which tightly curls a determined length of material, may be used on virtually any synthetic strands. To make a "curling rod" or "frizzle rod," simply bend a brass rod about .070" diameter, as shown in Fig. 3. The smaller the rod diameter, the tighter the curls. Brass rods are available in most craft or hobby stores. Point the butt of the curling rod as a tooth to comb out the strands. If desired, you may wish to attach a small plastic or wood handle to the rod.

To frizzle the fibers, tie a small overhand knot in the end of a modest fiber bundle. Remember that few strands are enough to make a plump fly. Divide the bundle into two equal sections. Catch the knot in the first rod loop. Then tightly wind one section (about four times) around the rod as illustrated. With the same number of turns, counterwrap the other section over the first section. This produces balanced and symmetrical curls. Then, while trapping the tailing fibers against the rod handle, immerse the tightly wound sections in boiling (or near-boiling) water for about four seconds. Then plunge the heated wraps into cold water and dry with a cloth. You can also pour boiling water over the wrapped strands.

Now, take the curled strands off the rod and gently tease them out with long strokes. Once combed, the strands will puff up to provide bulk for a fly. Due to the open lattice of the curled strands, air easily penetrates the fly and dispels water during casting.

FIG. 3

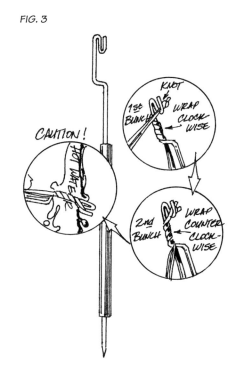

CAUTION!
HOT WATER

KNOT
1st BUNCH
WRAP CLOCK WISE

2nd BUNCH
WRAP COUNTER CLOCK WISE

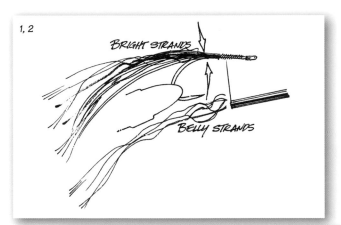

1, 2

BRIGHT STRANDS

BELLY STRANDS

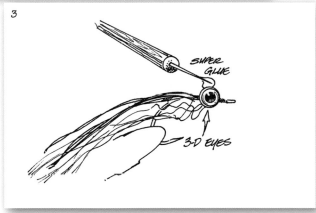

3

SUPER GLUE

3-D EYES

Hook: Daiichi X-Point or Trey Combs Big-Game hook, appropriate size
Thread: Uni Big Fly (Uni-Products) or Ultra Thread 140 (Wapsi)
Eyes & Inserts: Spirit River Real Eyes or Deep Sea Eyes with 3-D inserts. For ultralight patterns, use prismatic tape eyes
Belly strands (curled): Bright white Supremehair or Kinkyfiber
Underbelly strands (curled): Yellow Mirage Flashabou or silver Flashabou
Mid-strands (curled or straight): Red Holographic Flashabou
Topping (curled): Opal Flashabou Mirage

1 After attaching thread to the front third of the shank, mount the bright central strands. These may be curled or uncurled depending on the amount of bulk required (for a large fly, curl all the strands). If attaching a harness, mount it before adding the central strands.

2 Wrap the middle strands on the shank and, if desired, add some underbelly strands beneath the shank.

3 Securely mount the Real Eyes, adding a drop or two of superglue to the wraps. Mount the topping either in front of or behind the eyes. For greater bulk, mount the topping in front.

4 After mounting all the strands, trim the fly to length. Use Anvil's Taperizer scissors if you wish to thin and taper the tail.

One week from the day of this writing, I return to the Amazon. I can already see it: The long, clean cast. Then the glowing Tracer shooting past, arcing out and then dropping, burning brightly until extinguished by dark waters.

3

TOP STRANDS

4

The Kit & Caboodle
Making a home for your precious tying tools

Darrel Martin
July/Aug 2000

Most fly tiers collect tools that, with time, become familiar and useful friends. Tying with such comfortable and reassuring tools seems easier and more natural. For me, it is far more difficult to tie with strange tools than to cast a new fly rod. Tying tools can be remarkably intimate. And some may be unusual or expensive. In any case, your tools—your cherished, collected caboodle—should have a home.

Here is one way to make a serviceable roll-kit that protects and organizes those favorite tools. Materials for the kit are available at any fabric shop. Fine cotton twill or lightweight duck works well (some slick nylons may shift during sewing). Avoid stiff fabrics that do not roll easily. The outer pockets are made from fine leather, usually identified as "wallet grade," available through mail-order or special leather shops. The thin,

tough leather protects the points and blades of tools. Some modern sewing machines can accommodate the fine, light leathers as well as heavier, slick nylons, but make certain you use the appropriate needles and threads.

This pattern has four leather pockets—divided into two scissors pockets and eight small tool pockets. The fabric roll adds another 10 pockets, for a total of 20. Furthermore, the large fabric pockets hold many individual tools. To accommodate a variety of scissors shapes, I usually make the scissors pockets unusually wide at the bottom. The kit, which closes with a tab of Velcro or other hook-and-loop material, includes pockets designed specifically for each tool. You will want, of course, to design your kit according to your personal taste and tools; use the illustrations as a guide.

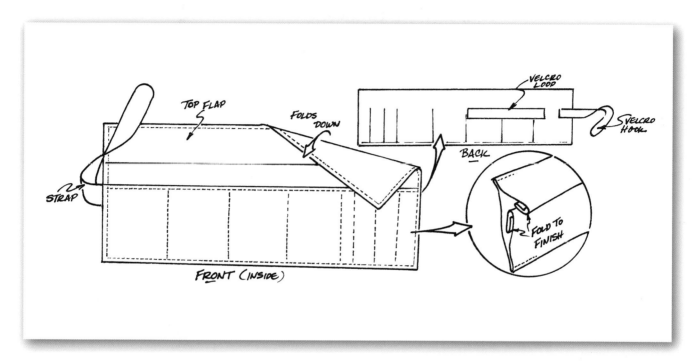

Making the kit

1 Lay out all those special tools that you'll want the kit to hold. Mine include three different pairs of scissors, a hair compressor, a whip-finisher, a spinning hook, a dubbing whirl, a small aluminum hair stacker, several sheathed X-Acto single-edge razor blades with Stanley Blade Holder, a plastic bull-dog clip, a bobbin threader, six mini bobbins, 20 or more plastic bobbin spools (sewing-machine spools) loaded with tying thread of various colors and sizes, two hackle pliers, a compact dubbing-wax stick, a dubbing rake, an extended-body/dubbing needle and a brush for fuzzing dubbing (made of the hook side of hook-and-loop material). I throw in other tools as required.

2 You'll need no more than a half-yard of fabric. Use chalk or marking pencil to draw the pattern on your fabric. Of course, you'll want to modify the pattern and the pockets to accommodate your special tools and needs. Take time to consider the pocket size and the position of each tool. Allow room for inserting and extracting the tool; avoid excessively snug pockets. Also avoid tool clash by judging what the kit will look like when rolled up.

3 Cut out the pattern, including width for the ¾" double-hem edge. Double fold the fabric edge for a narrow hem that hides the raw border. Before sewing, iron the fabric to flatten the folded hem edges. On some fabrics it may be necessary to finish the border with a zigzag stitch before double-folding the edge. Complete all folded hems at this time.

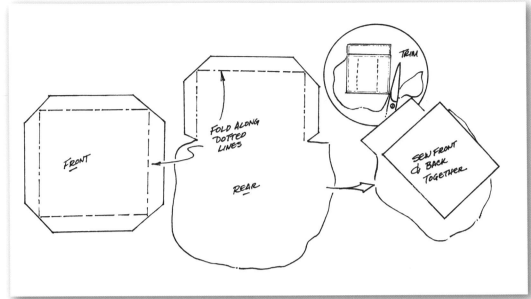

**Tool pocket pattern
& assembly**

❹ After hemming, fold—but do not sew—the kit together to determine the location and width of each pocket. Mark the pockets with chalk or pencil. Use the marked lines to determine the placement of the leather pockets.

❺ Make and mount the hook-and-loop closure tab. My closure tab is backed with leather. Mark the position and attach the "rug" strip to the back of the kit, making the tab long enough so that the roll-kit can be closed when empty and when stuffed.

❻ Now make the pocket templates by tracing each tool onto cardboard, allowing extra space or "free-bore" for the tool and extra width for the overlapped edges. For symmetrical pockets, fold the pocket template down the center and cut it out. To make a durable template for future use, transfer the pocket template onto a polystyrene sheet (from most hobby/craft stores). Sew the leather pockets by hand or with an appropriate machine and leather needle. For a modest fee, your local shoe or leather repair shop may sew the leather pockets on for you. Use a heavy Dacron thread for the leatherwork.

❼ Cut out and assemble the leather pockets. Trace the pocket template on the back side of the leather sheet. Add the single-fold edge,

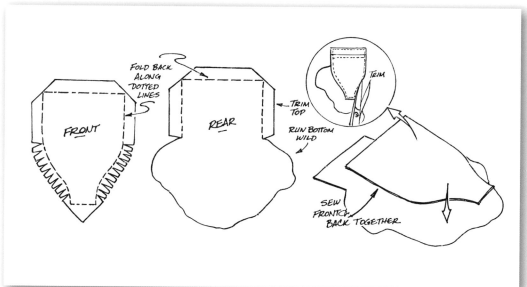

scissors pocket

about ½", to the pattern. Make gentle curves; avoid all abrupt or sharp curves that the leather cannot follow. Clip "V's" in the hem, as illustrated, to allow the leather to fold back and follow the curves. Make both the short front panel and the longer back panel. (I merely shorten the pocket template to make the front panel.) Apply rubber cement to the back folds and tabs to create a smooth line or curve. Mark the finished side edge with a leather creaser to imprint the sew line. After sewing all the edges, each leather pocket can then be sewn onto the fabric where marked. Complete the pockets before they are sewn onto the fabric. Take care that the pockets do not shift during sewing. Sew the pockets only on the sides and bottom to create an extra pocket at the top between the leather and the fabric.

8 Sew the leather pockets onto the front of the kit. Then fold the kit together, making certain that all side hems match, and sew the bottom and side-hems together.

9 Sew the top flap along the outer side edges of the kit front, forming a protective cover. This will help keep tools from falling out. Finally, carefully double-sew the divisions (previously marked) between the pockets. Remember that this roll-kit pattern only suggests some possibilities.

I have two other matching kits. One kit contains my vise, removable stem and bobbin cradle/gallows tool. The other kit, with a pull-string closure, carries a portable lamp and cord. To discourage straying tools when I teach classes, each tool is identified with a small, bright band of red thread coated with nail polish. I also attach a name and address tag to the roll kit.

Some tools have odd shapes or angles you must accommodate. The offset Anvil Signature Scissors, for example, do not readily fit into a standard flat pocket. Merely sheathe the blades in leather and stow such scissors in a larger pocket. The dubbing whirl, protected by a small film canister, also stashes in a larger pocket. Any pointed or bladed tool can be sheathed with a leather tip and then stowed.

Like most tiers, I have treasured tools collected over a lifetime of wrapping shanks—custom whip-finishers and bobbins, and other unusual tools. This roll-up kit protects and organizes. It lies flat when open, making each tool accessible. After tying, each tool returns to its special pocket. And, prior to roll-up, a quick glance determines if a tool is truant. When rolled up, the kit travels well and protects those friendly but inconspicuous tying tools. Designing and making a roll-kit is just another complementary pleasure of tying.

Wings & Things
Some thoughts on wings and wing-burners

Darrel Martin
March 2005

My son, Michael, recently wrote about his recurring dream: "As we drove through the desert, Dad lectured on the advantages of winged patterns, but I was more intent upon visions of rising trout. After hours of highway, we turned onto a dry track. Heavy dust swirled and floated behind us. Soon, Dad pulled off the track and parked, waiting for the dust to settle. Quickly armed with rod and vest, he said there was no need for waders. We made our way through scrub and channeled scabland down to a dry, ancient riverbed, scattered with rocks white in the sun. Always the first to fish, Dad tied on a winged Dust Devil and made a cast. It settled lightly on a rock. He slowly pulled it off onto the sand. Suddenly, dust and rocks exploded as a fish—half grayling and half mudskipper—struck the fly. Dad quickly landed the fish. Grinning, with fish in hand, he turned and said: 'Now it's your turn.'"

Wings—delicate and seductive wings—may be the only reason fish would rise in a dusty, dry riverbed. There are complete books devoted to wings and winging. Charles Walker's *Old Flies in New Dresses* (1898) focuses on mounting wings in the natural position. His explicit thesis is "to work out and bring down to a definite rule" the wing position of the various imitations. "The wings of a fly undoubtedly play an important part in forming the outline, and consequently the general appearance of the fly. Therefore, if they are not put in the natural

position, the whole contour of the imitation must be entirely different from that of the natural fly." Walker then catalogs the various wing positions of the naturals and the various winging methods. To Walker, the winged profile was far more important than pattern color.

Antique fly patterns, imitating the natural, often wore wings. Though wings are not always required, they somehow seem to complete many patterns. Colonel E. W. Harding, in *The Fly-fisher & The Trout's Point of View* (1931), would readily replace the traditional quill wing with a wrapped hackle: There is "a large and successful school of fly fishers who question the necessity for winging a fly at all.

"A hackle of a colour and density which represents the combined effect of the legs and wings of the natural fly is considered to represent the fly more accurately on the water and makes the fly lighter in weight and easier to fish." Nevertheless, he reluctantly adds, "but it seems to me that there are occasions when the general silhouette and colour effect of the wings can be obtained in no other way except by direct representation of wings in the conventional manner." Like most tiers, I would rather wrap a hackle than mount matched wings. However, wings are often attractive and functional. Moreover, some methods make winging as easy as wrapping.

Colonel Harding notes, "The suggestion of outspread wings is essential for a spent spinner pattern and how to obtain it is one of the most difficult problems in fly dressing." He rejects hackle-tip wings, claiming they are forced under the bend and, when wet, become useless for support. Despite Colonel Harding's censure, hackle-tip wings—when properly mounted—neither wrap nor sink. In any case, for transparent spinners, Harding wrapped double hackles. "In using two hackles, the first is wound and adjusted to simulate wings, the under fibres being cut away and not more than three turns of the second hackle." This method may have many variations for both dun and spinner.

Double-hackle wings

To tie double-hackle wings, such as the double-hackle dun (A and B), first mount the "leg" hackle (barb length equals ¾ shank length). Then mount the "wing" hackle (barb length equals shank length). Wrap a dense "wing" hackle, secure and trim excess. Next, carefully trim all underbarbs (A). Finally, wrap the "leg" hackle through the wing barbs, secure and trim excess. With standard hackles, the pale under-barbs melt into dark wings. When wrapping "hackle through hackle," do not avoid barbs by weaving through them. Rather, match the barb angle of the first hackle and then ignore the barbs as you wrap the second hackle. Trapped barbs usually snap back into place. Wrapping two different-color hackles creates a soft and subtle color blend that appeals to both tier and trout (B).

With modern micro hackles, this method also creates the swollen thorax of small spinners and duns. For double-hackle spinners (C), trim both top and bottom of the "wing" hackle and then wrap a short-barbed hackle to suggest the swollen thorax or legs. The thorax hackle increases flotation and visibility.

The CDC spinner (D) wears a quill body and CDC wings formed with a wing burner. Though not as durable as some spinners, the stiff stems and splayed barbs do float the fly well. Insert CDC barbs into a split-thread loop, spin and Figure-eight for hackle. This creates a gauzy and graceful spinner. Like a natural spinner wing, the CDC barbs imprint the surface with minute bubbles and sparkles.

flytying

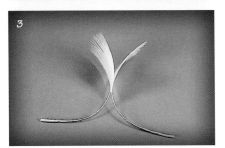

The fan wing

Usually regarded as niggling and annoying, mounting fan wings challenges many tiers. Finding quality fan feathers also poses a problem. The small, white breast feathers of a wood duck or Mandarin duck are often considered the best. Try this method for mounting fan wings for quill patterns and Coachmen:

❶ Select two breast feathers that have modest stem curvature. Reject those that have twisted or splayed barbs. The feathers should match in curvature, width and length. Feather matching is best done by selecting feathers that grow in close proximity on the bird. Strip surplus barbs so that wing length matches shank length. Match wing width at top of feather. Leave stems long for mounting.

❷ After matching and sizing the feathers, place a small dot of superglue gel at the base of the barbs on one feather as illustrated. Apply the gel "micro" dot with a fine needle. Avoid the thinner, "wicking" superglues; thin superglue, through capillary action, will invade the wing barbs.

❸ Next, carefully join the two feathers—convex side to convex side—and set aside to dry. The flat barb base keeps the feathers flat and parallel.

❹ When dried, "saddle" the wings on the shank: Straddle a stem on each side. No matter what the pattern, mount the wings first. Mount the wings with Figure-eight thread wraps (fore and aft) over the stems. Each wrap should capture both stems.

❺ After securing the wings, trim the stems to about ⅛" and fold back. "Lock" the wings with several wraps over the folded stems. Sometimes it is necessary to flatten thick stems prior to mounting or folding back. Flatten thick stems with small pliers.

❻ Finally, complete the fly with tail, body and hackle. The pattern is a Fan-Wing Quill.

Hackle-tip wings

Mounting hackle-tip wings for the ubiquitous Adams and its relatives requires a modified method. I like to select grizzly hen hackles that are rectangular, with high-contrast bands. The softer hen hackles are easily mounted and often have full width to their tips. This makes an attractive wing, unlike the more common pointed or tapered cock hackles.

If proper rectangular hackle tips are not available, wings may be burned from soft cock or hen capes. Hen grizzly hackle, especially the large hackles, usually lack the narrow, close bands or bars common in smaller cock hackles. When possible, always select those hackles that have narrow, contrasting bars and straight stems. Merely position the hackle within the wing burner and, with propane lighter, remove the excess. Mount burned hackle wings in the same manner as natural hackle wings.

You can also mount hackle-tip wings spinner style. J. Edson Leonard suggests a vibrating mount: "Hackle tips cocked so far forward they are nearly parallel with the shank, thus vibrating when the fly is set in motion by either the current or the retrieve." A secure spinner mount comes from Major Sir Gerald Burrard's *Fly-Tying: Principles and Practice* (1945). The hackle-tip stems cross the shank. Figure-eight wraps hold the wings in place. Cement the stem crossing and, when dry, fold forward and secure. It may be best, however, to crush the stems prior to mounting, and after mounting fold them back to become the underbody for the thorax.

❶ First, select matching (length and width) hackles. Strip off those barbs not required for wing length. For most patterns, wing length should equal shank length.

❷ Place a drop of superglue gel at the barb base and stem. Neck hackles and stems are usually flat, thus the stems may be cemented together. The glue should just enter, rather than invade, the barb base. Set the wing assembly aside to dry. When dry, place the doubled stem on top of the hook shank at wing position and overwrap. When mounting wings, position natural tips to the right: overwrap firmly to secure. Fold wings back to erect them. Note that the doubled stems create a shallow furrow for the hook shank. Trim excess stem length.

❸ Finally, fold the hackles back to erect them. Place three thread wraps in front of wing to preserve stance. Complete the pattern.

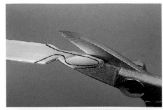

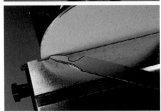

Burning wings

A wing burner is a metal template that holds feathers or fabric so that a flame, usually from a butane lighter, burns the surplus, thereby forming a shaped wing for fly-tying. Wing burners come in a variety of shapes for adult or nymph, mayfly, caddis and stonefly wings. Wing burners offer several advantages: 1) a wide variety of sizes; 2) realistic shapes; and 3) no blades to dull. Wing cutter blades eventually dull and may deform the feather.

For many patterns, commercial wing burners are either the wrong shape or the wrong size. To solve this, I often make wing burners by modifying commercial burners or by shaping brass strips. Depending upon the template size required, brass strips, in various lengths and thicknesses, are available from most hobby or hardware stores and catalogs. Burners for wings, legs and other pattern parts are readily made from brass strips, ½" or ¼" wide and .032" thick. Thinner strips, such as .016" thick, form more easily, but bend or deform readily.

Such strips are readily shaped with metal shears, files and grinders. Merely draw the desired shape on the end of the brass strip. Note: Remember to use protective eyewear and dust mask when shaping metal.

First, draw the wing shape and then rough-shape the template with metal shears. With files and grinders, take the metal down to within a couple of millimeters of the final desired shape. A small Minimite Dremel tool, mounted with ¼", ⅜" and ½" cap or drum sander/grinder works well in this close shaping. Select fine or extra-fine grit sanders. Cutting disks also quickly shape the template.

Once you have the shape close, fold and match both ends together. I generally fold the strip so that the burner is approximately 4" long. Short wing burners index, or match, better than long ones. Now, firmly tape the folded strip to match the ends for final shaping. Trim and rough-cut the other matched end.

Finally, bring the template down to final form with the Dremel and disk grinder. Polish when done. Grinders may heat the metal. If required, cool the metal by immersion in water. Make certain that both templates accurately match. Sometimes I inscribe a stem-line on both sides of the burner for wing replication.

For the Adams wing, I make a rather narrow wing shape with a slightly advanced wing tip. A narrow wing suggests a hackle-tip wing (rather than a natural wing shape) and reduces casting flutter. A single wing burner may accommodate two or more hook sizes. I also use burners to make delicate, wispy CDC wings. These wings float well and neither spin nor plane during the cast. For wing burning, select patterned hen feathers that have the barbs at right angles or nearly so. Acutely angled barbs may be burned through at the base, resulting in a truncated or angular wing. Match the wing-burner base with the barb angle. This creates an off-center wing stem and avoids a truncated wing base. When making or selecting a burner consider these following features:

- An appropriate wing size and shape
- A well-matched template edge for clean, sharp wing edges
- The proper metal thickness to prevent warped or fuzzed wing edges
- An adequate length for cool handling
- A secure clamping of the feather
- Variable feather positioning to accommodate dun, thoracic dun and spinner wings
- A template design that permits various stem angles

Imitating the precise wing shape is seldom, if ever, required. Wings, however, can be distinctive. Insect families often have a distinctive shape: the small circle (Caenidae); the small, elongated oval (Baetidae); medium, elongated oval (Ephemerellidae and Leptophlebiidae); medium triangle (Heptageniidae); large triangle (Ephemeridae and Potamanthidae) and so on. Some insects, such as the Ephemeridae, have a large hind wing that may be incorporated into the forewing shape. Size, however, is generally considered more important than the specific wing shape.

Rolled and divided wings

This antique method still creates some lovely flies. Rolled wings, also known as bunched wings, are merely barb fibers or hairs matched, bundled and mounted (A). Rolled wings may be mounted as a single wing on smaller patterns or divided to form paired wings on larger flies.

The natural tips are usually matched to create a sharp wing profile. J. Edson Leonard, in *Flies* (1950), advocated rolling soft breast-feather barbs back and forth between the fingers to quash their natural lay.

Long, soft barbs—such as woodduck breast-feather barbs—do not stack. The best method for aligning the natural tips is to remove a few barb "panels" at a time. Then carefully align the natural tips by pulling or rocking the panel with the fingers. Finger-stack several tip-aligned panels for mounting.

Reverse-mount the bundled wing, i.e., butts facing aft and natural tips over the hook eye. Erect the wings with fore-wraps and divide the wings with Figure-eights. Finally, complete the fly with tail, body and hackle (B).

From the March 2005 issue

10 Minute Ties

by A.K. Best

A production fly tier for decades, A. K. Best is also the guy who shows up periodically in John Gierach's work, up to some mischief or other. He's been a *Fly Rod & Reel* columnist since 2002.

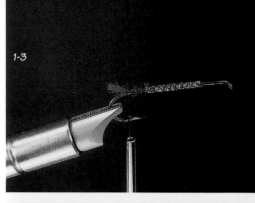

{**1O Minute Ties**} A.K. Best March 2007

The Black Nose Dace
A weighted streamer for the early season

One of my favorite streamer patterns is the classic Black Nose Dace. It imitates many species of minnow and baitfish from coast to coast and has undergone many variations during its long existence. I like to tie it as a weighted fly because I don't always carry a sink-tip line with me. For those of you who do a lot of lake fishing, an unweighted pattern on a sink-tip or full-sinking line will work fine. I have also made a couple of changes to the pattern that have proven to be successful.

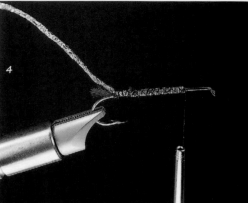

> **Hook:** Your favorite streamer hook in sizes 2 to 8. I prefer Mustad 79580
> **Weight:** Lead-substitute wire. Diameter same as hook shank
> **Thread:** Danville's black monocord
> **Tail:** Short (hook-point length) red yarn single strand
> **Body:** Silver woven tinsel
> **Under-wing:** Straight white bucktail
> **Over-wing:** Black bucktail or black bear
> **Throat:** Small, short clump of soft red hackle fibers, length to equal hook gap

❶ Attach lead-substitute wire over hook point and wind forward to within one hook-gap space behind the hook eye.

❷ Attach tying thread in front of wire, wind back and forth twice to anchor wraps and apply a liberal amount of head lacquer to fix the weight.

❸ Tie in single strand of red yarn immediately behind wire wraps. Trim length to be no longer than the distance of the hook point to the rear of the barb.

❹ Tie in braided tinsel immediately behind wire wraps, lash down to cover all thread wraps to the rear, bring the bobbin forward to hang down immediately in front of the lead wraps.

❺ Carefully and firmly wind the braided tinsel forward and tie off on top of the hook two hook-eye spaces behind the eye. Trim excess at an angle just behind the hook eye.

❻ Select a small clump (about the diameter of a wooden match) of rather straight white bucktail, pull out all the longest hairs, flick out all the shortest hairs and use the pinch-and-pull method of stacking the tips. (You don't want a square wing on a hairwing streamer).

❼ Tie on the clump so the tips extend beyond the hook bend by a distance equal to two hook gaps. Lash butts to rear of hook eye, lift butts and trim at an angle.

❽ Select a very small clump of straight black hair (no more than a dozen hairs), and tie on top of the white under-wing so that the tips of both are even. Do not allow the black hairs to separate or roll to one side. Lash down just behind clipped white wing butts. Lift butts and clip off at an angle.

❾ Tie in a small clump of red hackle fibers as a beard, trim butts, completely cover the head with thread wraps and lacquer several times to achieve a glassy head.

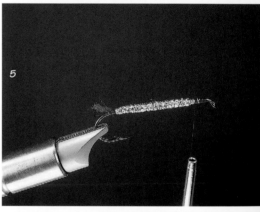

6, 7

8, 9

The BWO Sub Emerger
An ace-in-the-hole

There seems to be a Blue-Wing Olive hatch on every trout stream in every country around the world. I never leave home without them. One of my ace-in-the-hole patterns when fishing this hatch is what I call the Sub Emerger. It's a fly that imitates the nymph with the beginnings of wings. The beauty of this pattern is that it can be fished subsurface at any depth, as well as greased and fished in the surface film.

Hook: Your favorite dryfly hook, sizes 16 to 22
Thread: Danville's olive, 6/0
Tail: Three fibers of dark brown pheasant tail
Rib: Brown 6/0 thread
Body: Light green dubbing (color of split-pea soup or avocado flesh)
Emerging wing: Small loop of light gray poly yarn. Split the segment to suit the size of the fly
Wing case: Dark gray goose segment. Width to equal hook gap
Thorax: Dubbing one shade darker than the body

---

❶ Attach thread at mid-shank, wrap to the end of the shank and tie in three tail fibers. Lash to thorax area, clip off butts, attach rib and lash to the beginning of the bend.

❷ Tie in the goose segment by its tip with the dull side down.

❸ Apply thin and firmly dubbed tapered body and wind into thorax area. Fold the goose segment forward, tie down, reverse-wrap the rib and tie off in thorax area.

❹ Split a segment of poly yarn in half for size 16 flies and into thirds for size 18 and smaller. Stretch the yarn before splitting and liberally rub with dubbing wax to help straighten the fibers.

❺ Snip one end to even the fibers and tie in at the rear of the thorax area on top of the goose segment, with the remaining strand to the rear.

❻ Make a small loop in the poly yarn to the rear, tie down firmly and clip off remainder.

❼ Hold goose segment back to expose only the loop tie down, anchor with two or three turns of thread, and dub a fuzzy thorax.

❽ Carefully fold the goose segment forward over the thorax, tie off immediately behind the hook eye, clip off the remainder, whip-finish and apply a drop of head lacquer to both the head and the goose segment.

Note: On size 16 and 18 flies, I will often tie in a short segment of mottled brown hen back as a beard hackle. I don't think it's necessary on size 20 and smaller. Just tease the dubbing when you've finished the fly.

1-3

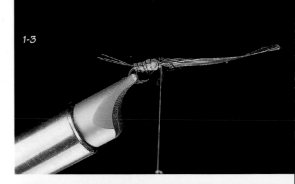

4, 5

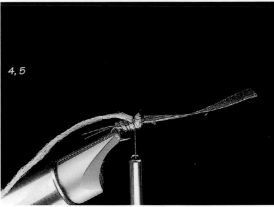

6

7

8

{**10 Minute Ties**} A.K. Best: April 2007

Olive Quill Duns
A favorite Blue-Wing Olive pattern

My favorite mayfly hatch is the Blue-Wing Olive. They can be found in sizes as large as 16 and as small as 26, appearing as early as March and as late as mid-November. Of course, nature is in complete control of this, and the emergence can vary by weeks or even a month. Some years ago, John Gierach and I went down to Colorado's South Platte River in February with the intention of fishing a midge hatch and ended up fishing a heavy emergence of BWOs during a snowstorm.

There are a number of Latin names for these little aquatic bugs, but I prefer to call any little mayfly that has a green body, and medium-to-dark-gray tail, legs and wings a Blue-Wing Olive, even though the green body is seldom olive and the wings aren't blue.

I used to fish the standard dubbed-body version of this fly, but Figured I was getting too many refusals from actively rising fish. So I began experimenting with quill-bodied BWOs and my success ratio climbed dramatically. I'm convinced that it has to do with the smooth, waxy appearance of the quill body and the segmentation effect that the wound quill exhibits. And I began to experiment with dyeing my own materials to match the colors of the natural's tail, legs and wings. They're not really gray, but sort of dirty gray, as though a little tan had been mixed in. The body colors are really a mixture of cream, green, gray and yellow—you wouldn't see this unless you magnified the natural fly until it was three feet long!

Since these flies are small, it sometimes helps to trim all the hackle off the bottom of the collar even with the bottom of the abdomen to get the fly to rest low on the water like the naturals.

❶ Attach tying thread one hook-gap distance behind eye and wind to beginning of bend, creating a tiny thread bump over the last wrap of thread.

❷ Tie in tailing fibers (whose length will be equal to the hook length) at the bend and wrap tying thread forward to the initial thread wrap and clip off the butts. This will be the shoulder of the body. Leave the thread here.

❸ Select a quill and clip off the tip at a point where the remaining diameter is equal to the diameter of the hook, tailing and thread. This will provide the correct segmentation width to the body of the fly.

❹ Place the clipped quill directly over and even with the clipped tailing butts and wind the thread over the quill toward the hook bend, keeping the quill on top of the hook shank. Bring the thread back to the shoulder and wind the quill forward in tightly nesting wraps to the shoulder. Bind it down on top of the hook and clip off the excess.

❺ Tie in a pair of matched hen-hackle tips (whose length will be equal to the entire hook) immediately in front of the shoulder of the fly. Separate and anchor.

❻ Tie in a trimmed hackle butt in front of the wings. Wind hackle first behind wings then in front for a total of no more than five turns of hackle.

Hook: Your favorite dryfly hook, sizes 16 to 26

Thread: Bright green Danville 6/0 for sizes 16 to 22; camel-color 8/0 Uni-thread sizes 24 and 26

Tail: Gray (to match the natural) spade hackle fibers or dyed Coq de Leon saddle fibers

Body: Stripped and dyed Chinese rooster neck hackle quill

Wings: Gray (to match the natural) hen hackle tips

Hackle: Gray (to match the natural) neck or saddle (sparsely wrapped)

1, 2

3, 4

4

5

{**1Ɵ Minute Ties**} A.K. Best July/Oct 2006

The *Callibaetis* Quill Dun
A must-have pattern even on streams

Although they are common on stillwaters, I've only been lucky enough to hit the *Callibaetis* hatch about twice a year on moving water, and when I do I'm damn glad I always carry an assortment of flies for rare events such as this. Trout seem to ignore anything else that might be on the stream when the *Callibaetis* begin hatching. When I find them, I usually come across them on slow-moving pools. We all know where insects are supposed to live; however, they can go any place that suits them.

Hook: Mustad 94840, size 14 to 18
Thread: Danville 6/0 #31 gray
Tail: Light-medium dun spade hackle fibers, length equal to entire hook
Wings: Pair of light-medium dun hen hackle tips, length to equal entire hook
Hackle: Light but well-marked grizzly hackle with enough web to simulate the large thorax

❶ Attach the thread to the hook one hook-gap space behind the eye and wind to the beginning of the hook bend. Cut off the tag and make a little thread bump with two or three turns of thread over the last one.

❷ Tie on tailing fibers immediately in front of the thread bump. This will cock them up slightly.

❸ For size 14 and 16 flies, use two quills. One quill should be twice the diameter of the other. Clip off the tips at a point where the combined width of both quills is about equal to the diameter of the hook eye. Tie them onto the top of the hook with the clipped tips aligned with the thread start.

❹ Wind the quills forward, making certain that the thicker one covers the thinner one. Tie off on top of the hook one hook-gap space behind the hook eye and clip off the butts.

❺ Tie on wings in front of the shoulder of the body, and leave just enough space for two turns of hackle behind the wings.

❻ Trim hackle butt and wind the hackle in your favorite manner. Take two turns behind the wings and three turns in front. Tie down the tip, clip it off, whip-finish, and apply a drop of head lacquer to the thread head only.

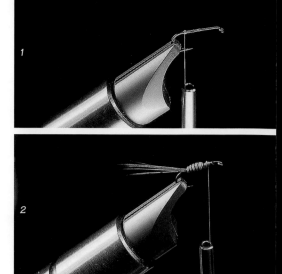

Easy Stonefly Nymph

Effective, simple . . . and no fussing with the details

There is a great temptation among all tiers (myself included) to try to include every possible detail when tying these large nymphs. If you're going to do that, I'd suggest you go all out, take a day or two to tie an exact imitation—and then save it in a glass case. Losing a true work of art on the first cast can be a maddening experience.

Tying stonefly nymphs for fishing can be a lot easier than most tiers suspect. There are some facts about stonefly nymphs and trout that will free your mind a bit when tying these large insects. For instance, when stonefly nymphs lose their grip and are free floating, their antennae are folded back over their bodies, so there is no need to tie them on. And, trout can't count the number of wing-case pads, so use only one long one. Finally, the stream is usually a little off color, so size, shape and general color are the main considerations. Forget the little details . . . .

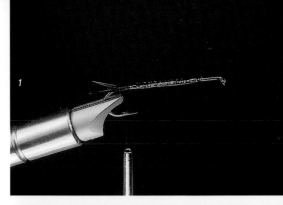

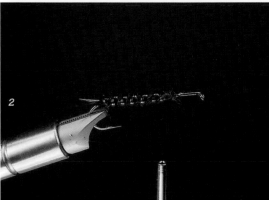

Hook: Mustad 79580, size 2 to 8
Thread: Danville black monocord
Weight: Length of lead wire on each side of hook
Tail: Black goose biots
Body: Black coarse wool sweater yarn
Ribbing: Black Swanundaze or V-Rib
Wing pad: Black goose or turkey segment
Legs: Black hen back feather
Thorax: Dirty orange dubbing

❶ Lash lead wire to each side of the hook and lacquer liberally. Dub a small ball at the end of the shank and tie in a goose biot on each side.

❷ Tie in black Swanundaze or V-Rib first, and then attach a thinned end of heavy, black sweater yarn. Twist the yarn and wind it forward to within one hook gap of the eye, tie down and clip off excess. Spiral wrap the Swanundaze forward in a similar manner.

❸ Tie in a hook-gap-width segment of black goose or turkey by its base on top of the body about one third back from the hook eye, shiny side down.

❹ Tie in one black hen back feather by its tip (with the shiny side up) immediately on top of the goose segment.

❺ Create a dubbing loop, insert dirty orange dubbing, spin the loop to form a rope and wind from behind the eye toward the rear of the thorax, and then forward again. Trim the top, sides and bottom of the thorax. This will create a properly shaped thorax as shown in photo.

❻ Stroke the hen fibers to the rear to create two V's, pull them forward over the thorax, tie down behind the eye and clip off the butts.

❼ Fold the wing-case segment forward over the hen back, tie down firmly and clip off the excess.

❽ Liberally lacquer the wing case, being careful to avoid the hen hackle fibers.

{1○ **Minute Ties**} A.K. Best Nov/Dec 2007

The Matuka

Big browns at twilight and dusk? Here's the fly . . . .

I occasionally enjoy going to the stream in the evening to look for deep holes and drop-offs where I'll fish a large, weighted Matuka in hopes of fooling a big, cannibalistic brown trout. I usually take a 6- or-7-weight 9-foot rod and fish a 7-foot leader with a 3X tippet. It's a meat-and-potatoes set up, but it's what I need if I have any hope of landing the big fish that come out in the evening looking for a mouthful. I prefer a mottled-wing Matuka-style fly for this kind of fishing because the wing of the Matuka is lashed to the hook shank, preventing the wing from separating from the weighted body of the fly. Some Coq de Leon rooster saddles have a few feathers at the butt of the pelt that are perfect for this and make a beautiful Matuka.

Hook: Mustad 79580, size 2
Wire: Diameter to match hook shank
Thread: Danville's black Monocord
Rib: Thin gold braid
Body: Tan yarn
Wings: Two pair of webby, mottled brown Coq de Leon butt feathers
Collar: One mottled Coq de Leon butt feather

---

❶ Place a size 2 streamer hook in the vise and wrap lead-substitute wire from just above the hook point to within a hook-gap space behind the eye.

❷ Attach tying thread just behind the eye and wind back and forth over the lead wire a couple of times. Liberally coat with head lacquer.

❸ Tie in the gold ribbing immediately behind the lead wraps.

❹ Tie in yarn immediately behind the lead wraps, and then wind thread forward to hang down immediately in front of the lead wraps.

❺ Carefully wind the tan yarn forward and tie it off on top of the hook immediately in front of the lead wraps.

❻ Carefully pair the wings, strip enough fibers from the tops to allow for tie-down behind the eye and enough fibers from the bottom to clear space for lashing to the top of the hook shank. Wing should extend beyond the end of the hook by at least a hook length.

❼ Wet top wing fibers with saliva and stroke them up to form Vs, and take the first turn of ribbing under the wings.

❽ Continue ribbing over the wings to the front of the body, then tie off the ribbing on top of the hook.

❾ Tie on the collar feather on top of the hook, with the shiny side forward.

❿ Carefully wind the collar hackle to lean to the rear, whip-finish and apply two or three coats of head lacquer.

{**1⊙ Minute Ties**} A.K. Best Jan/Feb 2004

The *Callibaetis* Spinner
The preferred food of finicky fish

I love it when I find a *Callibaetis* hatch, because trout seem to prefer this bug to many others that may be hatching at the same time. However, it's not a colorful fly: It is a delicately gray insect with a prominently segmented body, long tails and speckled wings. It also has an enormous hump in its thorax.

Sometimes, if there is a stream near a pond or lake, you can find *Callibaetis* landing on the stream. This can be a little confusing until you net the water to find what all those rising trout are eating. The spinner fall often occurs at the same time the duns are on the water; it all happens during daylight hours and seems to last a very long time. In fact, if you know there has been a *Callibaetis* hatch, you can often tie on a spinner and bring fish up to it.

❶ Attach the thread to the hook about two hook-eye spaces behind the eye and wind to the beginning of the bend. Take two or three turns over the last wrap to create a tiny thread bump that will cock the tails up slightly.

❷ Tie in the tail fibers to be at least hook length plus half a hook gap. Clip off the butts two hook-eye spaces behind the eye.

❸ Select one dyed quill and clip off the tip at a point where its remaining diameter is equal to the diameter of the hook, thread and tailing butts.

❹ Lash the clipped tip down at the clipped tailing butts and wind the thread over the quill to the last turn of thread holding the tailing. Bring the thread forward.

❺ Wind the quill forward in tightly nesting turns to within three hook-eye spaces of the eye. Lift the butt and clip it off on top of the hook. Cover the butt with thread.

❻ From the side of the neck select a light but well-marked grizzly hackle whose fibers are two sizes larger than the hook you're tying on. For example, use a size 12 hackle for a size 16 hook. These side hackles are often referred to as spades and should contain no web.

❼ Trim away all the softer fibers near the butt and tie the butt on top of the clipped-off body quill with the shiny side down.

❽ Take only three turns of hackle, tie down the tip and clip it off. Use your right thumb and forefinger to press the hackle collar into two halves.

❾ Carefully wrap thread in a Figure eight around the two halves, forming horizontal wings.

Hook: Your favorite dryfly hook in sizes 14 to 18

Thread: Danville's 6/0 #31 Gray (Note: if you want 8/0, spin the bobbin!)

Tailing: Light smoky-dun spade hackle or Coq de Leon fibers

Body: One stripped-and-dyed-to-light-smoky-dun rooster-neck hackle quill.

Wing: Oversize grizzly hackle

Thorax: Light-to medium-dun dryfly dubbing. I prefer rabbit with no guard hairs

Hackle: None

1-8

8b

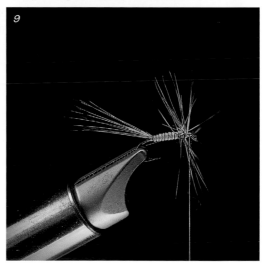

9

{**10 Minute Ties**} A.K. Best July/Oct 2002

Durable Beetles
Finally, a really tough terrestrial

I love to fish beetles mid-day in late summer. It's a time, usually long after the morning hatch and hours before the evening spinner fall, when most people leave the stream to take a nap. It's a lazy hour during a laid-back portion of the summer. About the only things that are active are terrestrial insects and me. Ants and hoppers are always the flies of choice at this time, but beetles don't seem to get the attention I think they deserve.

If you should happen to see a rise, chances are some terrestrial insect just became a snack, and a well-presented beetle pattern will probably bring a repeat performance from the same trout. Even if you don't see any rises, the beetle is always a good choice as a prospecting fly, especially next to a bank in those slow-moving, shady pools where trout always seem to be looking up.

I think one of the reasons beetle patterns aren't more popular is the durability problem. The old deerhair shellback patterns worked well, but didn't last long. Some of the newer sponge-back beetles suffer from the same weakness. But now there is a relatively new product called Bugskin on the market that will allow you to tie beetles that will endure many trout and lots of rough handling. Bugskin is a product of the leather industry and is practically indestructible when used on a fly. A Bugskin beetle that has been thoroughly saturated with a silicone-base flotant will stay on top all day!

❶ Cut the Bugskin into strips as wide as the hook gap.

❷ Shape one end of a strip into a spear point.

❸ Tie in the pointed end of the strip just behind the end of the hook shank.

❹ Wrap a small ball of dubbing over the strip tie-down.

❺ Tie in a stiff hackle feather by its tip.

❻ Dub the remainder of the hook shank. Keep the body full but remember to maintain as much hook-point clearance as you can, and save room for the palmered hackle tie-down and shell back tie-down just behind the hook eye.

❼ Palmer-wrap the hackle forward, clip off the butt and trim all the hackle from both the top and bottom of the fly.

❽ Fold the Bugskin strip forward, pull it tight and tie it down with firm wraps of thread. Clip off the tag as close to the thread as you can, cover the clipped strip with thread, whip-finish and carefully apply head lacquer to the head only. The leather strip will readily absorb head lacquer, which will prevent it from absorbing any fly flotant.

7, 8

Hook: Your favorite dryfly hook, size 14 to 20
Thread: Black 6/0
Shell Back: Black for black beetle, bronze for bronze beetle
Body: Dubbed black for black beetle, brown for bronze beetle
Hackle: (Palmered) black for black beetle, brown for bronze beetle

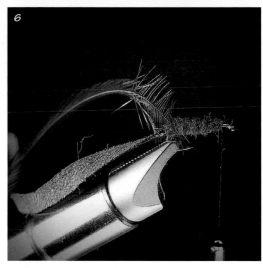

1, 2

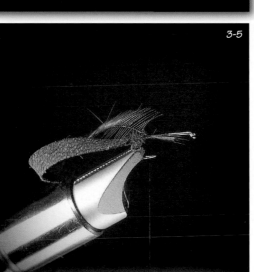

3-5

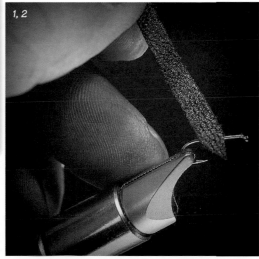

6

{**1O Minute Ties**} A.K. Best Jan/Feb 2005

The Floating Hare's Ear Nymph

Not easy to see on the water, but that just adds to the drama

It doesn't happen often, but when it does, you had better be prepared. I'm sure you've all heard that admonition before. I'm referring to those days when, for reasons known only to them, the trout will not eat any of your dry, parachute, emerger, sub-emerger, wetfly or spinner patterns. Yet, you can see them feeding at the surface with their noses barely breaking the film. Invariably this is a time for a floating nymph.

You can adapt the following floating nymph pattern to imitate any mayfly nymph in sizes 12 and smaller by altering the color of the dubbing—even ones down to 20 and 22. For those of you who (like me) prefer tying flies without the use of manmade materials, my floating nymph pattern can be accomplished without the use of foam balls or sponge rods.

Visibility can be a problem with these flies, but I prefer to avoid hi-vis materials in order to preserve as much of the drama of fly-fishing as I can. I believe that as the drama decreases, so does the thrill.

1 Start the tying thread one hook-eye space behind the eye and tightly wrap the entire hook shank with thread. Leave the thread hanging at the bend.

2 Stack a small bundle of elk body hair and tie it on top of the hook with the tips extending beyond the bend by one hook-gap distance.

3 Spiral wrap thread forward over the elk to within two hook-eye spaces of the eye. Leave the elk butts pointing over the eye.

4 Bring the thread forward toward the bend in one open spiral wrap under the hook to hang down one hook gap behind the eye. This will form the thorax area.

5 Fold the elk hair to the rear, tie down with two turns of thread, make another open spiral wrap of thread forward under the thorax and let the thread hang down at the front of the thorax.

6 Fold the elk hair forward and tie down with two turns of thread. Bring the thread back toward the rear of the thorax in another open spiral wrap beneath the thorax and continue toward the hook bend. Lift the elk hair butts and carefully trim.

7 Tie in ribbing if you desire, and very finely and tightly apply dubbing for the abdomen and wrap it forward to the rear of the thorax.

8 Tie in a goose segment at the rear of the thorax, dub the thorax, fold the goose segment forward, tie off, clip off the butt, whip-finish and apply a small drop of head lacquer (to the thread head only).

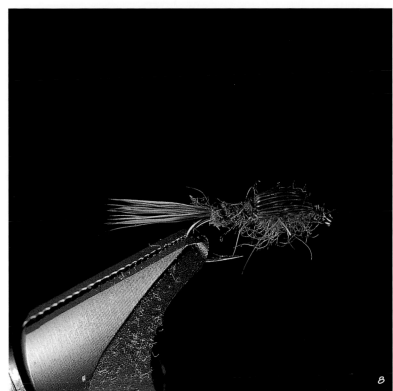

8

Hook: Dryfly, size 12 to 22
Thread: Black, brown or tan 6/0 or 8/0
Tail: Small clump of stacked elk body hair
Underbody: Layered elk hair
Overbody: Very fine dubbing, color to match naturals
Wing pad: Medium dun to black goose quill segment
Thorax: One shade darker dubbing than abdomen, loosely applied and teased

1-3

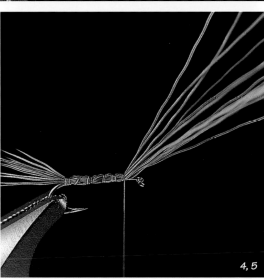

4, 5

6

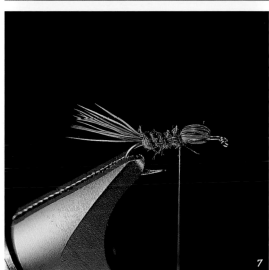

7

{**10 Minute Ties**} AK Best Jan/Feb 2007

The Hare's Ear Soft-Hackle
A versatile imitation

Lately there has been a lot of discussion about tying and fishing soft-hackle flies. This is a fly every angler should carry and know how to tie. My favorite is the Hare's Ear Soft-Hackle because it's easy to tie and imitates a host of emerging or drowned insects. Although a tier can vary the body and hackle color to suit their needs, I haven't found it necessary to carry a whole box of color variations for this basic weighted pattern. They can be tied with tails or without. Again, I haven't found a single version to be more effective. The biggest controversy seems to be about how the fly should be hackled and what to use. I say, again, it really doesn't matter as long as you achieve the desired result, which is catching fish.

Hook: Your favorite dryfly hook, sizes 12 to 18
Weight: Lead-substitute wire. Diameter to equal hook shank diameter
Thread: Danville red, 6/0 or 8/0 (I use red for weighted flies and black for unweighted)
Rib: 28- or 32-gauge brass wire
Body: Thin, but slightly tapered, hare's mask dubbing
Hackle: Mottled brown hen neck or back feather. Coq de Leon hen backs make beautiful hackle collars when dyed to a light brown or olive. The natural shade is gray

---

❶ Attach lead-substitute wire at mid-shank and wind to within two hook-eye spaces behind the eye. Attach tying thread in front of the lead wraps, wind back and forth twice to secure lead wraps and apply a liberal amount of head lacquer to this assembly.

❷ Firmly tie in a length of brass wire on your side of the hook immediately behind the lead wraps. Very firmly dub a small amount of hare's mask dubbing to the thread to create a small-diameter bump to the rear of the body. Keep adding dubbing to create a slightly tapered dubbing rope.

❸ Carefully wind dubbing rope forward and stop immediately on top of the last turn of lead wraps behind the hook eye. This is to create a shoulder immediately behind the hackle collar.

❹ Reverse-wrap the brass wire forward in evenly spaced turns and tie off on the bottom immediately in front of the lead wraps. Select a hackle feather whose fibers will not extend beyond the hook point. I use my dryfly hackle gauge for this. Strip off all the marabou-like fibers from the butt and all the fibers from the side of the feather that will be touching the hook. Tie the feather on by its butt immediately in front of the shoulder of the fly.

❺ Wind forward the hackle feather for two turns, stroking the fibers to the rear after each wrap. Tie off the tip, trim, whip-finish, and apply a drop of head lacquer.

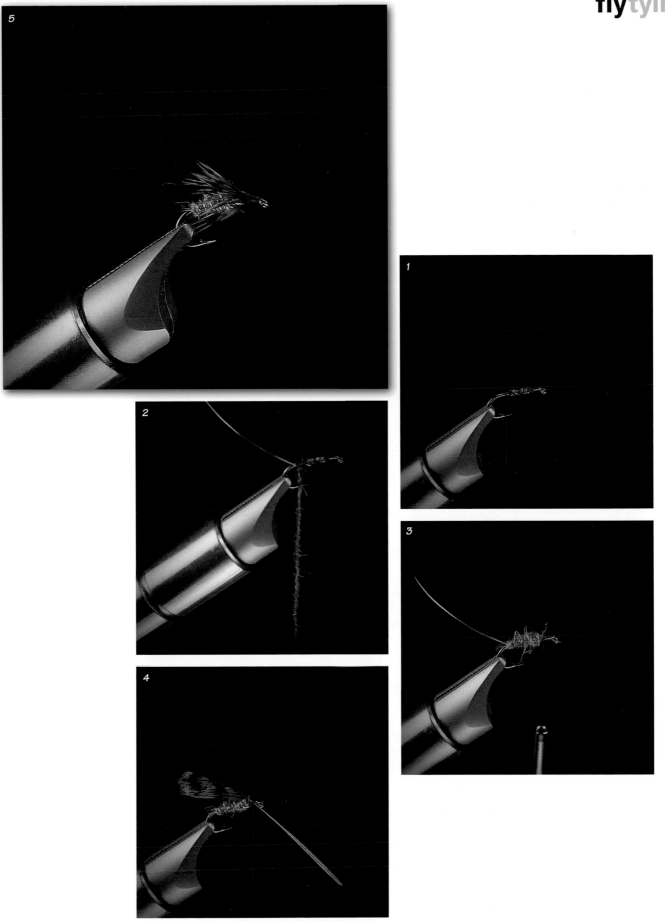

{**1⊙ Minute Ties**} AK Best June 2007

The Mickey Finn
A classic streamer that still catches fish

The first streamer fly I tied over 40 years ago was the Mickey Finn. I chose it because I thought it was a pretty fly and was an old and well-established classic pattern. The neat thing about many classic flies is that they work quite well on today's supposedly "educated" trout. Since we have some new materials to work with, we can make them more durable and a little easier to tie. These days I weight them and use woven gold Mylar tinsel for the body, but that's the only change I think needs to be made.

Hook: Your favorite streamer hook. I prefer Mustad 79580, size 2 to 8.
Thread: Danville's black monocord
Tail: None
Weight: Lead-substitute wire. Diameter to equal hook shank diameter
Body: Woven gold tinsel
Underwing: Bright yellow bucktail
Midwing: Bright red bucktail
Overwing: Bright yellow bucktail
Throat: Optional red soft hackle fibers

---

❶ Attach lead-substitute wire over the hook point, wind forward to within three hook-eye spaces behind the eye and clip off the tag. Attach tying thread immediately in front of the lead wraps and wind back and forth two

❷ Tie on one end of the woven gold tinsel immediately behind the lead wraps and lash down to the end of the shank.

❸ Carefully wind the woven tinsel forward, tie off immediately in front of the lead wraps, but lash down up to the rear of the eye before clipping off at an angle.

❹ The wing is the tricky part. The total mass of the wing should equal the diameter of a wood kitchen match; less for size 6 and 8 hooks. I try to aim for 50 percent on the bottom layer, 30 percent on the middle and 20 percent on the top layer of hair. This will prevent the top yellow layer from completely covering the middle red layer.

a Select a clump of straight yellow bucktail not quite the diameter of a wood kitchen match. Use the pinch-and-pull method to even the tips and tie on so that the tips extend beyond the hook bend by two hook-gap spaces. Lash down almost to the eye, lift the butts and clip off at an angle.

b Select a slightly smaller clump of straight red bucktail and repeat the above steps, except do not lash down all the way to the hook eye. Stop and clip off at an angle so the front taper of the head is in line with the angle of the first clump.

❺ Select a slightly smaller clump of straight yellow bucktail and repeat step 4b. Carefully wind thread around the head to cover all the hair butts, apply a couple of layers of thick head lacquer and set aside to dry.

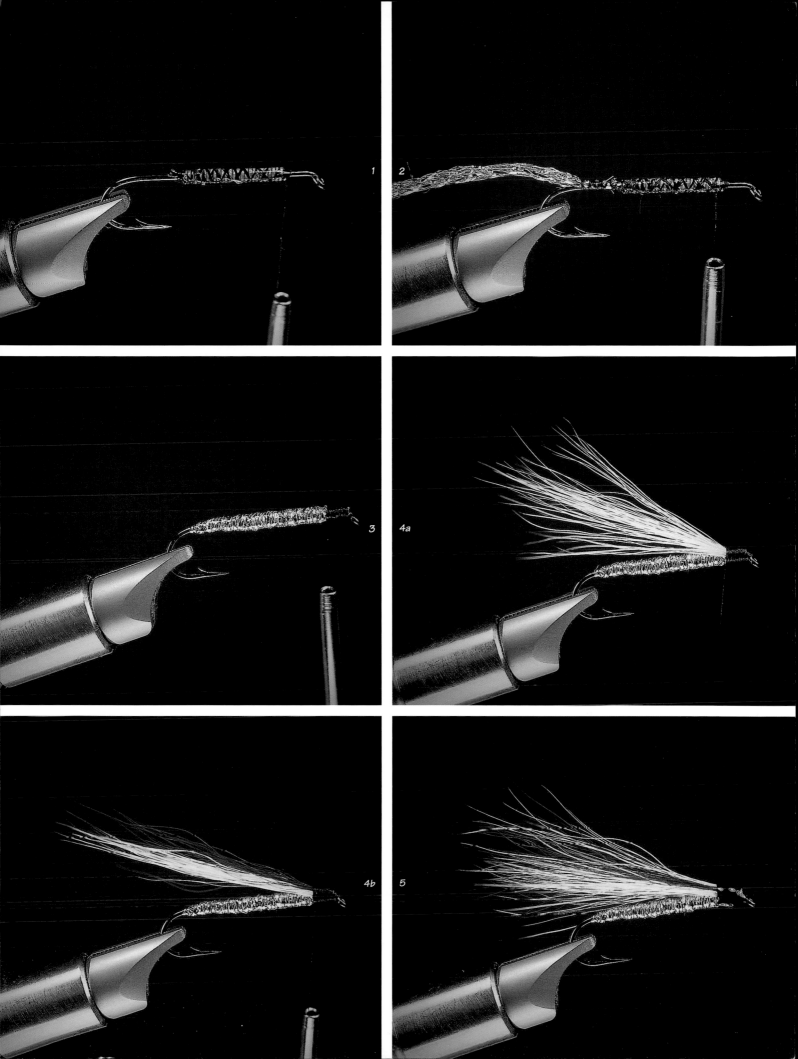

{**10 Minute Ties**} A.K. Best Nov/Dec 2006

The Pheasant Tail Nymph
The classic all-purpose nymph—with a modification or two

My "go-to nymph" is nearly always the Pheasant Tail. I carry them in sizes 14 through 22, unweighted.

I've always felt that the original Sawyer pattern appeared a little too clean around the thorax area, so I have added a fuzzy hare's ear thorax in place of the trim-looking pheasant thorax of the original. The hare's ear dubbing is a little darker in color than the pheasant tail fibers and provides the appearance of gills and legs. For those of you who like flash in the wing case, try using dyed black wild turkey tail segments. Tie in the segment with the shiny side down. The fibers in the turkey tail are quite flat and when pulled forward over the thorax will twist to one side and provide a nice, shiny surface.

❶ Attach tying thread above the hook point and wrap to the beginning of the bend.

❷ Tie in pheasant tail fibers, lash them to the middle of the thorax area and clip off the butts.

❸ Tie in the wire here and lash it to your side of the hook all the way to the beginning of the hook bend. This will prevent the wire from cutting off body fibers as you reverse-wrap the wire over the body later.

❹ Select an appropriate number of fibers for the body, clip off the tips to even them, tie them down with the tips at mid-shank and lash them down to the end of the shank.

❺ Carefully wind the fibers forward to create a smooth and slightly tapered body well into the thorax area. This is to provide a platform on which to tie the wing case.

❻ Reverse-wrap the wire over the body in evenly spaced turns, tie down and clip off the excess in the thorax area.

❼ Tie in the turkey segment with the shiny side down and tip to the rear.

❽ Loosely dub the thorax to create a diameter about twice the size of the shoulder of the body. Save two hook-eye spaces for tying down wing case and head.

❾ Carefully fold wing case forward, tie down firmly, clip off excess, whip-finish and apply a drop of head cement.

❿ Tease the dubbing for a fuzzier thorax.

9, 10

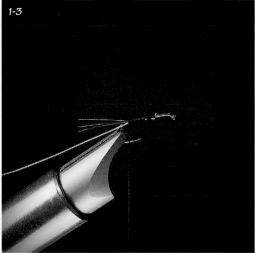

1-3

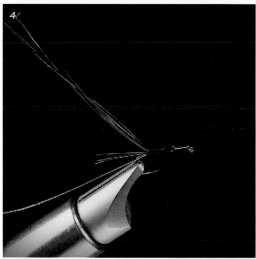

4

Hook: Use your favorite dryfly hook, size 14 to 22 (I prefer dryfly hooks because I occasionally want to grease the fly to make it float)

Thread: Thompson's 6/0 on sizes 14 through 18, and 8/0 on sizes 20 and 22

Tail: Three light- to medium-brown pheasant tail fibers, hook-gap length

Rib: Soft brass wire from your local craft store. 28- to 32-gauge

Body: Fibers from the center tail of a rooster ringneck pheasant. Size 14: 6 or 7 fibers; size 16: 5 or 6 fibers; size 18: 4 or 5 fibers; size 20 and 22: 3 or 4 fibers

Wing case: Hook-gap-width segment of dyed black wild turkey tail. Spray liberally with Krylon Workable Fixatif before separating

Thorax: Loosely dubbed hare's ear dubbing

5, 6

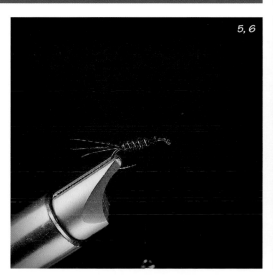

7, 8

{1⊙ **Minute Ties**} A.K. Best June 2004

The Quill Body RS 2
Simple to tie, effective on fish

One of the simplest nymphs to tie, and one of the most effective to fish, is the RS 2. It's the nymph to use during either a Baetis or midge hatch. Besides looking very much like the nymphal stage of either insect, it can be fished not only down near the bottom but anywhere between the bottom and the surface—and you can grease it and present it as a surface emerger. It has become a classic pattern.

I'm like a lot of other fly tiers in that I'm always trying to make a change or two to established flies to suit my needs. For example, I like the traditional gray RS 2 to have a green body for some Baetis hatches or a tan or black body for some midge hatches. I want to improve on the visibility when fishing it as a floating emerger, and I like to add to the buoyancy of the fly. Some experimenting with basic materials substitutes and a few years of field-testing has led me to the Quill Body RS 2.

❶ Attach the tying thread just above the hook point and wind to the beginning of the bend.

❷ Stroke a well-marked hen back or mallard flank feather to even the tips and clip off a segment that is no wider than the hook gap.

❸ Tie the segment to the top of the hook with the tips to the rear and extending beyond the hook bend by the distance of the hook-shank length. Lash the tailing down to within one hook-gap space of the eye, lift the butts and clip them off.

❹ Trim off the tip from a quill at a point where the remaining diameter is equal to the hook and tailing, and tie it onto the hook about a hook-gap space behind the eye.

❺ Lash the quill down with tying thread to the beginning of the bend and bring the thread back forward to the starting point.

❻ Wind the quill forward in tightly nesting wraps to within one hook-gap space behind the eye, tie it off on top of the hook and clip off the butt.

❼ Tie on a segment of light gray poly yarn that has been split to be no larger in diameter than about twice the size of the hook eye and clip it to a length of no more than ⅛". Be sure to tie in the poly yarn immediately in front of the quill body. This will make it stand up slightly.

❽ Dub a fuzzy thorax area immediately in front of the post. Whip-finish, tease the dubbing a bit and apply a drop of head lacquer.

Hook: Your favorite dryfly hook, size 16 to 22
Thread: Color to match body, 6/0 or 8/0
Rib: None
Tail: Mottled brown hen back segment or Rit Tan-dyed or natural gray mallard flank segment.
Body: One stripped and dyed rooster neck hackle quill. Dye to tan, green, black or gray.
Wing Post: Split segment of gray poly yarn
Thorax: Gray, tan or black rabbit with some guard hairs left in

1-3

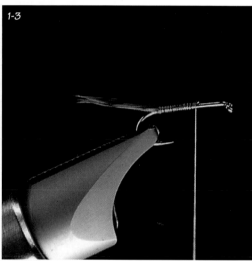

6

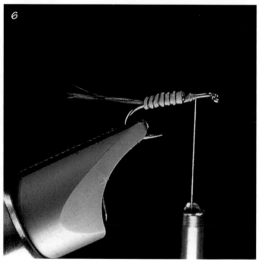

4, 5

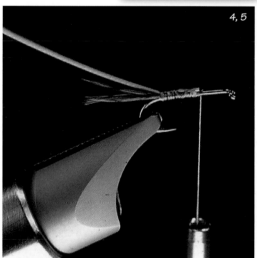

7

8

{**1O Minute Ties**} A.K. Best Jan/Feb 2006

The Spent Cream Caddis
Stand out in the crowd

You've been there before: Blanket caddis hatch, fish rising, some jumping out of the water. You're getting good drifts, even some looks, but no takes. Why? (Actually: Why God, WHY!?)

Here's my thought: The trout have seen flies like your Elkhair or Goddard Caddis many times before and won't be fooled again. Maybe they want something a little easier to eat—maybe something like a spent caddis, for instance. Try it. It works.

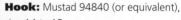

Hook: Mustad 94840 (or equivalent), size 14 to 18
Thread: Danville 6/0 #8 yellow
Body: Fine cream dryfly dubbing
Wing: One clear blond tip of a hen pheasant breast feather
Hackle: Creamy ginger dryfly hackle

❶ Place the hook in the vise and attach the tying thread one hook-gap space behind the eye, wind to the end of the shank and clip off the tag.

❷ Apply tiny puffs of dubbing to the tying thread, and dub a thin body that tapers slightly toward the thread starting point.

❸ Prepare one hen pheasant breast feather by removing the fibers from each side until the remaining feather tip is as wide as the hook-gap space and will extend beyond the hook bend by one hook-gap space.

❹ Place the feather tip flat on top of the hook and make the first turn

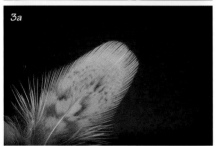

of thread over the feather tip one hook-gap space behind the eye. Be certain the feather tip does not roll to one side. Lash feather quill toward the eye and clip off one hook-eye space behind the eye.

❺ Attach a dryfly hackle by its butt immediately in front of the wing tie-down point and wind forward to create a trim hackle collar.

Note: A Spent Olive Caddis works well, too. Simply use black thread, olive dubbing, partridge back feather for the wing, and brown hackle. Sometimes it's a good idea to trim all the hackle from the bottom of the collar, but always apply a liberal amount of flotant to the fly before making your first cast.

The Sulphur Quill Dun
A springtime standby

We're not supposed to have Sulphurs here in the West, but they are taking up residence in the Frying Pan River in Colorado. At least I think they are; while I'm no entomologist, they are the same sizes and color as the Sulphurs I've seen on Pennsylvania spring creeks. Bugs can't read, so they don't know where they are supposed to live. In both places, trout seem to prefer them to whatever else may be on the water. I prefer the quill-body version of this fly because of the reflective and buoyant qualities of a stripped and dyed rooster-neck hackle quill.

Hook: Mustad 94840 or equivalent, size 14 to 18
Thread: Danville 6/0 #8 yellow
Tail: Medium-ginger spade-hackle fibers, length to equal entire hook, tied splayed
Body: Stripped and dyed lemon-yellow rooster-neck hackle quill. Note: Some hatches will have a little orange tint to them, so experiment by adding a pinch of orange to the yellow dye bath
Wings: Pale, smoky-dun hen hackle tips
Hackle: Medium ginger

---

❶ Attach the thread one hook-gap space behind the eye, wind to the beginning of the bend, snip off the tag and create a tiny thread bump over the last turn of thread. Clip a sparse segment of spade hackle fibers, measure for length to equal entire hook, plus one hook-eye space, tie on immediately in front of the thread bump, and lash forward to the thread start. Clip off butts.

❷ For size 14 and 16 hooks, use two quills (one quill for size 18). One quill should be twice the diameter of the other. The smaller quill will function as an underbody to provide for a proper body taper. Clip off the tips at a point where the remaining quills will have a combined diameter of the hook eye. Tie the clipped tips directly on top of the thread starting point, lash to the rear,

bring the thread forward to the starting point, and wind the quills forward, being certain that the thicker quill covers the thinner one.

❸ Select two hen hackle tips with widths equal to the hook-gap space and cut them to a length that is equal to the entire hook plus one hook-eye space. This is for the tie down. Tie in the wings just in front of the shoulder of the quill body, saving enough space behind the wings for two or three turns of hackle.

❹ Select one hackle, trim the butt and attach it to the hook in your favorite manner. Take two turns of hackle behind the wings and three in front. Tie off the tip, clip off the excess, whip-finish and apply a small drop of head lacquer.

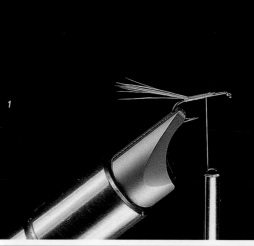

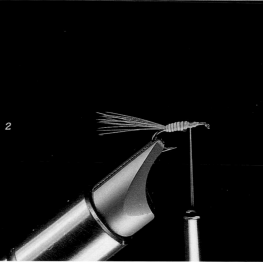

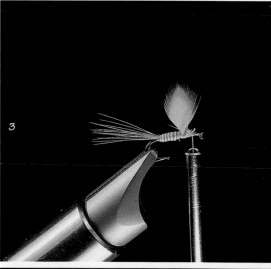

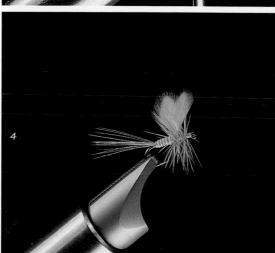

{1☉ **Minute Ties**} A.K. Best July/Oct 2006

The Winged Beetle
It just works

Every beetle I've ever seen on the water has its wing tips visible just behind the shell back halves. This usually amounts to about 25 percent of the insect's total silhouette. Yet all the beetle patterns I see in catalogs and in fly shops have no wing tips showing. I think it's another case of taking photos of an insect the way it isn't seen by the trout and then tying a fly to look like that. It's pretty easy to photograph a beetle when it's on a rock or a stick, but that's not where trout feed, is it?

I've caught trout on the Winged Beetle in every stream I have fished it in. From the Frying Pan River in Colorado to the Henry's Fork in Idaho during Green Drake hatches, as well as on the Tiber River in Italy to a small feeder stream in Denmark. Try it—I'm sure you'll catch fish on it, too.

Hook: Mustad 79580, size 14 to 18
Thread: Danville 6/0 black
Tail: Pair of medium-dun hen hackle tips
Underbody: Black or brown rabbit dubbing
Palmer Hackle: Black or brown saddle
Shellback: Black or brown Bugskin strip, or 1mm black or brown Razor Foam strip
Note: Match dubbing and hackle colors to the shellback color

---

❶ Attach tying thread above the hook point and wind thread slightly into the bend. Firmly attach a very small pinch of dubbing to create a tiny ball no larger then the hook eye, just after the end of the shank.

❷ Select two hen hackle tips, width not quite equal to the hook-gap space, and tie them in immediately in front of the dubbing ball in a Delta wing formation. The length should be about ⅓ the hook-shank length.

❸ Cut a strip of Bugskin or Razor Foam as wide as the hook-gap space. Trim one end to an arrow shape and tie the tip on immediately in front of the wings. Be sure the shiny side is down when you tie it on the shank.

❹ Create a dubbing ball whose diameter is about half the space of the hook gap, then tie in the butt of a saddle hackle in front of it. Continue dubbing to within one hook-eye space behind the eye.

❺ Palmer the hackle forward, tie it down and clip off the excess. Trim all the fibers from the top of the body. Fold the shellback forward, tie it down immediately behind the hook eye and clip off the excess thread. Turn the fly over and clip off all the hackle from the bottom of the fly.

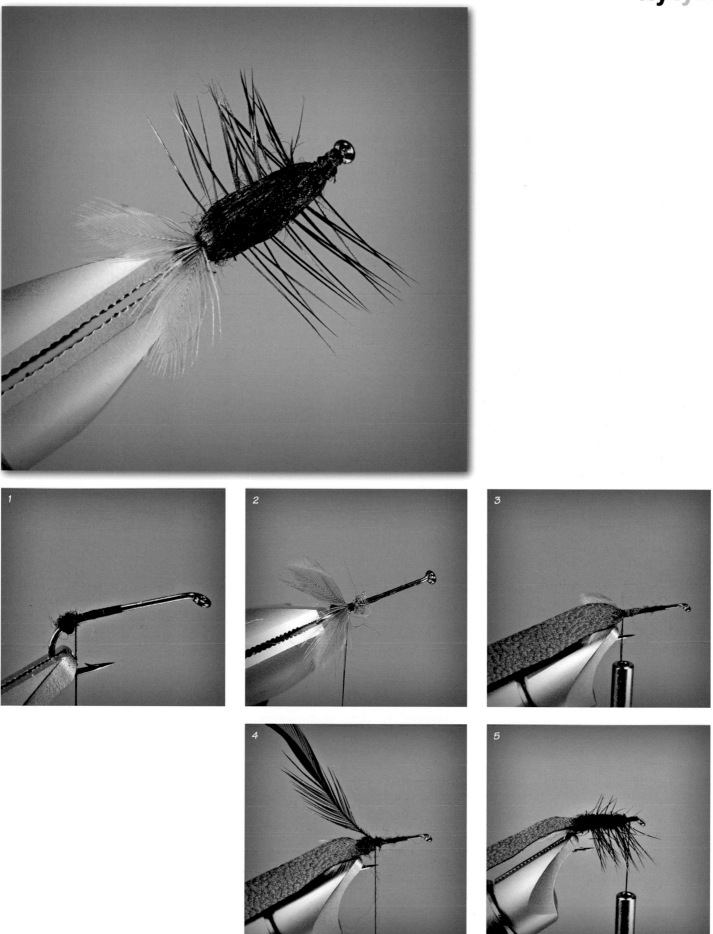

{**10 Minute Ties**} A.K. Best March 2006

Easy Wulff Wings
Finally, a solution to the tedium of tying with calftail

I always carry a couple of dozen Royal Wulffs in one of my fly boxes. They range in size from 12 to 16. It can be the fly of the day when I'm fishing some little high-mountain stream where the fish are eager to eat almost anything that floats over them. When I get a chance to go to Labrador to fish for giant brook trout, I'll tie up some 6s and 8s, and this seems to be the dryfly size of choice. Whatever the size, the white wings are easy to see and they float like little corks.

I used to hate tying Wulffs because of the white calftail or white bucktail wings. It seemed to take forever to stack the hair to make a neat-looking pair of wings, and there was always a huge bump at the spot where I tied in the wing butts. Plus, the hair always seemed to me to be a little top-heavy.

I started playing around with white turkey T-base feathers as a wing-material substitute about 15 years ago. I only tied them for my personal use, thinking that no one would buy a Royal Wulff if it didn't have white hair wings. But just for the hell of it, I tied up a few dozen for a local shop . . . and they sold like hot cakes!

❶ Attach the tying thread to the hook at mid-shank and wind to the beginning of the bend. This will establish the front shoulder of the body.

❷ Tie in hook-shank-length tailing material (moose or elk) at the bend of the shank, wind the thread over the tail fibers to mid-shank, lift and clip off the butts. Wind the thread forward to the hook eye and back to the shoulder.

❸ Select a white turkey T-base feather whose quill is centered in the middle of the feather.

❹ Clip out the center quill to a distance equal to the length of the entire hook.

❺ Fold back (do not strip off) each side of the remaining feather until each side's width is equal to the hook-shank length (this is a good measurement for any size hook).

❻ Fold the feather halves together into a single post.

❼ Place the post immediately in front of the tailing butts against your side of the hook at a 45-degree angle, with the tips below the hook eye.

❽ Very firmly lash the post to the hook, using thread torque to roll the post on top of the hook on the second and third turns of thread.

❾ Take seven or eight very firm turns of thread in the same spot, lift the butt of the feather and clip off at an angle. Save the remainder for a parachute post or some other smaller fly.

❿ Cover the clipped butt with thread, bring the thread forward and build a thread dam in front of the post.

⓫ Divide the post into equal halves. Form a Figure eight with tying thread and wrap the base of each wing with five or six turns of thread. Apply a tiny drop of head lacquer to the base of each wing. Hold and squeeze the wings flat with your thumb and forefinger.

⓬ Construct the body of peacock herl and floss.

⓭ Wind on lots of hackle and go fish whitewater!

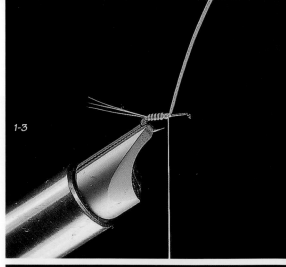

1-3

{1O Minute Ties} A.K. Best Jan/Feb 2008

The Trico Quill Dun
Carry a dozen for early morning fishing

If you haven't fished the Trico hatch, you're missing out on some of the finest dryfly fishing to be had, no matter what part of the country you live in. Most fly fishers get very excited about the Trico spinner fall, which can be a lot of fun, but the actual hatch is even better. Get to your favorite stream before dawn, because that's when these little guys begin to hatch. Chances are you'll have a lot of stream to yourself and all the action you could hope for. These are little insects, so casting accuracy is mandatory, as is about four feet of 6X or 7X tippet. Total leader length should be at least 12 feet.

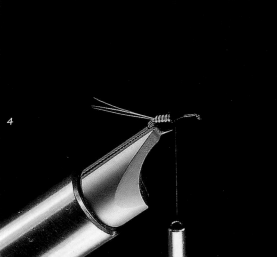

4

Hook: Mustad 94840 or equivalent, size 16 to 22. Use a ring-eye or up-eye hook for smaller sizes.

Thread: White 6/0 or 8/0 for abdomen; black 6/0 or 8/0 for the thorax and head

Tail: Small clump (5 or 6) white spade hackle fibers, length to equal hook shank

Abdomen: Light green to dark green stripped and dyed rooster neck hackle quill. The body color of the natural will vary from stream to stream.

Thorax: Charcoal gray to black fine dryfly dubbing

Wings: Pair of slightly oversize white hen hackle tips (use size 16 for a size 18 fly). The wings are larger than proportion charts indicate.

Hackle: Check your local hatches. Some have cream legs, some have medium- to dark-gray legs. THE DUNS DO NOT HAVE BLACK LEGS! (Even though the spinners do.) Use only three or four turns of the hackle that matches the color of the legs of your hatch

5

❶ Attach the white tying thread to the hook at mid-shank and wind to the beginning of the hook bend.

❷ Tie in tail fibers and clip off butts at mid-shank.

❸ Tie in one stripped and dyed quill and wind to mid-shank.

❹ Change to black thread and dub a short, thin thorax. Leave at least a hook-gap space for wings, hackle collar and head.

❺ Tie in a pair of white hen hackle tips in front of the dubbed thorax.

❻ Tie in and wind the hackle collar. One turn behind the wings and two in front is all that's needed.

❼ Clip off hackle tip, whip-finish and apply a tiny drop of head lacquer.

6, 7

{**10 Minute Ties**} A.K. Best Jan/Feb 2009

The Flash Fly
An easy one for steelhead

Some years ago, I tied a lot of steelhead flies for Bill Hunter when he still owned Hunter's Angling Supplies, in New Boston, New Hampshire. Flies tied in Colorado, sent to New Hampshire and fished in Alaska. Go Figure. One of the favored patterns was called the Flash Fly. It's an easy fly to tie, as steelhead flies go, and I was told it was very effective. It might come under the heading, "Something old is new again."

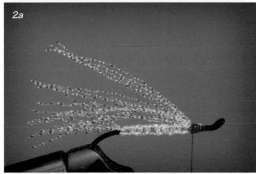

❶ Attach the white thread and tie in a small clump of pearlescent Krystal Flash. Lash the clump to the end of the hook shank and bring the thread forward to the starting point. Taper the tailing tips. Tie in the pearlescent Body Braid above the thread starting point and lash it to the top of the hook, wrapping to the start of the hook bend. Bring the thread forward and wind the Body Braid forward to create a slight taper to the rear of the body. Tie down and trim off the excess. This will be the beginning of the base of the tapered head.

❷ Switch to fluorescent red thread and tie in a clump of pearlescent Krystal Flash immediately in front of the body. Trim the length of the wing material to extend beyond the end of the tail by half a hook-gap length. Tie in a smaller clump of red Krystal Flash on top of the pearlescent material. Snip a slight taper in the ends of the wing materials.

❸ For the collar, select a small clump of light blue Krystal Flash, clip to even the tips and tie the first clump to the bottom of the fly. Allow the individual fibers to spread around the hook slightly.

❹ Continue tying in small clumps until you've formed a complete collar. Create a tapered thread head and apply several coats of lacquer for a glassy head.

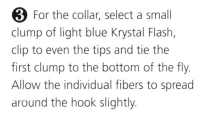

Hook: Mustad Salmon 36890, size 4
Thread: Danville 6/0 #1 white for the body; Danville 6/0 #505 fluorescent red for the head
Tail: Pearlescent Krystal Flash
Body: Pearlescent Body Braid
Wing: Under-layer of pearlescent Krystal Flash; top layer of red Krystal Flash
Collar: Light blue Krystal Flash

{**10 Minute Ties**} A.K. Best July/Oct 2005

A. K.'s Hopper
A hybrid that's both durable and easy to tie

I think there are three "classic" hopper patterns: the hackle-collared Joe's Hopper (known as the Michigan Hopper before Joe Brooks popularized it); Ed Shenk came up with the simple Letort Hopper; and Dave Whitlock created Dave's Hopper, complete with kicker legs. Each of these flies has an attribute that I think is very important. I like the palmer-hackle body of the Joe's Hopper, the clean wing design of the Letort Hopper, and the trimmed spun-deerhair head of the Whitlock. I put the three together to form what I call A.K.'s Hopper. It's relatively easy to tie and extremely durable.

Hook: Mustad 94831, size 6 to 12
Thread: Yellow Monocord
Tail: None (ever see a grasshopper with a red butt?)
Body: Yellow 4-strand yarn (Lion Brand Sayelle-100% Orion Acrylic)
Palmer Hackle: Stiff brown neck or saddle
Underwing: Sprayed wild turkey secondary wing-quill segment
Overwing: Sparse natural deer body hair
Head: Natural deer body hair, spun and trimmed to shape

❶ Attach the thread to the hook one hook-gap space behind the eye and wind to the beginning of the bend with very firm tension. Bring the thread forward to the starting point. Directly even with the thread start, and using only five turns of thread, tie in the squarely trimmed tip of the yellow body yarn. Firmly lash the yarn to the beginning of the bend and take seven very firm turns of thread.

❷ Twist the yarn tag to form a hook-gap-length loop as a body extension and tie down with six very firm turns of thread.

❸ Tie in the tip of a long hackle feather directly over the loop tie-down, then wind the yarn forward to the beginning tie-down to complete the body. Anchor with seven very firm turns of thread wraps (noticing a pattern here?). Clip off the yarn tag to create an abrupt vertical shoulder. (This last step is crucial!)

❹ Spiral-wrap the hackle forward, tie it down on top of the shoulder and clip off the butt, being certain to maintain the abrupt vertical shoulder. Trim off all the hackle on top of the body.

❺ Clip a hook-gap-width segment from a wild turkey secondary wing feather, and fold it lengthwise. Clip off the tip to form a "V," clip off the two bottom points, place it on the hook to align the tips with the end of the body loop, and cut off the butt immediately in front of the shoulder

of the body. Tie it down with only three turns of thread and apply a drop of lacquer.

❻ Clip and stack a small bundle of hard and shiny deer hair (about 12 hairs) and tie the hair clump on immediately over the turkey wing with only four turns of thread. Apply a drop of lacquer. DO NOT CLIP OFF THE HAIR BUTTS, but fold them back. (We'll cut them off when we trim the head.) Bring the thread forward to hang immediately in front of the body.

❼ Tie in a small bundle of hollow hair, BUTTS TO THE REAR, spin and firmly pack. Tie in a second small bundle of hollow hair, BUTTS TO THE REAR, spin and pack. Tie in a third small bundle of hollow hair, BUTTS FORWARD! Spin and firmly pack.

❽ Carefully trim with a razor blade, making the first cut along the bottom of the head, then each side, and finally shape the top to a slight sloping angle as shown in the photo. Trim away the hair butts from the overwing.

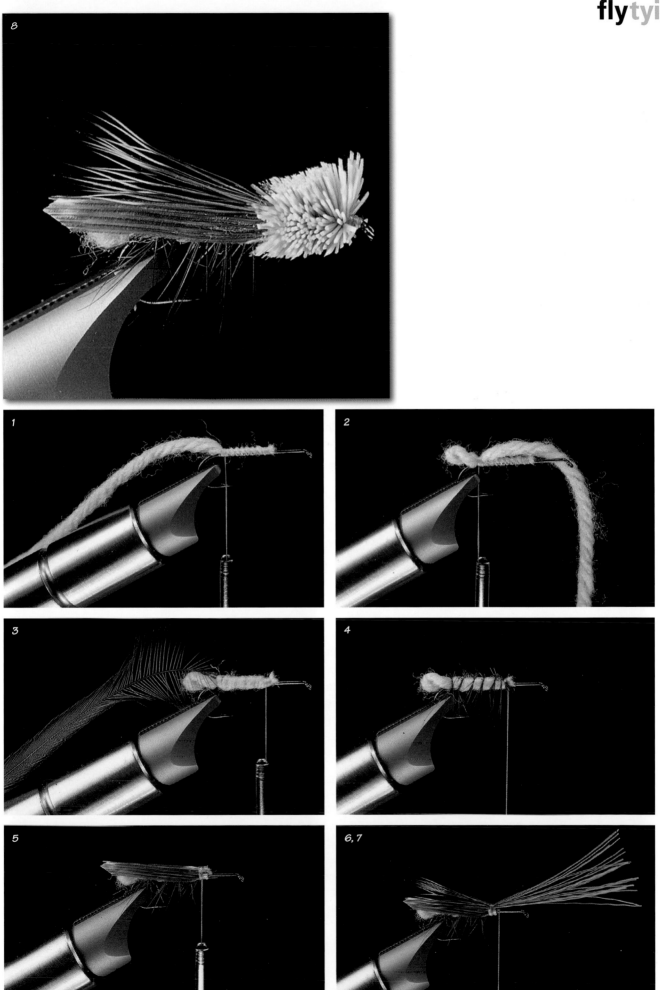

{**1O Minute Ties**} A.K. Best April 2005

The Red Quill Spinner
Right for a variety of mayfly species

I wish I had called this pattern the "Rusty Quill Spinner" about 20 years ago when I first began tying it. The idea came to me while I was fishing a PMD spinner fall on the Harriman Ranch portion of the Henry's Fork. I was getting way too many refusals with the standard dubbed-body Rusty Spinner and, after carefully observing the naturals, I rediscovered the fact that no mayfly has a fuzzy body. So back to camp I went, to tie some quill-body spinners using a light tan rooster-hackle quill for the body. I still got some refusals because of bad drifts, but I had far more confident rises and hookups than before. It isn't often that we can use one pattern for a variety of mayfly species (not counting the Adams, of course), but the Red Quill Spinner closely imitates Blue-Wing Olive spinners and the prolific Western Red Quill. I carry them in sizes 14 to 22, with 16s and 18s making up the bulk of my spinner box.

❶ Start the thread on the hook three hook-eye spaces behind the eye, wind to the beginning of the bend, clip off the tag, and make two or three turns of thread over the last turn to create a tiny thread bump.

❷ Tie in the tailing fibers just in front of the thread bump. Length should be about two hook-eye spaces longer than the entire hook. Wind thread over the butts to the thread starting point and clip off the excess butts. Splay the fibers by pushing them up slightly with your left thumbnail. Apply a tiny drop of head lacquer at the base of the tail fibers and they will stay in their splayed position forever!

❸ Select a stripped and dyed quill whose length and diameter will allow you to create a suitable body on the size hook you're using. That is to say, clip off the tip to a point where the remaining quill-tip diameter is equal to the hook, tailing butts and thread already on the hook. Tie the quill onto the hook as shown.

❹ Wind the quill forward in tightly nesting wraps and tie it off on top of the hook immediately over the tied-in clipped tip. Clip off the remaining butt and smooth down with thread wraps.

❺ Select a pair of white hen hackle feathers whose tips are slightly wider than the hook-gap space. Clip off the butts at a point where the remaining tips will be two hook-eye spaces longer than the entire hook, tie them to the hook, divide and flatten.

❻ Thinly and firmly apply dubbing to the thread and create a Figure-eight dubbed thorax that is twice the diameter of the shoulder of the body of the fly.

Hook: Your favorite light-wire dryfly hook, size 14 to 22
Thread: Tan 6/0
Tail: Light tan or medium ginger hackle fibers
Body: Quill from light tan stripped neck hackle
Wings: Pair of white hen hackle tips
Thorax: Any kind of rust-colored dryfly dubbing

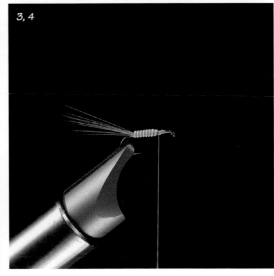